THE POWER OF POWERLESSNESS

A Story of Alcoholism and Recovery

by
Billy Steel

Bright Pen

A Bright Pen Book

Text Copyright © Billy Steel 2010

Cover design © Jamie Day 2010

British Library Cataloguing Publication Data.
A catalogue record for this book is available from the British Library

ISBN 978-07552-1255-2

Authors OnLine Ltd
19 The Cinques
Gamligay, Sandy
Bedfordshire SG19 3NU
England

This book is also available in e-book format, details of which are available at www.authorsonline.co.uk

CONTENTS

PART ONE

The Problem

PART TWO

The Solution

ACKNOWLEDGEMENTS

This book would never have been written without the help and encouragement of a select few people. I wrote the first draft manuscript in 1995 when I had been sober for twelve years and it was then that I first developed my theory of 'The Power of Powerlessness'. But the draft was not the way I wanted it to be largely because even though I then thought I knew it all, my understanding of alcoholism and recovery was nothing like as well developed and comprehensive as it has since become. Consequently it lay on the shelf gathering dust until 2007 when I was inspired, encouraged and indeed challenged by a member of the Fellowship, who wishes to remain anonymous but whom I shall call Jack, to pick up my pen again and rewrite it. Because, however, of extremely debilitating and painful arthritis, both osteo and/or rheumatoid, throughout 2008, I did not feel well enough to actually start writing until the spring of 2009.

In addition to Jack, I should now like to thank the following for their generous support, help and advice: Huw T., Jeremy Best, my son Charles Steel and my old friends of over fifty years Christopher Normand, John Littlewood and Nicky Winter. I must thank too Roddy Bloomfield for his kind and much appreciated professional advice following completion of the unedited draft manuscript.

I must also specifically mention and thank Ed Lindsey who not only was the first sober alcoholic to meaningfully carry the AA message to me back in December 1982, but who also kindly agreed to write the Foreword to my book. There can surely be no one in the UK who is better qualified to write the Foreword because apart from being sober for well over thirty years, Ed additionally spent most of his sober working life as a counsellor, CEO and/or Trustee of Broadway Lodge, the first Minnesota model treatment centre in Britain.

I want also sincerely to thank Frances Kavanagh first for editing my manuscript to a state fit for publication but secondly and as importantly for the great encouragement and advice she gave me as, chapter by chapter, she read through the draft manuscript as it was being written. From the beginning she manifestly had an interest in and knowledge of alcoholism which I found most unusual and unexpected. I did not understand why until I had almost finished the draft when she told me that some years ago she had been married to an alcoholic who sadly died from the illness. So like Ed with the Foreword, there surely could have been no one better suited to editing my book.

Lastly I want to thank my wife Sarah not only for her encouragement but also for having her dining table used as a rather cluttered desk for over six months and for the most part cheerfully tolerating a husband very much preoccupied with writing.

WHAT OTHERS HAVE SAID

I enjoyed reading the book and found it very readable, informative and an offer of hope to the countless other alcoholics/drug addicts out there who at times may feel hopeless.
Peter Smith, Development Director, Broadway Lodge.

Thank you for being an alcoholic! Another AA paradox perhaps or just an irony, but certainly serendipity, for you have helped me understand Michael, 'my' alcoholic, in a way that could not have happened except by being 'immersed' in the whole subject of alcoholism from an alcoholic's point of view. I thought I already understood. In actual fact, I just knew a lot, and as we know, knowledge doesn't always equate with understanding. Although Michael is no longer here physically, I feel he's happy about all this, and perhaps had something to do with it. And feeling that, it is as if he's making amends from wherever he is, even as I realise there is nothing to forgive him for. So when I say thank you for being an alcoholic, I could not mean it more sincerely, because you've given me a very special gift.
Frances Kavanagh, Editor.

I think this idea of seeing the healing offered by AA lived in practice is probably the key message of the book. Additionally, the focus on the role of spiritual virtues and principles of belief in the chapter 'Miscellany' gives the whole book a holistic and more rounded foundation – that there is spiritual nourishment in here. The fact that the manuscript shows the 12 Steps in action, and grounds the AA principles in a very real spiritual and social context that can help other alcoholics and their families to see it in practice and understand its workings is I think the most distinguishing and powerful feature of the book – for me, at least.
Anon.

I have spent the past 2½ hours reading – and I am profoundly moved by what you have written. You describe so graphically the dangers, misery and disastrous consequences of alcoholism not only for the alcoholic but also for family members and other close friends. You also show, however, that a normal sober life is possible. Seeing you (and your own serenity) today so many years after you stopped drinking is the most inspirational proof that alcoholism need not be a life sentence if the "problem" is faced with honesty and humility.

Christopher Normand.

I have finished reading your excellent book. Great title and sound, mature AA exposition combined with interesting autobiographical material. I particularly liked your intertwining treatment of powerlessness, love, forgiveness, resentment and serenity. Unsurprisingly, I agree with you entirely regarding the woefully misconceived and inadequate approach to chemical dependency adopted by the Government and the NHS.

Martin, Lord Noel-Buxton Author of 'ARRESTING DESTRUCTION – Recovery from Alcoholism'.

Your experience has been one hell of an eye opener into a world to which, thankfully, I have never been exposed. I am sure your book will be of great value to both warn off others as well as help those in trouble. Your own letter written to yourself is truly illuminating.

Rene Maby.

You clearly have a comprehensive understanding of the disease concept and an ability to communicate that I am unable to do except in a one to one situation. You must finish this book and get it published as I believe it could be used as a text. There is so little published information that is reliable and even more rubbish printed in so called self help books. A definitive account from someone with your experience is desperately needed. I know you said that you made plenty of notes but your memory of 1982 is remarkable; most of us had lost not but a few brain cells by the time we got into Broadway.

Ed Lindsey.

I very much enjoyed reading your book, at one point couldn't put it down (made me late for dinner).

Ed Lindsey.

FOREWORD

At last a book from one who has walked the walk. Billy Steel provides an insight into alcoholism rarely seen. It is the story of one man's journey into chronic alcoholism and subsequent recovery. Today most people who know anything about alcoholism, which unfortunately very few do, would accept that alcoholism is a progressive and incurable illness. While it may well be self-inflicted, no alcoholic sets out with the intention of ending up homeless on the embankment, on a park bench or dead. Nor does it happen overnight; it can take many years and even several decades to reach the final chronic stages. To those who maintain it is not an illness, I can only say that anyone who has seen the depth of suffering of a chronic alcoholic at rock bottom could in no way maintain that he or she has any degree of 'wellness'. On the contrary, such an alcoholic is a very sick person in the terminal stages of a physical, mental and spiritual disease.

As Billy asserts, alcoholism is the most untreated treatable disease in the western world, making this book even more welcome because, unlike most books written by alcoholics, the greater part of it is not about drinking but about recovery. The first part, which includes an account of Billy's early life – the sort of person he was and the life he led from the very beginning –, describes his journey from moderate consumption to obsessive drinking, explaining the factors that led to the obsession, his addictive personality and many years of denial before finally accepting that alcoholism is an illness for which there is no cure but from which 100% recovery is possible through (in this case) the AA programme.

The second part of the book relates his progress from treatment and his first AA meeting, twenty-seven years ago, to the present day, his total acceptance of the condition and how recovery can be achieved if the AA programme is strictly followed. He gives a clear insight into what sobriety is like and the very different person he has become, showing that, if one wants to, and no matter how low one may have sunk, it is perfectly possible to recover from this very misunderstood, progressive, incurable and otherwise killer disease.

Billy also looks at the roles both alcoholism and drug addiction play in today's society and questions the controlled drinking model and 'substitution treatments' favoured by many alcoholic counsellors, doctors and the government. He states that the *proven* method of recovery from chronic alcoholism is the abstinence method which is the AA programme.

This book will be an inspiration to alcoholics not yet on the AA programme and those in early recovery on the programme. Additionally, it will be an invaluable tool for anyone working in the field of alcoholism and drug addiction.

Ed Lindsey
Former Trustee and CEO of Broadway Lodge
For 18 years, counsellor and head counsellor at Broadway Lodge

INTRODUCTION

This is the story of how, from a privileged and promising beginning, I descended over a period of some thirty years into the sheer hell of alcoholism. It is also the story of how I was helped and managed to turn my life around; how, for the last twenty-seven years I have lived a worthwhile and generally happy life in recovery, without drinking or, much more importantly, without wanting to drink. As such the book is a memoir of my life particularly as it has been affected by my alcoholism and to a lesser extent by my chronic addiction to nicotine.

I hope that my account of how I have got well may help other alcoholics to realize that if I can recover, so too can they, if they do the same simple things as I have done and continue to do; namely, follow the Twelve Step recovery programme of Alcoholics Anonymous (AA). My intent is to pass on my experience and what I have learned more widely than is possible in AA alone and with this in mind, I have five main objectives, all of which are important though the greatest emphasis is perhaps on the first three:

1.   To help, encourage and motivate alcoholics and other AA members who are newcomers or who may be in early recovery.

2.   To support and help AA members who may be sponsoring or about to sponsor newcomers.

3.   To inform and educate non-alcoholics, including family members and close friends, as to the precise nature of this very subtle and confusing disease.

4.   To instruct/educate doctors and other health professionals, most of whom regrettably receive little or no training in alcoholism, drug and other addictions.

5.   To make everyone, including doctors and politicians, much more aware of AA (it currently has well over two million members worldwide), of how it came into being, what it actually is and how and why its Twelve Step programme of recovery is by far the most widespread and successful treatment available in the world today.

The exact nature of the illness is covered in the following chapters, but essentially the experiences of all alcoholics and other drug addicts are the same, and, while their circumstances may differ greatly, the one factor which they all have in common is the progressive deterioration and eventual disintegration of the human personality. In 1943 Dr E.M. Jellinek, who was then a leading authority of scientific research on alcoholism and director of the School of Alcohol Studies at Yale University, conducted studies of the 'Phases in the Drinking History of Alcoholics'. He illustrated the phases in chart form, 'A Chart of Alcohol Addiction and Recovery'. (Fig 1)

I am a very visual person and when I first saw the illness and recovery explained in this graphic way, it enormously helped me to picture and hence to better understand just what alcoholism, addiction and recovery were all about. One point I would like to stress, however, is that in my experience not all the symptoms listed in the chart necessarily occur in the order in which Dr Jellinek places them and that the time taken to travel from the first drink to 'obsessive drinking continuing in vicious circles' at the bottom of the chart can vary hugely from one alcoholic to another. The same is true for recovery, for those relatively few alcoholics who eventually find it.

After a great deal of thought I have decided to break my anonymity as a member of AA and to own the book by writing it in my own name, because to have written it anonymously would have substantially weakened the credibility of my story of the last seventy four years. I also have a nagging feeling that hiding behind the cloak of anonymity could indicate a withholding of some of the truth about myself, or the shame of being an alcoholic, neither of which is the case. Back in 1982 I was ashamed, but not any more.

I have altered the names of a few people in order to protect their identities and, with the exception of four who have given permission for their full names to be used, I have referred to other past and present members of AA by their first names and the first initial of their surnames.

One of the most noticeable and to some perhaps most interesting changes in the Fellowship since I became a member has been the increase in the numbers of women members, to the point where, if they have not already done so, they are rapidly approaching parity with men. In the book, however, I have referred to alcoholics in the masculine form simply to avoid the continual and irksome repetition of 'he' or 'she', 'his' or 'her' etc. It is not in any way meant to be sexist and if it should appear so, I would ask your forgiveness.

Finally, I did not write my heartfelt 'Plea for Common Sense' to politicians, doctors and the NHS as a member of, or on behalf of AA, which has no opinion on outside issues, but rather as a British citizen who happens to be an alcoholic with some sixty years' experience of the illness, of which twenty-seven have been in continuous recovery. I wish to make clear beyond any doubt that the experiences, views and opinions which I have expressed in the book are, except where otherwise stated, mine and mine alone, and do not necessarily represent the views of other members of AA or of the Fellowship itself.

NB: All AA material in this book is reprinted with the kind permission of the General Service Board of Alcoholics Anonymous (Great Britain) Limited.

Addiction and Recovery

(Fig 1)

OCCASIONAL RELIEF DRINKING

CONSTANT RELIEF DRINKING COMMENCES

INCREASE IN ALCOHOL TOLERANCE

ONSET OF MEMORY BLACKOUTS

SURREPTITIOUS DRINKING

INCREASING DEPENDENCE ON ALCOHOL

URGENCY OF FIRST DRINKS

FEELINGS OF GUILT

UNABLE TO DISCUSS PROBLEM

MEMORY BLACKOUTS INCREASE

DRINKING BOLSTERED WITH EXCUSES

DECREASE OF ABILITY TO STOP DRINKING WHEN OTHERS DO SO

GRANDIOSE AND AGGRESSIVE BEHAVIOUR

PERSISTENT REMORSE

EFFORTS TO CONTROL FAIL REPEATEDLY

PROMISES AND RESOLUTIONS FAIL

TRIES GEOGRAHICAL ESCAPES

LOSS OF OTHER INTERESTS

FAMILY AND FRIENDS AVOIDED

WORK AND MONEY TROUBLES

UNREASONABLE RESENTMENTS

NEGLECT OF FOOD

LOSS OF ORDINARY WILLPOWER

TREMORS AND EARLY MORNING DRINKS

DECREASE IN ALCOHOL TOLERANCE

ONSET OF LENGTHY INTOXICATIONS

PHYSICAL DETERIORATION

IMPAIRED THINKING

INDEFINABLE FEARS

MORAL DETERIORATION

DRINKING WITH INFERIORS

OBSESSION WITH DRINKING

UNABLE TO INITIATE ACTION

ALL ALIBIS EXHAUSTED

VAGUE SPIRITUAL DESIRES

COMPLETE DEFEAT ADMITTED

CRUCIAL PHASE

CHRONIC PHASE

OBSESSIVE DRINKING CONTINUES IN VICIOUS CIRCLES

HONEST DESIRE FOR HELP

TOLD ADDICTION CAN BE ARRESTED

LEARNS ALCOHOLISM IS AN ILLNESS

STOPS TAKING ALCOHOL

MEETS FORMER ADDICTS NORMAL AND HAPPY

ASSISTED IN MAKING PERSONAL STOCKTAKING

RIGHT THINKING BEGINS

SPIRITUAL NEEDS EXAMINED

PHYSICAL OVERHAUL BY DOCTOR

ONSET OF NEW HOPE

START OF GROUP THERAPY

APPRECIATION OF POSSIBILITIES OF NEW WAY OF LIFE

REGULAR NOURISHMENT TAKEN

DIMINISHING FEARS OF THE UNKNOWN FUTURE

REALISTIC THINKING

RETURN OF SELF-ESTEEM

FAMILY AND FRIENDS APPRECIATE EFFORTS

DESIRE TO ESCAPE GOES

NEW CIRCLE OF STABLE FRIENDS

ADJUSTMENT TO FAMILY NEEDS

FACTS FACED WITH COURAGE

NEW INTERESTS DEVELOP

INCREASE OF EMOTIONAL CONTROL

REBIRTH OF IDEALS

FIRST STEPS TOWARD ECONOMIC STABILITY

APPLICATION OF REAL VALUES

PERSONAL APPEARANCE

CONFIDENCE OF EMPLOYERS

RATIONALIZATIONS RECOGNIZED

GROUP THERAPY AND MUTUAL HELP CONTINUE

CONTENTMENT IN SOBRIETY

INCREASING TOLERANCE

ENLIGHTENED AND INTERESTING WAY OF LIFE OPENS UP WITH ROAD AHEAD TO HIGHER LEVELS THAN EVER BEFORE

REHABILITATION

OVERTURE

Dr. Jung, Dr. Silkworth, and AA

The article that follows comprises excerpts from Bill's talk at his 33rd AA anniversary sponsored by New York Intergroup. He was the third and final speaker, preceded by Jim from Long Island and Kirsten from Scarsdale.

January 1968

As Kirsten said so poignantly just now, "The years laid waste by the locusts are over...." And as Jim so simply remarked, "There is a God and there is a Grace...."

Tonight I think I would like to tell you my own story in terms, first, of the "years laid waste" and the reasons I now see this was so – what in my early life contributed to my alcoholism – and then, in terms of my belief that "there is a God and there is a grace" and what the outcome has been for me and for so many because of that belief.

Our chairman tonight remarked on the wonderful friends that AA has had from the start. He might have said the wonderful friends we have had since before AA was even a gleam in the eye of any of us!

Long before I was sober, long before there was any idea that there would be this AA way for alcoholics to help themselves, certain men and women were gaining skills and insights that were to make all the difference to us in later years. The thing that characterized all of these early friends of ours who were to donate their skill and wisdom to us in AA was this: In each case where telling contributions were made, the man or woman was *spiritually centred, spiritually animated.*

Tonight I would like to sketch just one of the historical situations out of which our Fellowship sprang. Many of you have heard parts of the story before, the story of how Rowland H., an American businessman, was getting progressively worse in alcoholism – undergoing one treatment, one so-called cure after another, with no result. Finally as a refuge of last resort, he went to Europe and literally cast himself upon the care of a psychiatrist, Dr. Carl Jung, who was to prove, in the event, a great and good friend of AA.

You will recall Dr. Jung as one of the three first pioneers in the art of psychiatry. The thing that distinguished him from his colleagues, Freud and Adler, was the fact that he was spiritually animated – something that was to make all the difference to each and every one of us now here, and will make all the difference for all yet to come....

I never realized what a very great man in spiritual dimensions Carl Jung was until, in 1961, I wrote him a very belated letter of gratitude for the part that he played in originating our Society of Alcoholics Anonymous.

This was the last year of Dr. Jung's life. He was old. Nevertheless, he sat down and wrote me a letter. It looks like he tapped it out on a typewriter with one finger. It is one of my most cherished possessions. Lois framed it and it will always be with us.

We ought to note very carefully what Dr. Jung said in that letter, so obviously written in profound love and understanding – in the language of the heart. His insight into what was needed for recovery from alcoholism, an insight that came through Rowland and Ebby at a crucial point in my own deterioration, meant everything for AA when it was still in embryo. His humble willingness to speak the truth, even when it meant disclosing the limitations of his own art, gives the measure of the man.

There was another spiritually animated man, Dr. William D. Silkworth, whose contribution to AA paralleled Dr. Jung's. Unlike Jung, Dr. Silkworth was a man in obscure position, but he was spiritually centred – he had to be! He declared to all comers, after twenty years of almost absolute defeat in trying to help alcoholics, that he did love alcoholics and wanted to go on working with and for them. Every alcoholic who came his way felt that love. A very few recovered. He thought I might recover. Then came the day when it was clear that I would not, that I could not.

By this time Dr. Silkworth had defined alcoholism as a sickness of the emotions, coupled with a sickness of the body which he loosely described as an allergy. These words of his are to be seen in the foreword of the Big Book, *Alcoholics Anonymous*, entitled, "The Doctor's Opinion," and over the years they have been incorporated into the consensus that is AA.

As Jung had told Rowland that his case was hopeless and that medicine and psychiatry could do nothing more for him, so Silkworth told Lois on a fateful day in the summer of 1934: "I am afraid that Bill will have to be committed. There is nothing that I can do for him, or anything else that I know." These were words of great humility from a professional.

They scared me into sobriety for two months, although I soon resumed my drinking. But the message that Ebby had brought me from Dr. Jung and from the Oxford Groups, and the sentence that Dr. Silkworth pronounced over me, continued to occupy my mind in every waking hour thereafter. I began to be very resentful. Here was Dr. Silkworth, who had defined alcoholism – the obsession that condemns you to drink against your will and true interests, even unto destruction, and the bodily sensitivity that guarantees madness and death if you drink at all. And here came Dr. Jung via Rowland and Ebby confirming that there was no way out known to doctors. My god, science, the only god I had then, had declared me hopeless.

But Ebby had also brought hope. Not much later, I was back in the hospital, in Dr. Silkworth's care after what proved to be my last drunk. Ebby came to visit me again. I asked him to repeat once more what he had said over my kitchen table in Brooklyn that first time he told me how he had gotten sober.

"Well," he said, "you know, you get honest with yourself; you make a self-survey; you talk it out with the other guy; you quit living alone and begin to get straight with the world around by making restitution; you try the kind of giving that demands no reward either in approval, prestige, or money; and you ask whatever higher power there is, even if it is just an experiment, to help you to find the grace to be released from alcoholism."

As Ebby put it, it was quite simple, quite matter-of-fact, and said with a smile. But this was it.

So Ebby finally took his leave. Now the jaws of the dilemma really crushed. I hit an all-time block. I can only suppose that any particle of belief that there was a single thing I could do for myself alone was for the moment rubbed out. And I found myself as a child, utterly alone in complete darkness. And I cried out as a child expecting little – indeed, expecting nothing. I simply said, "If there is a God, will he show himself?" Then I was granted one of those instantaneous illuminations. The sort of thing that really defies description. I was seized with great joy and ecstasy beyond all possible expression. In the mind's eye, it seemed to me I stood on a high mountain. I was taken there. I had not climbed it. And then the great thought burst upon me: "Bill you are a free man! This is the God of the Scriptures." And then I was filled with the consciousness of a presence. A great peace fell over me, and I was with this I don't know how long.

But then the dark side put in an appearance, and it said to me, "Perhaps, Bill, you are hallucinating. You better call in the doctor."

So the doctor came, and haltingly I told him of the experience. Then came great words for Alcoholics Anonymous. The little man had listened, looking at me benignly with those blue eyes of his, and at length he said to me, "Bill, you are not crazy. I have heard about this sort of thing in the books but I have never seen it firsthand. I don't know what it is you have, Bill, but it must be some great psychic event, and you had better hang on to it – it is so much better than what you had only an hour ago."

So I hung on, and then I knew there was a God and I knew there was a grace. And through it all, I have continued to feel, if I may presume to say it, that I do *know* these things.

Then, of course, being trained as an analyst of sorts, I began to ask myself why this had happened to me. And why had it so seldom happened to drunks before? Why shouldn't this be the heritage of any drunk? And while I was wondering, Ebby came again the next day and he had in his hands a message from another great man, William James, and the message came to me in a book called *Varieties of Religious Experience.* I read the book cover to cover, and naturally I found experiences corresponding with my own. I found other experiences, however, that were very gradual. I found experiences that occurred outside of any religious association.

But nearly all these experiences that were capable of transforming motivations had common denominators over and above any explanation by associations, or common discipline, or faith, or what have you. These gifts of grace, whether they came in a rush or very gradually, were all founded on a basis of hopelessness. The recipients were people who in some controlling area of life found themselves in a situation that could not be gotten over, around, or under. Their defeat had been absolute, and so was mine

Then I wondered about that defeat, and I realized what part my god of science, as personified by Dr. Carl Jung and Dr. Silkworth, had played in it. They had transmitted to me the very bad news that the chance of recovery on my own unaided resources or merely by medication was just about nil. This was deflation at depth – this made me ready for the gift when it came.

Now, actually, although this is the great experience of my life, I do not think it in any way superior or in its essentials very different at all than the experience which all AAs have had – the transforming experience – the spiritual awakening. They are all from the same source: the divine peace.

So, with my own experience had come the possibility of a chain reaction. I realized nothing had happened to me until certain messages had been transmitted, striking me at great depth, by another alcoholic. Therefore, the thought came of one alcoholic talking to another just as Oxford Group people were talking to each other - in the language of the heart. Maybe this could be the transmission belt. So I started working among alcoholics.

I went to a few Oxford Group meetings and to the missions. Dr Silkworth let me work with a few people in the hospital at the risk of his reputation. And lo and behold! Nothing happened. Because – some of my old grandeur had come back, I had thought my experience was something very special. The old ego had begun to boom again. I was destined to fix all the drunks in the world – quite a large order.

Naturally nothing happened until – again – the deflation came. It came on that day when, in the Mayflower Hotel in Akron, I was tempted to take a drink for the first time since my hospital experience. That was when I first realized that I would need other alcoholics to preserve myself and maintain the original gift of sobriety. It was not just a case of trying to *help* alcoholics. If my sobriety were to be maintained, I *had* to find another alcoholic to work with. So when Dr. Bob and I sat down for the first time face to face, it was a very different act. I said, "Bob, I am speaking because I need you as much as you could possibly need me. I am in danger of slipping back down the drain."

So there is the story. There is the nature of the illness as explained by Dr. Jung and Dr. Silkworth – and there is one drunk talking to another, telling his story of recovery through reliance on the Grace of God.[1]

(NB. *Bill was one of the two co-founders of AA in 1935 and the text of his correspondence with Dr. Jung is reproduced in full in Chapter 8.*)

THE DOCTOR'S OPINION

We of Alcoholics Anonymous believe that the reader will be interested in the medical estimate of the plan of recovery described in this book. Convincing testimony must surely come from medical men who have had experience with the sufferings of our members and have witnessed our return to health. A well-known doctor, chief physician at a nationally prominent hospital specializing in alcoholic and drug addiction, gave Alcoholics Anonymous this letter:

To Whom It May Concern:
I have specialized in the treatment of alcoholism for many years.

In late 1934 I attended a patient who, though he had been a competent businessman of good earning capacity, was an alcoholic of a type I had come to regard as hopeless.

In the course of his third treatment he acquired certain ideas concerning a possible means of recovery. As part of his rehabilitation he commenced to present his conceptions to other alcoholics, impressing upon them that they must do likewise with still others. This has become the basis of a rapidly growing fellowship of these men and their families. This man and over one hundred others appear to have recovered.

I personally know scores of cases who were of the type with whom other methods had failed completely.

These facts appear to be of extreme medical importance; because of the extraordinary possibilities of rapid growth inherent in this group they may mark a new epoch in the annals of alcoholism. These men may well have a remedy for thousands of such situations.

You may rely on absolutely anything they may say about themselves.

Very truly yours,

William D. Silkworth, M.D.

The physician who, at our request, gave us this letter, has been kind enough to enlarge upon his views in another statement which follows. In this statement he confirms that we who have suffered alcoholic torture must believe – that the body of the alcoholic is quite as abnormal as his mind. It did not satisfy us to be told that we could not control our drinking just because we were maladjusted to life, that we were in full flight from reality, or were outright mental defectives. These things were true to some extent, in fact, to a considerable extent with some of us. But we are sure that our bodies were sickened as well. In our belief, any picture of the alcoholic which leaves out this physical factor is incomplete.

The doctor's theory that we have an allergy to alcohol interests us. As laymen, our opinion as to its soundness may, of course, mean little. But as ex-problem drinkers, we can say that his explanation makes good sense. It explains many things for which we cannot otherwise account.

Though we work out our solution on the spiritual as well as an altruistic plane, we favour hospitalization for the alcoholic who is very jittery or befogged. More often than not, it is imperative that a man's brain be cleared before he is approached, as he has then a better chance of understanding and accepting what we have to offer:

The doctor writes:

The subject presented in this book seems to me to be of paramount importance to those afflicted with alcoholic addiction.

I say this after many years' experience as Medical Director of one of the oldest hospitals in the country treating alcoholic and drug addiction.

There was, therefore, a sense of real satisfaction when I was asked to contribute a few words on a subject which is covered in such masterly detail in these pages.

We doctors have realized for a long time that some form of moral psychology was of urgent importance to alcoholics, but its application presented difficulties beyond our conception. What with our ultra-modern standards, our scientific approach to everything, we are perhaps not well equipped to apply the powers of good that lie outside our synthetic knowledge.

Many years ago one of the leading contributors to this book came under our care in this hospital and while here he acquired some ideas which he put into practical application at once.

Later, he requested the privilege of being allowed to tell his story to other patients here and with some misgiving, we consented. The cases we have followed through have been most interesting; in fact, many of them are amazing. The unselfishness of these men as we have come to know them, the entire absence of profit motive, and their community spirit, is indeed inspiring to one who has laboured long and wearily in this alcoholic field. They believe in themselves, and still more in the Power which pulls chronic alcoholics back from the gates of death.

Of course an alcoholic ought to be freed from his physical craving for liquor and this often requires a definite hospital procedure, before psychological measures can be of maximum benefit.

We believe, and so suggested a few years ago, that the action of alcohol on these chronic alcoholics is a manifestation of an allergy; that the phenomenon of craving is limited to this class and never occurs in the average temperate drinker. These allergic types can never safely use alcohol in any form at all; and once having formed the habit and found they cannot break it, once having lost their self-confidence, their reliance upon things human, their problems pile up on them and become astonishingly difficult to solve.

Frothy emotional appeal seldom suffices. The message which can interest and hold these alcoholic people must have depth and weight. In nearly all cases, their ideals must be grounded in a power greater than themselves, if they are to re-create their lives.

If any feel that as psychiatrists directing a hospital for alcoholics we appear somewhat sentimental, let them stand with us a while on the firing line, see these tragedies, the despairing wives, the little children; let the solving of these problems become a part of their daily work, and even their sleeping moments, and the most cynical will not wonder that we have accepted and encouraged this movement. We feel, after many years of experience, that we have found nothing which has contributed more to the rehabilitation of these men than the altruistic movement now growing up among them.

Men and women drink essentially because they like the effect produced by alcohol. The sensation is so elusive that, while they admit it is injurious, they cannot after a time differentiate the true from the false. To them, their alcoholic life seems the only normal one. They are restless, irritable and discontented, unless they can again experience the sense of ease and comfort which comes at once by taking a few drinks – drinks which they see others taking with impunity. After they have succumbed to the desire again, as so many do, and the phenomenon of craving develops, they pass through the well-known stages of a spree, emerging remorseful, with a firm resolution not to drink again. This is repeated over and over, and unless this person can experience an entire psychic change there is very little hope of his recovery.

On the other hand – and strange as this may seem to those who do not understand – once a psychic change has occurred, the very same person who seemed doomed, who had so many problems he despaired of ever solving them, suddenly finds himself easily able to control his desire for alcohol, the only effort necessary being that required to follow a few simple rules.

Men have cried out to me in sincere and despairing appeal: "Doctor, I cannot go on like this! I have everything to live for! I must stop, but I cannot! You must help me!"

Faced with this problem, if a doctor is honest with himself, he must sometimes feel his own inadequacy. Although he gives all that is in him. It often is not enough. One feels that something more than human power is needed to produce the essential psychic change. Though the aggregate of recoveries resulting from psychiatric effort is considerable, we physicians must admit we have made little impression upon the problem as a whole. Many types do not respond to the ordinary psychological approach.

I do not hold with those who believe that alcoholism is entirely a problem of mental control. I have had many men who had, for example, worked a period of months on some business problem or business deal which was to be settled on a certain date, favourably to them. They took a drink a day or so prior to the date, and then the phenomenon of craving at once became paramount to all other interests so that the important appointment was not met. These men were drinking to escape; they were drinking to overcome a craving beyond their mental control.

There are many situations which arise out of the phenomenon of craving which cause men to make the supreme sacrifice rather than continue to fight

The classification of alcoholics seems most difficult, and in much detail is outside the scope of this book. There are, of course, the psychopaths who are emotionally unstable. We are familiar with this type. They are always "going on the wagon for keeps." They are over-remorseful and make many resolutions, but never a decision.

There is the type of man who is unwilling to admit that he cannot take a drink. He plans various ways of drinking. He changes his brand or his environment. There is the type who always believes that after being entirely free from alcohol for a period of time he can take a drink without danger. There is the manic-depressive type, who is, perhaps, the least understood by his friends, and about whom a whole chapter could be written.

Then there are types entirely normal in every respect except in the effect alcohol has upon them. They are often able, intelligent, friendly people.

All these, and many others, have one symptom in common: they cannot start drinking without developing the phenomenon of craving. This phenomenon, as we have suggested, may be the manifestation of an allergy which differentiates these people, and sets them apart as a distinct entity. It has never been, by any treatment with which we are familiar, permanently eradicated. The only relief we have to suggest is entire abstinence.

This immediately precipitates us into a seething caldron of debate. Much has been written pro and con, but among physicians, the general opinion seems to be that most chronic alcoholics are doomed.

What is the solution? Perhaps I can best answer this by relating one of my experiences.

About one year prior to this experience a man was brought in to be treated for chronic alcoholism. He had but partially recovered from a gastric hemorrhage and seemed to be a case of pathological mental deterioration. He had lost everything worthwhile in life and was only living, one might say, to drink. He frankly admitted and believed that for him there was no hope. Following the elimination of alcohol, there was found to be no permanent brain injury. He accepted the plan outlined in this book. One year later he called to see me, and I experienced a very strange sensation. I knew the man by name, and partly recognized his features, but there all resemblance ended. From a trembling, despairing, nervous wreck, had emerged a man brimming over with self-reliance and contentment. I talked to him for some time, but was not able to bring myself to feel that I had known him before. To me he was a stranger, and so he left me. A long time has passed with no return to alcohol.

When I need a mental uplift, I often think of another case brought in by a physician prominent in New York. The patient had made his own diagnosis, and deciding his situation hopeless, had hidden in a deserted barn determined to die. He was rescued by a searching party, and, in desperate condition, brought to me. Following his physical rehabilitation, he had a talk with me in which he frankly stated that he thought the treatment a waste of effort, unless I could assure him, which no one ever had, that in the future he would have the "will power" to resist the impulse to drink.

His alcoholic problem was so complex, and his depression so great, that we felt his only hope would be through what we then called "moral psychology", and we doubted if even that would have any effect.

However, he did become "sold" on the ideas contained in this book. He has not had a drink for a great many years. I see him now and then and he is as fine a specimen of manhood as one could wish to meet.

I earnestly advise every alcoholic to read this book through, and though perhaps he came to scoff, he may remain to pray.

William D. Silkworth, M.D.[2]

NB: This opinion appeared in "Alcoholics Anonymous" (the Big Book) when it was first published in 1939. It has remained in the Big Book unchanged ever since.

PART ONE
The Problem

Chapter 1

How It All Began
Childhood and School Days
1936 - 1954

On 17th December 1982, after some thirty years of alcoholic drinking, I found myself at the age of almost forty seven being diagnosed for the first time as a chronic alcoholic. I had lost everything. A very frightened, broken man, I entered treatment for my illness of chemical dependency and alcoholism. Miraculously, I have not had a drink since that day. How then, from a promising start in life, did I manage to get into such a dreadful state? How did I manage to turn my life around? How have I been able to stay sober for the past twenty seven years and recover from this frightful, incurable and otherwise killer disease?

My earliest memory is of accompanying my father to collect his new 2 Litre MG motor car from University Motors just off Piccadilly in London. This was over seventy years ago in 1939, very shortly before the outbreak of war, when I was some three and a half years old. Even then I had a great interest in cars which persists to this day. With the advent of war, however, the lovely MG had to be put up on bricks and, for the duration of the war, my father and the family had to put up with a much smaller and more modest second hand Standard 8. In fact, we were very lucky to have a car at all, but my father was a doctor and needed it for his work. Petrol, though, was strictly rationed and almost all his mileage had to be accounted for.

My father, a Scot, met my English mother (they were both born in 1900) in the early thirties at the Edgware General Hospital in Middlesex where he was deputy medical director and she the sister tutor. They married in 1934 when my father was appointed the first medical director of the then brand new Hillingdon Hospital, also in Middlesex.

I was born in January 1936 in Hillingdon, in the same house in which we were to live for the next twenty-two years. My brother Donald followed seventeen months later in August 1937. As we were so close in age, I don't ever remember not having a brother. From quite early on, though, he was bigger than me and in the difficult war years, and for sometime thereafter, I do remember regularly having to wear the clothes that he had grown out of!

Throughout the war my father worked very long hours and we really only saw him for short periods and at weekends, although he did like to spend as much time with us as possible, and encouraged my brother and me to try most things, particularly games, in which he loved to take part. As was common in those days, my mother was a devoted full time wife and mum and, in spite of the war, we were a very happy and loving family. In the twenty-nine years I knew them both, I never heard my parents rowing. They did not agree on everything but if they did have rows they were never in front of Donald or me and they were both capable of laughing at themselves.

Yet despite all of this, there was a tension in the house which, quite simply, was due to the war. My earliest recollections, particularly during the Blitz, are of the 'black out', air-raid sirens, search lights flitting across the sky, sleeping night after night in the Anderson air raid shelter at the top of the garden, bombs dropping nearby (one night a part of the hospital only a quarter of a mile away was hit) and, towards the end of the war, the flying bombs or 'doodle-bugs' as they were commonly known. I remember one of them flying quite low in broad daylight and as it passed in front of the house its engine cut out; shortly thereafter, we heard it crash less than a mile away. Although living to the west of London we did not get anything like the bombing that hit the East End, it was all nonetheless quite frightening for a young boy still only nine years old when the war ended. As a result I learned that it was best always to play it safe, to stay below the parapet and not stick my head out further than was necessary. Yet I also always had the feeling that somehow no real disaster would befall us, a feeling that, despite all the apparent disasters that have since happened to me, I still have. I am inclined to optimism, a state of mind which is unusual in most alcoholics!

Throughout the war, food and clothes were strictly rationed and by today's standards life was very austere. There were no new toys or books so that what few Donald and I possessed were valued, treasured and well looked after. Even so, Christmases were keenly anticipated and very much enjoyed. The presents we received were mostly second hand, yet it did not seem to matter, probably because we did not know any differently. What I remember the most clearly about the war, however, was the great sense of community spirit, with people for the most part extraordinarily cheerful, united as we were against the common enemy, Adolph Hitler. Even for a child, this cheerfulness was typified by wireless programmes such as *It's that Man Again* (ITMA) with Tommy Handley and Mrs Mop with her catch phrase: 'It's bein' so cheerful as keeps me goin'.' And of course, the singing of Vera Lynn, with her still famous hits, *It's a Lovely Day Tomorrow, We'll Meet Again, There'll be Blue Birds Over the White Cliffs of Dover,* and many more. Other songs which come to mind were *Colonel Bogey* and *We're Going to Hang Out Our Washing on the Siegfried Line* (a reference to the second Siegfried Line, which was a defensive line of fortifications built in the 1930s by the Germans on their Western border opposite the similar French Maginot Line).

Each night, my parents would listen to the nine o'clock news on the wireless (as the radio was then called) and in the early part of the war it was generally bad. I was not able to fully understand it all, but I do remember how my parents seemed to be uplifted whenever Winston Churchill spoke to the country. There is absolutely no doubt in my mind that Churchill was the inspiration behind all of the war effort. Even in the darkest days, it was he who gave us hope and united us behind his leadership. I am sure we could not have won the war without the Americans, Russians and our other allies, but in those early days when we stood alone, it was Churchill whose indomitable spirit enabled us to avoid losing it – something which is not generally appreciated and which, if it is, is all too easily forgotten.

The war ended in May 1945, but, strangely, with the onset of peace, for which everybody had been fighting, the community feeling disappeared almost overnight, quickly to be replaced by greed, crime, strife, turbulence, disharmony and great malcontent, which in many ways, and in spite of huge material and technical advances, is still the case today. As a nine year old boy, I could not understand why peace, which we had so looked forward to, seemed to bring out the worst in people. Today, I believe it was because we had lost our common sense of primary purpose, our common enemy. The crisis of war, which had brought us all together, had passed. (I was to experience this sense of community in the face of a common foe again, however, nearly forty years later, when I became a member of Alcoholics Anonymous.)

My father was a member of Denham Golf Club some four or five miles away from our home. He first took Donald and me there soon after the war and we met the newly appointed golf professional, John Sheridan. There are a few people we have the good fortune to meet, who have a profound effect on us and are instrumental in making a difference in our lives; one such was John, not only on me but also on Donald. John had learnt his trade before the war as an assistant professional at Sunningdale, where his father was caddie master for over fifty years. He was of the old school and, having served in the army during the war, there was also a bit of the sergeant major about him. As young boys, Donald and I called him 'Sir'! He was, however, a kind and generous person as well as a very good golfer. In short, he was the perfect mentor for two young boys keen to learn how to play golf. It was he, more than anyone, who nurtured my love of the game which, despite my subsequent alcoholism, was to give me so much pleasure and enable me to make so many good lifelong friends. He himself was also to become a great friend until his sad death at the age of eighty six in 2005. He was professional at Denham for an astonishing fifty two years before he eventually retired in 1998, and never has a golf club been more faithfully served by one man. For me, Denham Golf Club *was* John Sheridan and I never went into the clubhouse without first going to his shop to say 'hello' to him if he was there. Throughout our teens, Donald and I used to cycle up to Denham to play golf almost every day during the school holidays. As a result we both became pretty good golfers.

But from a small boy, my greatest interest in life was anything with wheels on it. I treasured the second hand pedal car I had during the early part of the war, followed by several bicycles, culminating in my teens with a brand new Raleigh, fitted with cable brakes and Sturmey Archer three speed gears. Most of all, though, it was cars. I have always been passionate about them and from a very early age, when I was with my father as he drove on private roads, one of which he regularly used twice a week, I was allowed to lean across and steer the car for him. Later, I would always get the car out of the garage for him and in most instances put it away too. He also let me drive it on private roads whenever there was a chance. In short, I was crazy about cars and driving and could not wait to pass my test when I was seventeen. It was a long wait, during which I only ever had one driving lesson; it was on the day before my test, and was mainly to receive one or two tips about the *Highway Code* and go over the test course. At the end of the lesson my instructor told me, 'You should be fine; there's nothing I can teach you.' I duly passed and obtained my licence which, despite almost thirty years of alcoholic drinking, I have never lost.

I am sure that what I liked, and continue to like, so much about driving is that I am in total control of the vehicle. Assuming it is roadworthy, a car is one of the very few things that will, within certain limits, do whatever I tell it to do and go wherever I tell it to go. Whilst I have never been able to afford my dream car, I have owned or have had first use of no less than thirty-six different cars, some of which were classics. And when it comes to cars, it could be said that I have been very promiscuous; certainly I have fallen in and out of love with far more cars than I have women! I get a lot of pleasure out of them and great thrills and enjoyment from driving, especially in beautiful places which I would not otherwise be able to visit or see.

I remember very little of my earliest school days, but at age seven I went to Gayhurst Preparatory School for boys in Gerrards Cross, some seven miles from Hillingdon. My father took me and later my brother to school by car, picking up a number of boys along the way, and then we would return home on the bus. I was academically quite bright and invariably in the top half of the form in all subjects. By the time I left in 1949, I was also a member of the first eleven cricket and football teams and the first fifteen rugby team. I enjoyed school life and games and I still look back at those days with affection. Having easily passed my Common Entrance Exams (100% in arithmetic, algebra and geometry!), I left Gayhurst at the age of thirteen to go to Fettes in Edinburgh, where I was to spend the next five years, boarding.

My father had come to London after he graduated from St. Andrew's University in 1926. However, being Scottish, there was never any question about where he would send Donald and me to be educated. For my first few days at Fettes I felt quite homesick and abandoned which was natural, being away from home for the first time; it did not last long and I soon made one or two friends. However, I was a shy boy, reluctant to take risks (a result of the war years), and this was not helped by a sense of rejection I felt from the clannishness of the Scots boys. I had always been proud of my Scottish ancestry and ancestors (some of whom I believe originally came from the Western Isles). It therefore came as a great surprise to me that as an 'Anglo' I was somewhat looked down upon by most of the Scottish boys. I came to realize that for the most part the Scots do not like the English. Though kind and 'generously thrifty' as individuals, as a nation they have little affection for us, particularly 'Anglos' whom they seem to regard as being neither one thing nor the other. Nevertheless, I prospered relatively well. Schoolwork presented me with no undue problems, and though I would not say that there was no bullying, in my experience it was rare and I personally was never bullied.

I always felt an inner sense of superiority, however, whenever England beat Scotland at Murrayfield. When I was at Gayhurst I was considered a very promising rugby player, indeed I was vice-captain of the first fifteen, but at Fettes I disliked it and certainly did not excel at it. It is, of course, very much a macho, contact game, and it was this more than anything that I shied away from. (Even now, when I see it played on the television,

I cringe at the roughness and violence, and the physical punishment the players put their bodies through. I do not believe the human frame was designed to withstand this sort of treatment.) However, being a very good, proud and intense rugby school, we Fettesians always had to go to all the internationals at Murrayfield and I must confess that it gave me some pleasure and satisfaction to watch Scotland lose every match they played there during the five years I was at Fettes!

Perhaps I was mistaken in my opinion of the Scots, but nothing has since happened to cause me to alter my mind. And as a result of that early experience, I have always thought of myself as very much English first and Scottish second, although I love Scotland, which overall, and the weather apart, is the most varied and beautiful country I have ever been to.

By today's standard, life at Fettes was very tough. There was no central heating and even in winter we had cold showers every morning. In addition, rules were rules and discipline was very strict: there was fagging for the first two years and beatings as a form of punishment were common. Though it was not by any means an everyday occurrence, very few boys went through their school careers without being beaten at least once, but if we were caught doing wrong and were accordingly punished (I was beaten twice in five years) it was regarded as a fair cop and very much part of the game. It did us very little harm and by no stretch of the imagination do I consider I was abused by corporal punishment; on the contrary, I strongly believe that overall we emerged very much the better for experiencing this way of life.

We had to attend chapel every morning on weekdays, and every Sunday evening for the weekly service. Additionally, in house, we sang a hymn and said prayers every weekday evening for which I played the piano, being the only boy in the house who could do so. Being quite musical, I thoroughly enjoyed the congregational singing at chapel and occasionally the odd good sermon; and like many other boys of age fifteen or sixteen, I attended Church of Scotland confirmation classes. I did not particularly want to be confirmed but as almost everybody else seemed to be doing it, I went along with the crowd. But then, as confirmation day approached, the school chaplain made it clear that once confirmed I would be required to attend church every Sunday. That would interfere with my Sunday golf. I decided, therefore, that I was not ready to make the sacrifice and hence was not confirmed. At least, I thought, I am not being hypocritical. It was not that I did not believe but simply that I could not accept the terms. And so I turned my back on God and for the next thirty years or so 'did it my way'.

[7]

It was during one of the school holidays that I first tasted alcohol. There was always drink in the house as my father was regularly given bottles as presents from grateful patients, but my parents seldom drank and then only the smallest of amounts on social occasions. Indeed I think Mother positively disliked the stuff for I don't ever remember her fully emptying her glass. One Sunday lunch time, however, perhaps because there were guests present, drink was produced at the end of the meal and Father asked me if I would like to try some. Out of curiosity and probably to feel grown up I said I would. He poured me a thimbleful of Tia Maria, a coffee liqueur, and I shall never forget the effect that that one drink had on me. It gave me the most astonishing and wonderful WOW feeling of wholeness, euphoria, contentment and general well being; so much so that I not surprisingly asked for another, which Father gave me. And so from the very beginning, one drink led to another! It was a feeling – a high – that I have tried to recreate many times since, without success. (I know now that you can never recreate any initial high, because the wow factor, the element of surprise, can only present on the first occasion. Would that I had known that then!)

As I was to learn thirty years later, alcoholism is in part a disease of perception and my perception was changed with those first two drinks. It would have been no use to talk to me then about making sensible and informed choices (which today the so called alcohol and other drug experts are forever asking the young to make) because my mind was already made up. I had quite logically concluded that, because of its effect, drink was the answer to all my problems. I was brought up both at home and at school in a disciplined environment in which we were taught to have great respect for our elders and betters. (I dislike this term as very often it simply is not true. They may have been older and they may well have been more experienced and wiser, but they were not necessarily better.) 'Little children should be seen and not heard' was the mantra of the day, though to be fair to them, it was not one my parents used. We also had great respect for people in authority and consequently, like many others, I unconsciously put myself down by putting others up, which led to a certain degree of unjustified low self-worth. Although I knew I had talent, I did not have sufficient belief in myself to overcome serious self-doubt.

Low self-worth is a sense of inadequacy and all feelings of inadequacy are to greater or lesser degrees emotionally painful. My first drink took away that pain: briefly at least, I felt the equal of the grown-ups at that lunch table and in asking Father for another drink what I really was asking for was more of that feeling. Without my realising it, alcohol was acting as a *pain killer,* as it does for countless others who may be unaware of that aspect or won't admit it. Alcohol is an addictive drug, a pain killer from the same family of narcotic drugs as tranquillisers and heroin. And if it works, it is addictive!

In the nineteen fifties drinking and smoking were illegal for those under the age of eighteen and, unlike today, this law was much more strictly enforced and observed: no one would serve alcohol or cigarettes to anyone underage and certainly we were not allowed in pubs unaccompanied. It did not occur to me to question this and so, having tasted that first Tia Maria, I knew I would have to be patient and wait another two or three years before I could openly drink and smoke as much as I liked. Because of this, and little realising how stupid and immature I was being, I associated drinking and smoking with pleasure and being grown up. I would not say that I craved alcohol and nicotine or was in any way obsessed by them, but they were always there in the back of my mind as something to look forward to, and I really wanted to be eighteen. In the meantime those feelings of inadequacy and lack of self-belief continued to persist.

My main interests at school, rugby apart, were games, particularly cricket and to a lesser extent hockey; also golf, but I could really only play that in the holidays. At cricket I developed a passion for wicket keeping, probably because it involved having to concentrate on every ball when fielding. Godfrey Evans, the England wicket keeper of the day, was my mentor and it was his technique that I studied most. Inwardly I resolved to be in the school first eleven as soon as possible, but unfortunately there was a boy one year ahead of me who became the first eleven wicket keeper when he was only fifteen. He was the 'man in possession' and he was blocking my selection. Each year I tried hard to dislodge him and eventually in my penultimate year at school (and his last) I got my chance. I was selected to play in the two day match at the Founder's Weekend against the Old Boys. In the match I made no mistakes, had a total of eight victims behind the stumps and allowed no byes. For good measure I also scored twenty-four and twenty-five not out with the bat. I was delighted with my performance and was pretty certain that I had done more than enough to become a permanent member of the side. But at assembly the next morning, it was the other boy's name that was called out by the captain of cricket, and, with the whole school applauding, it was he who was awarded his first eleven colours. It was a huge disappointment, the more so as I very much wanted to join my younger brother Donald, who had already been justifiably selected for the team for the second year running as an opening batsman. I felt devastated, as if the stuffing had been knocked out of me. I hid my feelings, of course, but it was my first real experience of rejection and only one person, who some years later was coincidentally to die from alcoholism, sought to console me in any serious way. I wondered what on earth was the point of trying. Surely I had succeeded way beyond reasonable expectations. Of course, I was selected in my last year but even though I was then written up in *The Scotsman* newspaper as the best schoolboy wicket keeper in Scotland, it was little consolation for the rejection I, even then, still felt.

In 1953, when I was seventeen, I played golf in the Scottish Boys Championship at North Berwick and in the British Boys Championship at Dunbar. I lost in the second round on both occasions, though at Dunbar I beat a boy from Edinburgh Academy who was about to go up to Oxford and who won his 'blue' there in 1957.

At Fettes we all had to join the Combined Cadet Force in one of the three armed services. My first preference would have been for the air force but as my eyesight was not up to scratch for flying I opted for the army. In those days, we all had to face the prospect of doing two years compulsory National Service after leaving school or in some cases after university. Many Fettesians opted for one of the famous Scottish Infantry regiments but in 1953 we received a visit from a troop of the Royal Horse Guards, 'The Blues' (The Blues), as they were then known [in 1969 the regiment was amalgamated with the Royal Dragoons to become The Blues and Royals], who were on a recruiting drive for potential officers. We were taken by bus to somewhere in the Pentland Hills where we were shown their armoured cars and scout cars. With my love of all things on wheels, I was immediately won over. I was not daunted by the fact that they were the second senior regiment in the British Army and together with the Lifeguards formed the Household Cavalry and part of the Brigade of Guards; nor, for that matter, the fact that I had then never ridden a horse. The important thing was that they were not the infantry and that they were an armoured car regiment. Accordingly, I applied to join them as a prospective officer and was subsequently summoned for an interview with the Silver Stick, Colonel John Ward, in Whitehall. It all seemed very grand but he immediately put me at my ease, the interview went well and I was duly invited to join the regiment in September 1954 shortly after I was due to leave school.

I had always greatly admired and secretly envied my father and from quite an early age I had wanted to follow in his footsteps and be a doctor. Accordingly, at Fettes, I studied physics, chemistry and biology at both 'O' and 'A' level. My father, however, was not keen on the idea, mainly because, like many doctors at the time, he was not much in favour of the then relatively new National Health Service. If I understood him correctly, as a doctor in charge of a large general hospital, he considered the bureaucracy and general inefficiency to be unnecessarily expensive and not always in the best interests of the patients. So he did nothing to encourage me to go into medicine; but to be fair to him, he did not discourage me either.

My school housemaster duly arranged an interview with Dr C.L.G. Pratt, the Senior Tutor at Christ's College, Cambridge, in charge of undergraduate admissions, with a view to my reading medicine after I left school. The interview was shortly after my seventeenth birthday and what sticks in my mind most about the occasion was that, having obtained a provisional driving licence, it gave me the much longed for first opportunity to drive my father's car legally on public roads. So with the 'L' plates on the car and Father in the passenger's seat, I drove all the way from London to Cambridge. It was a great thrill and it made me feel more confident than perhaps might otherwise have been the case when I faced the formidable Dr Pratt.

'How did you get here?' was one of the first questions he asked.

'I drove up with my father,' I replied.

'Why didn't you bring him in?' he retorted.

'Because I did not think you would want to see him,' I said.

'Quite right!' he said. 'I don't!'

We both laughed and I was off to a good start. I remember little else about the interview except that I quite enjoyed it and felt that I had done all right, as was subsequently borne out when I was offered a place. (My brother was interviewed a year later by the same Dr Pratt. He was applying for a place at Christ's to read agriculture. As he was entering the room, Pratt threw some learned and obscure book at him saying, 'Have you ever read that?' Donald passed the first test by catching the book and the second by replying 'No'. 'Thought so,' said Pratt, 'you're a Fettesian aren't you?'! As I write in April 2009, Donald has just told me that only last month Dr Pratt died at the age of one hundred and two. He was some character.)

The more I studied physics, chemistry and biology, however, the more I began to realize that these subjects did not 'grab me'. The 'how' of science was of much less interest to me than the 'why' of human behaviour. I was also daunted, if not appalled, at the prospect of having to study for seven years before qualifying. It was a price I was not prepared to pay for something I did not really want to do anyway. As Cambridge were not prepared to offer me a place to read anything other than medicine, my housemaster quickly arranged for me to read politics, philosophy and economics at St. Edmund Hall, Oxford, in 1956, after I had completed my National Service.

There was a classroom at Fettes on one of the upper floors of the main college building which had a splendid and spectacular view over Edinburgh. During my last year at Fettes, I remember looking out at this view of the castle, Arthur's Seat and the Pentland Hills beyond and wondering what the future held for me. I had had quite a successful school career, far more so than many of my contemporaries, yet I still felt shy and, though it might outwardly have looked otherwise, I still lacked a sense of wholeness, of belief in myself. I had wanted to be grown up for a long time, mainly so that I could drink and smoke, and yet, now that I was eighteen and about to leave school, I was not quite so sure. How would I cope and what would become of me? Looking back, I can see that these feelings of uncertainty were made far worse because I had no real idea of what I wanted to do in life.

In his bestselling book *The Road Less Travelled*, first published in 1978, Dr M. Scott Peck writes: *'Of the thousands, maybe millions of risks we can take in a lifetime the greatest is the risk of growing up. Growing up is the act of taking a fearful leap into the unknown, undetermined, unsafe and unpredictable. It is a leap many people never really take in their lifetimes.'* Certainly it would seem to me that the world is full of adults who have never grown up! What I did not know, as I was about to leave school, was that alcoholism was to prevent me from growing up until I eventually began to risk doing so when I put down the drink in my mid-forties. In my final school report, my housemaster, Tom Goldie Scott, concluded with the words **'Billy is a survivor'**. I doubt he realized just how prophetic this comment was. Nonetheless it was, as, by the grace of God and despite my alcoholism and everything else, I am still surviving over fifty five years later.

Chapter 2

Learning to Drink
National Service
1954 - 1956

At the appointed hour on a sunny afternoon at the end of August 1954, Tony Pyman –another Old Fettesian who had been in the cricket eleven with me and who was joining The Lifeguards – and I duly reported for duty at the Household Cavalry's Combermere Barracks in Windsor. After being shown our barrack room over one of the stables and unpacking, we were told, much to our surprise, that we could go out for the rest of the evening provided we were back at 2200 hours. It was a lovely summer's evening so we walked the mile or two to Datchet where we had a few drinks in one of the pubs before walking back again. So far so good, I thought as I went to bed.

We were to spend a day or two at Windsor having medical checks, being issued with uniforms and other personal kit before being taken by truck to join the Brigade Squad at the notorious but long since defunct Guards' Training Depot at Caterham, where we were to receive six weeks' initial basic training. The Brigade Squad was a squad of twenty or so potential National Service officers who were hoping to be commissioned in one of the seven regiments making up the Brigade of Guards. All were exclusively from major public schools and some were titled nobility.

I knew that our training would be tough and intense, for the Guards training was and still is second to none. Just how tough, I was about to find out. On our first evening, we were introduced to Trained Soldier Smith who was to be responsible for helping us, generally keeping us in order, and ensuring that our barrack room was kept clean and tidy. He was also to show us how to clean our kit and how to do 'small circles' (a little polish and a lot of spit!) to shine our boots so that you could see your face in them. We were then introduced to our Drill Sergeant, one Sergeant Lewis of the Welsh Guards. Sergeant Lewis, though not as tall as many guardsmen, was, nonetheless, a formidable character whose first words to us, spoken in a very Welsh accent, were, 'You're not going to see your mummies for a very long time.' Like so many NCOs in the Brigade of Guards, his bark was worse than his bite but he stood no nonsense and by the end of our six weeks he had moulded us into a pretty impressive drill squad. Apart from a weekend leave half way through the six weeks, we were confined to barracks the whole time.

The Officer in charge of the Brigade Squad was Captain Erskine of the Scots Guards. We saw very little of him, but what I remember most about him was his brand new dark grey Jaguar XK 120 hardtop, in which he used to drive the short distance from the Officers' Mess to our barrack room hut. How I envied him the XK 120, which was then my dream car!

Almost every day consisted of two periods on the drill square and most of the time in the early days we were not drilled at the more normal speed of 120 paces to the minute, but at 180 paces to the minute. This pace is very fast and if you don't believe me, I suggest you go and try doing it. We also did some automatic weapons training with Bren and Sten guns and I seem to remember we threw a few hand grenades as well. This training was taken by an Irish Guards NCO who showed definite symptoms of hitting the bottle pretty hard on most evenings. We spent every evening cleaning our kit to an incredibly high standard.

Though far from being outstanding, I was a pretty good average and generally coped quite well and without getting into much trouble. On one particular day, though, which will remain indelibly in my memory until the day I die, we were being taught by the good Sergeant Lewis how to change arms on the march. This was an awkward and unnatural manoeuvre involving, while marching, the transfer of our 303 Lea Enfield rifles from the left shoulder to the right shoulder and then, later on, back again. Going from left to right was easy enough but getting it back again was for me an altogether more difficult proposition. The first time we tried it I ended up looking ridiculous with the rifle back on my left shoulder but held in my right hand. Having brought the squad to a halt, Sergeant Lewis slowly and patiently explained to me where I had gone wrong. We then tried it again, unfortunately with the same result.

'Squaaaad haaaaalt!' screamed the very irate Sergeant. '*YOU* are a waste of a good *FUCK*!

What are you?!' he yelled, his face only inches from mine.

'I am a waste of a good fuck,' I replied.

'*LOUDER! LOUDER*!' he screamed.

By this time the whole squad was laughing and although I could see the funny side of it, my ego was humiliatingly deflated and I felt very small. I have never since heard that expression, nor did I ever tell my mother about it!

The six weeks at Caterham went by pretty quickly and at the end I was as fit I have ever been before or since. If you can survive Caterham, you can survive anything! From Caterham we were transferred to Pirbright, also in Surrey and also a Guards' camp, which concentrated on aspects of training other than drill.

The commanding officer at Pirbright was Colonel A.A. Duncan of the Welsh Guards. He had been runner up in the British Amateur Golf Championship in 1939 and was a Welsh amateur golf international and many times former champion. He was also a member of the Oxford and Cambridge Golfing Society. Later on, I was to meet him on the golf course and play with him on a number of occasions. Although I knew who he was when I was under his command, he certainly did not know me.

Much of our time at Pirbright was spent doing route marches, training runs and assault courses, all of which I hated, while thanking the Lord that I was going on to an armoured car regiment and not the infantry. After a few weeks, we had to take our War Office Selection Board (W.O.S.B) exams at a camp in Barton Stacey, near Andover. There we underwent a series of tests designed to demonstrate our leadership qualities and general suitability as officer material. The tests concluded with an interview and as luck would have it, the colonel who interviewed me was a keen golfer. He must have been relieved to find someone else who played golf because we talked about Sunningdale and the Berkshire, where he was a member, and also about all the well known courses along the Forth Estuary east of Edinburgh, such as Gullane, Luffness, Muirfield and North Berwick. Suddenly the allotted time for the interview was up and there was no time to talk about anything else. As I saluted and left the room, he wished me luck. My golfing knowledge must have done enough to impress him as I was later informed that I had duly passed my W.O.S.B. tests, which meant that the time had then come to leave Pirbright and the Brigade Squad and transfer to Mons Barracks in Aldershot, the Officer Training School for National Servicemen in non-infantry regiments.

At Mons we became Officer Cadets and met up with cadets from other armoured corps regiments and other non-infantry corps. Our particular squadron was under the command of Major Fane Harvey of the Royal Tank Regiment, a somewhat humourless man who took himself and his soldiering very seriously, though, funnily enough, he too played golf. On one occasion he invited three of us to play golf with him at the North Hants Golf Club in Fleet where he was a member and which I had never previously played. So, armed with borrowed clubs and plimsoll shoes, we set out. At one hole I asked him for the best line to take off the tee, to which

[15]

he replied in typically military fashion, 'You see that bushy topped tree on the horizon, come left and minus of it and there is a hut, go three o'clock right and you'll see a large bush. That's your line.'! It was difficult to keep a straight face but it was kind of him to ask us to play and afterwards we had 'high tea' which he paid for, unless of course he was able to charge both the tea and the green fees to military expenses. An added bonus was that I felt we knew him better and, more importantly, that he knew us better.

Our Regimental Sergeant Major was RSM Smy of the Coldstream Guards. Two weeks earlier, he had succeeded the notorious RSM Britain, who had retired after many years in the job. On the first or second day he addressed our new intake and at the end of his talk he told us that we were 'a lot of idle, lazy, good-for-nothing gentlemen. I call you "Sir" and you call me "Sir". The only difference is that you mean it!' I suspect that this anecdote is as old as the hills but this was the first time I had heard it and I thought it was quite funny.

One of the good things about Mons was that we had weekend leave and Tony Pyman, Christopher Normand and I used to spend most weekends at my parents' home in Hillingdon. Christopher was another old Fettesian who was in the Royal Signals. Tony and I met him late one night when on our guard duty rounds we found him with his light on. Typically, and putting it politely, he remonstrated, but after a few laughs we did persuade him to put it out. On many weekends we were joined by Kenny MacKinnon, another Old Fettesian from Oban, who was then in the navy, training to become a mid-shipman. Mother and Father were very good hosts and the weekends were a lot of fun but for me it was lovely simply to be back in civilisation again, if only for forty-eight hours. The worst thing about the weekends was arriving back in Aldershot. There is nothing more depressing than waiting for a taxi around midnight at Aldershot railway station on a cold, wet, winter Sunday evening.

Fast forwarding a little, speaking of Kenny MacKinnon reminds me of 'McTavish' (see photograph), an everlasting greetings card which has gone backwards and forwards between us every Christmas since 1960, with a couple or so of exceptions when he must have got mislaid. So this last Christmas (2009) was his fiftieth – a remarkable record especially in view of my alcoholism. There are a number of boxes apart from 'Christmas' that can be ticked, Kenny's ruby wedding anniversary in 2003, for instance. But mostly it is at Christmas that he makes his annual journey between Oban and London and vice versa. In the early days we would write messages in pencil but, over the years, he got worn thin from the previous year's message being rubbed out, so this practice has long since had to cease. We also had to patch him up with Sellotape to keep his two halves together and the Sellotape has now become dark sepia in colour. He has become a treasured joint possession whose care and safe keeping is lovingly entrusted each to the other every alternate year. Now that Kenny and I are both well into our seventies, I am pretty certain McTavish is going to outlast us both. Like me, McTavish is a survivor!

At Mons much of our training was on tanks and gunnery. At that time, I believe the Lifeguards and The Blues were the only armoured car regiments left in the British Army, so we had no armoured car training at all. Part of the Mons training was a visit to the ranges at Lulworth Cove in Dorset to fire twenty-five pounder shells from a Centurion tank. I was looking forward to this but when my turn came to fire the gun, I carelessly got the sequence wrong and fired at the wrong moment with my shell probably ending up in the sea. This was not good news and even though it was the first major mistake I had made, I was nonetheless put back for two weeks and made to do it all again. One of the Blues' officers from Windsor came down to see us and when it came to my turn to see him, he told me in no uncertain terms that if it were to happen again I would go straight back to Windsor, *as a trooper!* Second time around all went well and I managed to hit the right target, having diligently followed the correct firing procedures. I duly passed out (I use the term advisedly and in the strict military sense) and received my commission on the fifth day of the fifth month, 1955, just three days before the tenth anniversary of the ending of the Second World War in Europe.

A couple of weeks later, after some well earned leave, I joined the regiment at Windsor and was introduced to my servant or batman as they were more commonly called, whom I shared with two of the other subalterns. I was also introduced to my brother officers, only a few of whom I knew. I was put in charge of an armoured car troop in B Squadron and my Squadron Leader was Major Dick Dickinson, with whom I got on well. He was a very keen games player and that summer I played a lot of cricket, keeping wicket for the regiment, which I very much enjoyed. Our military activities were strictly limited as it was nearly impossible to take armoured cars out on public roads without prior approval from the local authorities. We did, however, have a couple of days camping at Climping near Goodwood and twice we went to the races. It was my first experience of racing and to this day, Goodwood remains by far the most beautiful race course I have been to.

Soon after I arrived at Windsor we received a lecture on etiquette from an incredibly pompous captain. Some of the best bits I remember him mentioning were that The Blues was the only regiment in the British Army who could carry swords in Royal Palaces and also the only regiment who could salute without having a hat on. (This was something that I had earlier enjoyed being picked up on at Mons as it was rather like being breath tested when one hadn't had a drink!) When wearing plain clothes in London, – he refused point blank to call them 'civvies' – we must wear a plain dark grey suit, stiff white collar and bowler hat, and carry a rolled umbrella. Nor were we on any account to push perambulators! I wonder how the Princes William and Harry would have coped with some of that lot.

Prior to being commissioned, I hardly drank at all as there was little opportunity for it. Smoking was a different matter and I was soon on at least twenty cigarettes a day and well and truly hooked. At Windsor, however, at 12.30 pm on most days, we would repair to the Officers' Mess for a couple of glasses of sherry before lunch; drinking sherry seemed to me to be so very civilised. It was here that my drinking career really began, since most evenings were spent in the mess and I rarely went out. My pay as a 2nd Lieutenant or Cornet as we were called in The Blues was thirteen shillings and sixpence a day, the equivalent of sixty seven and a half pence in today's money – less than £250 per annum. It did not go far and not for the first time I found it a struggle to live within my means. Even so, I managed to do more than my fair share of drinking and I very quickly developed a high tolerance for alcohol. I sometimes got drunk but no more so than many of the others and it rarely seemed to matter. Drinking was very much a part of the culture in those days and for all I know, it probably still is. The two glasses of sherry or gin and tonic at lunchtime always made me feel relaxed and at least the equal of the more senior and far richer officers. As I have already said, I loved drinking from the word go and quickly was secretly very proud of the amount I could drink without appearing drunk. Unlike some who drink for oblivion, and it would seem that nowadays this is more and more the case, I hated going one over the eight as I loved the feeling, as I thought, of being in control and one under the eight. If I got really drunk I regarded it as failure – a failure to drink the other person under the table.

Although Windsor was only seven or so miles from home, I deemed it essential to have a car and managed to persuade my father to buy me a lovely but well used 1933 Riley 14/6 Stelvio from a fellow Old Fettesian for

£100. This does not seem a lot now but looking back it might well have been too much. Never mind, it was a vintage car and, in its way, a classic one as well. As well as a starter motor, it had an often used crank handle, a long bonnet, a windscreen which opened, cable brakes, a spare wheel mounted on the back, inflatable leather seats and a four speed crash gear box having no synchromesh of any of the gears. Having to double de-clutch was mandatory when changing down and as often as not I did it changing up as well. The 'H' gate for the gear lever was also unusual in that it was the reverse way round to practically all other cars, so that first gear was where third gear normally is and vice versa. This I soon mastered and what I loved about the car was that I felt that nobody could get in it and immediately drive it anything like as well as I could. I remember Father having a go one day and making an awful mess of it.

The Riley was looked after for me by Corporal of Horse Young who was a wizard with cars and this was probably why he was in charge of all regimental vehicle maintenance. One day, whilst driving home, the brake cable connecting the brakes on all four wheels snapped so that I was completely without brakes apart from a rather feeble hand brake. In 1955 there was nothing like the traffic on the roads that there is now but even so, it is extraordinary how little you need to use your brakes when you know you don't have any. I easily got back to home and then to Windsor by looking well ahead, making judicious use of the gear box and occasional use of my feeble hand brake. Actually it was great fun!

Occasionally, one or two of us would go up to London in the evenings and one of our regular haunts was a night club just behind Liberty of London in Regent Street. It was called the Bag of Nails or, as we sometimes referred to it, the Sack o' Tacks! It was a membership only club but the girls were extremely attractive and well spoken. It was with one of these girls, Susie, that at the ripe old age of nineteen, I lost my virginity, or as you might say in cricketing parlance, I broke my duck and got off the mark. She was a lovely girl and having taken her telephone number, I saw her two or three times subsequently but unfortunately I lost touch with her after I came back from Cyprus. I well remember one evening there when our colonel was also in the club with a lady who certainly wasn't his wife, and the following day, back at Windsor, he bollocked us because we were wearing suits and not dinner jackets! How times have changed!

Throughout my time at Windsor, I knew that in January 1956 the regiment was due to be stationed in Cyprus and take over from the Lifeguards, who were then stationed both there and in Suez. Prior to our departure, we had a regimental farewell ball to which the young Queen, our Colonel in Chief and then not four years on the throne, Prince Philip and the Princesses Margaret and Alexandra were invited. The Officers' Mess in which the ball was duly held was a somewhat scruffy venue, badly in need of re-decoration and general refurbishment. Nevertheless, it was deemed to be fit for the Queen. Although dress was white tie and tails, I suppose the ball was about as informal as it could be with the Monarch present. Certainly with the low level of lighting, perhaps to hide the scruffiness of the mess, it could in no way be described as a glittering and grand occasion. I remember thinking how young and stunning Princess Margaret looked as, glass in hand, she drew on her trade mark cigarette holder, though personally I thought that Princess Alexandra was overall the more attractive. As for me and my 'princess', we managed to accidentally bump into Her Majesty on the dance floor and I don't suppose there are many people who can say that! For the record, we were not locked up in the Tower; indeed, the Queen seemed quite unconcerned.

Two or three days after the ball we were off to Cyprus. It was a fine January morning and I well remember the regiment marching proudly through the streets of Windsor to the station. There we embarked on a specially chartered train to go to Liverpool, where the troopship, MV Devonshire, was waiting to take us to Cyprus. On the train one of the subalterns produced a bottle of whisky and we had a few drinks. I was careful not to drink too much but by the time we reached Liverpool I was feeling distinctly woozy. There are good days and bad days with alcohol and to my surprise this was certainly not one of my better ones as I really had not drunk very much. I gritted my teeth, kept myself together and by the time I boarded ship, I was feeling fine again. The voyage was to take twenty-one days, a long time to be cooped up in a crowded ship with little in the way of entertainment. It turned out to be both memorable and enjoyable for me, however, because the ship's doctor was a Scottish bridge international who very kindly took me and two other subalterns under his wing and taught us Acol and how to play bridge. Each day we would spend two or three hours playing in the morning, afternoon and evening. He was very kind and patient and it was a marvellous way to spend what would otherwise have been a very boring and excessively boozy trip. We were not, however, by any means abstinent, having a couple or so drinks during each playing session. Nevertheless, by the time we reached Cyprus, we were pretty good players, and this was to stand me in good stead for later on.

Shortly after crossing the Bay of Biscay, I went up on deck at around midnight to find that for some reason we had dropped anchor off Gibraltar. From my vantage point on the Devonshire in the bay, affording me an unusual view from the south looking northwards, I was astonished and surprised by the truly magnificent sight of the floodlit rock. It was a sight I shall never forget. I have been to Gibraltar many times since but it never has it looked as stunning as it did that first time.

At the end of the twenty-one days we docked at Famagusta and disembarked. At this point the regiment split up, with Headquarters and A Squadron going to Nicosia while C Squadron stayed in Famagusta and we in B Squadron went to Limassol. The journey to Limassol took a couple or so hours and on the way we passed the Lifeguards' convoy coming in the opposite direction to pick up the Devonshire which was to take them back to England. I clearly remember seeing Tony Pyman sitting in the front of one of the trucks. Also travelling in the convoy was Nicky Winter whom I had not then met but of whom more later.

Our camp in Limassol, where we slept under canvas, was a short distance from the town proper. As officers we had quite large tents with proper beds and they were quite comfortable, apart from the sun bearing down on them in the mornings, which made them very hot, becoming almost unbearable in the summer.

It was the time of EOKA terrorists, and Cyprus was rightly classified as a war zone. Archbishop Makarios and Colonel George Grivas were in their element causing a lot of trouble. Today it is often forgotten that during the Cyprus campaign 371 British Servicemen were killed in Cyprus. This compares with 255 in the Falklands War and, as of May 2010, 179 in Iraq and 285 in Afghanistan. Of course, we did not have the publicity that troops have today and certainly there was nothing like the television coverage.

There were about four times as many Greek Cypriots as there were Turkish Cypriots and their respective villages were all mixed up and dotted around in the same numerical proportions. I found it impossible to tell a Greek Cypriot from a Turkish one, individually, but in the villages it was very clear: when we drove through a Greek village, the villagers appeared hostile and were liable to throw stones at us; whereas, in a Turkish village, they waved flags and cheered us. To one lot we were the enemy and to the other we were friends.

Now that we were in Cyprus my pay as a 2nd Lieutenant amounted to one pound, seven shillings and sixpence a day, which included 'danger money', and, for the first and last time in my life, I had more money than I knew what to do with, mostly because the opportunities to spend it were limited: when we first arrived, everywhere outside of barracks was out of bounds and in any event, except on military duty, we rarely if ever got out of our barrack camp. Our messing fee (food) was two shilling and sixpence a day (twelve and a half pence), a red tin of twenty Benson & Hedges cost a shilling (five pence) and a tot of whisky sixpence (two and a half pence). You could smoke all you liked and drink yourself silly and still you would not have spent anything approaching a pound.

After a week or so, I was seconded with my troop to No. 45 Commando, Royal Marines, who were stationed an hour or so away quite high up in the Troodos Mountains in a village called Platres, which was not far below the snow line that existed in the winter months – in early spring it was easily possible to ski and swim both in the same day. Our function with the Marines was to provide reconnaissance and escort support. I had received training in neither! No matter, we learned on the job, which is always the best way. My troop was billeted in a hut which, under the direction of my gallant Corporal of Horse Sampson, they repainted and in Guards' tradition made to look very smart. Though he was newly promoted to the rank of Corporal of Horse (In the Household Cavalry, a Corporal of Horse is equivalent rank to a Sergeant elsewhere in the British Army.) Sampson was a veteran of the war and I was happy to leave him to take care of most things. He was a Geordie, could and often did knock back a few in the N.C.O.'s mess, and we got on pretty well. He never actually said, 'Forget all you have been taught, Sir, and listen to me.' But as I was a twenty year old subaltern on active service for the first time, he might just as well have!

I lived in a separate hut next to Costa's Bar and spent most of my time in the Royal Marine's Officers' Mess, which was in a small requisitioned hotel called the Splendide. The first time I entered the mess I was greeted by a red faced captain who told me that the Marines knew how to drink and that I should be careful. This of course was like a red rag to a bull and thereafter I settled down to drink as well as they did! And as we were often confined to barracks for quite long periods, I spent a lot of time playing bridge and drinking in the mess.

I enjoyed being with 45 Commando but I missed my own mates in Limassol and looked forward to Dick Dickinson's weekly visit to see how we were getting on. We would usually spend a good hour or more in Costa's Bar nattering about things in general. While I was in Platres, I also had a visit from our colonel, the then Marquess of Douro and now Duke of Wellington. It was the first time I had really talked to him and I found him much nicer and less intimidating than he was at Windsor. We also had a visit from the Chief of the Imperial General Staff, Field Marshall Sir John Harding (later to become Lord Harding) who was the recently appointed Governor of Cyprus. He was a lovely man and in the mess before lunch he ignored the more senior officers in favour of spending his time talking to the subalterns.

Being up in the natural terrorist country of the mountains where it was easy for them to hide, ambushes were quite common. On one occasion the marines had got word that they were planning one at a certain time and place and, as we had armoured protection and there were also members of 45 Commando hiding in the hills to protect us, we were ordered to drive along the road where the proposed ambush was to take place. I remember thinking that in these circumstances it was most unlikely there would be any ambush, though there was always the possibility of being blown up by a road side bomb. Nevertheless, feeling a bit scared, I gave the order for my troop to proceed and, with guns loaded, we drove slowly through the ambush point only to come out the other side completely unharmed. There was not a terrorist anywhere in the vicinity and I was quickly learning that fighting terrorists is very, very difficult. Unless intelligence is absolutely spot on, you always have to wait for the terrorist to strike first and even then you have no idea when or where this going to be. In Cyprus they were probably everywhere and they were unrecognisable.

One night, we were awakened and called out to the scene of an ambush in the unrealistic hope of capturing the terrorists. They had already bolted, but one of the casualties was a Marine I knew quite well and with whom I had played bridge. He was seriously injured and we did not know whether he would survive. One of the terrorists had been killed in the attack and later the next morning I saw him; with rigor mortis having set in, his legs were sticking straight out of the back of a Land Rover. His was the first dead body I had ever seen. As I looked at him, I saw evil and, to my surprise, I could not find an ounce of sympathy for him. On the contrary and for the first and last time in my life, I felt real hatred in me and I did not like it. War is a terrible thing and can do strange things to people. In some ways I can understand why people might react badly to violence and then do terrible things themselves; I am now much slower to condemn or to apportion blame. In 1956 the Greeks and Turks were at war with each other and 54 years later, they still are. Although the island is now partitioned and both sides want to join the European Union, they still can't really get on with each other. I find this very sad and I often wonder why it should be so difficult for man to live in peace and harmony. The expression 'live and let live' seems pertinent. If everyone were to do this, there would be few if any problems.

Shortly after this experience, my appendix flared up and I was taken to BMH Nicosia to have it removed. It had grumbled a bit before I went to Cyprus but the doctors thought it would be all right and they could deal with it when I got home after being demobbed. My surgeon was an army doctor who funnily enough knew my father. The operation went well but two days later I was joined in hospital by two members of my troop who had been wounded in an ambush the previous night. Happily they were not seriously hurt. Call it fate that I was not there, but in many ways I was sorry to have missed the ambush in this way. In other ways, of course, I was very glad.

I was in hospital for a week and then I was given two weeks' convalescent leave. The problem was, where to go: Suez was out because of the political situation (Nasser was about to seize the canal) and somehow Beirut did not appeal at that time. In the end I decided to fly home as, even taking the cost of the flight into account, it was probably the least expensive option. Having got a seat on the twice weekly evening flight, I somehow managed to get word to my parents that I would be arriving at Heathrow the following morning. I was very excited because I was flying for the first time and the aircraft was the brand new BEA Vickers Viscount four engined Turbo Prop. During the eleven hour flight, the plane was almost empty and I was waited on royally by three very attractive and flirtatious air stewardesses. We stopped to refuel at Athens and Rome. Leaving Rome just after dawn we flew low over the Alps and I shall never forget the sight of the snow just beneath us glistening pink in the rising sun. It was very beautiful, indeed it was magical. No flight that I have ever made since has compared with my first one.

I duly arrived at Heathrow, which then amounted to little more than a few pre-fabricated huts, where my anxious parents were awaiting me. I had forgotten to tell them why I was coming home and they were quite relieved when I told them I had had my appendix out. They naturally were pleased to see me and I them and as it happened I had a very good fortnight. They were about to go to Scotland to see my brother at Fettes for the Founder's weekend. Donald by that time was in his last term but he was Head of School and Captain of Cricket for the second year running. It was two years since I had last played in the two day match of the school against the Old Fettesians and I almost wished that I was playing too. For the record, Donald made a hundred and it was good to see him again. For some reason that I can't now remember, we went home via Wales and I was well enough to play golf with Father at Royal Porthcawl, where Donald was later to play for England. Porthcawl is a very fine golf course and it has the added bonus of some beautiful views across the Severn Estuary to Somerset.

My two weeks' leave flew past and I was soon back at Heathrow for the flight back to Cyprus and my last few weeks in The Blues. The aircraft was again the beautiful Viscount, but this time it only flew as far as Athens, where we were transferred to an aging Dakota. Still, the Dakota was a very famous aircraft and had been a real work horse during and after the war, especially during the Berlin blockade. I am glad, now, that I had the opportunity to fly in one, though after the Viscount it was decidedly slow, bumpy and uncomfortable. By the time we reached Cyprus, it was dark and as we flew low over the mountains on our approach to Nicosia airport, we saw the strangely beautiful yet terrifying sight of forest fires (in which a number of Gordon Highlanders lost their lives) raging bright orange just below us.

When I got back to the Regiment it seemed that as I was due to be demobbed anyway in a few weeks time, I had become surplus to requirements, so I went up to Kyrenia for a few days and stayed in a flat rented by the regiment and overlooking the famous harbour. I also managed to contact Christopher Normand who was serving in the Royal Signals in Nicosia, where his parents lived and had a house. It was good see him again a year or more after Mons and I particularly remember a very good picnic we had with his parents in the foothills of the Troodos Mountains.

The day came to return home and be demobbed, but as we arrived at Akrotiri airport for the flight home, it was evident that all was not well and that something was afoot. What had happened, of course, was that troop movements were being planned prior to Sir Anthony Eden's eventual decision to invade Suez; consequently, all troop planes were being grounded. There was a lot of confusion but we eventually took off for Tripoli in Libya, where we were due to refuel. Having reached Tripoli, however, we were informed that we were well and truly grounded and would be delayed indefinitely. We were put up in one of the British camps and for almost two weeks, while the British Government made a fool of itself over Suez, we daily awaited news as to when we might get home. It was very hot and we tended to stay in bed until lunchtime, and then go the Officers' Club in the afternoon, prior to going on the town in the evening. We played snooker, one day, and had a few drinks before going out to dinner. I really don't think I drank all that much but after arriving in a restaurant for dinner, all I can vaguely remember before waking up in bed the following morning is being in the back of a Military Police Land Rover and then being delivered to the camp where we were staying, mumbling to one of the Blues officers to 'fix the M.P.s'. It was the first time that I had ever completely passed out. In reality I had over-dosed on alcohol; it was an ominous warning, and it gave me a big fright which, of course, I subsequently ignored, denied and forgot about. It was not something I wanted to remember – and for many years I did not.

Eventually, we managed to get on a flight and we arrived back in England at Blackbush Airport in Hampshire, thus ending two very interesting and at times exciting years in the British Army. Overall, it had been a great experience that I would not have missed for the world. I had seen active service and although I had known it was possible to be killed, - a number of my comrades were - I somehow had never believed it would be me; indeed it later came as quite a surprise to hear my mother saying how worried she and Father had been.

Chapter 3

Alcoholism in Disguise
Oxford
1956 - 1959

In the month or so between leaving the army and going up to Oxford, I spent much of my time at Denham, playing golf, as more than anything I wanted to get a 'Golf Blue' out of Oxford.

Early in October 1956 I arrived at St Edmund Hall to begin three years at the university. St Edmund Hall or 'Teddy Hall' as it was and still is more affectionately called, has one of the smallest but most beautiful quadrangles of all the Oxford colleges. I was given a room on the second floor in a relatively newly converted residential block which directly overlooked the High Street. In those days there were no by-passes around Oxford so, for much of the night, heavy lorries would noisily rumble past on their journeys through the town. I did not sleep a wink the first night and I wondered how I was going to cope with this intolerable noise. Strangely enough, however, that first night was the only night I noticed them and thereafter I slept very well. You can get used to almost anything!

It had been agreed at school that I would read politics, philosophy and economics (P.P.E.) probably for want of anything better to read. But I found little interest in any of them and because of this work was pretty tedious and boring. What I was most interested in was golf and straight away I entered for the university golf trials at Southfield, where the first golf club was formed in 1875 by university graduates. The course itself is a good one with two or three very good holes, though back in the nineteen fifties it was very muddy in winter and, like many courses, was nothing like as well maintained as it is today. The golf professional was F.H. (Fred) Taylor, a relative of J.H. Taylor, one of 'The Great Triumvirate'. I only ever had one lesson from him and he told me I had lazy feet! To this day I am not quite sure what he meant and I certainly did not take much notice.

Although I did not do as well as I had hoped in the trial, which consisted of thirty-six holes medal play, I was subsequently invited to play for the Divots, the university second team. As eight of the 1956 Blues side were still up at Oxford, I had no real chance of getting into the first side anyway, so I was not too disappointed. What really did disappoint me was that having played for the Divots in three fixtures against outside clubs and winning all six of my matches, I was never asked to play again. This disappointment was all the more intense because I also played for Teddy Hall in the inter-collegiate 'Cuppers' competition against Brasenose and I beat Harvey Douglas, the captain of the university golf team, by one hole. (Walking round with us that day was Harvey's flat mate Michael G. who I was to meet again in the mid-eighties in AA since when we have become old friends.) It seemed like Fettes all over again when I was trying to get into the first eleven cricket team as a wicket keeper. Perhaps my face did not fit, and although I felt the same sense of injustice, this time I did not let it get to me. It was the Blues side I really wanted to play in and there was no realistic chance of that until the following year.

In my second year, after practising and playing a lot in the summer vacation and getting my handicap down to 1, I won the university golf trials. As I stood on the tenth tee in the second round level par, I was approached by John Littlewood, who was Secretary that year. Instead of asking how I was getting on, he said, 'Have you got a car?' I knew then that I would get an invitation to play the following weekend against Royal Wimbledon and, if memory serves me correctly, against Temple near Maidenhead, where the trees were magnificent in rich shades of red and gold in the autumnal sunshine.

Incidentally, the car that I then had was a 1939 Standard Nine, the Riley Six which I had at Windsor having suffered a cracked cylinder block when I was in Cyprus and to my disappointment Father had disposed of it without my knowledge. Still, I managed to persuade him that a car was essential at Oxford, particularly if I were to play golf, and the Standard 9 was the result. Being second hand it had seen better days, but although it was very slow with a practical maximum speed of around forty miles per hour, it was nonetheless quite reliable and I can't recall it ever letting me down. Like the Riley it had no heater so in the winter when the university played their golf, it could be very cold. Overcoats, gloves and occasionally rugs were the order of the day, something one is inclined to forget as we drive around in our modern cars of today, taking for granted all their climate controls, automatic transmissions, sat navs and other luxury equipment.

Though I took it seriously, playing golf for Oxford was the greatest possible fun. Every weekend throughout the winter we would play two matches against most of the best clubs in the London area. We also played the Oxford and Cambridge Golfing Society and 'The League', a very strong scratch side assembled each year by Raymond Oppenheimer, (himself an old pre-war Oxford Blue) to play ourselves and Cambridge. Not only did we play on these very good courses but we played against some of the best amateurs in the country. All of this was the build up for the Varsity Match against Cambridge in late March. On a historical note, both university golf clubs were founded in 1875, three years before the first match was played between them on 6th March 1878 at Wimbledon Common. Since then it has been played in the spring of every year except for 1881 (an exceptionally hard winter) and the war years, 1915 to 1919 and 1940 to 1945. The historical significance of the Varsity Match in the context of amateur golf is important as the match can claim the distinction of being the oldest established amateur event in the golfing calendar. In spite of the seriousness with which the match is taken, a great camaraderie develops that extends through the Varsity Match to the Oxford and Cambridge Golfing Society, whose members comprise the old blues of both universities. The Society celebrated its centenary in 1998 and commemorated the event with the publication of a book, *100 Years of Serious Fun*. To my mind this title encapsulates the nature of university and society golf: serious, yet fun, and occasionally very funny!

In 1958 the match was at Rye and my brother Donald was playing for Cambridge. Each side consisted of ten players and on the first day we played thirty-six holes of foursomes followed by thirty-six holes of singles on the second day. Being the first and only brothers ever to have been on opposing Oxford and Cambridge golf sides, Donald and I attracted quite a lot of Press comment, the more so because we were drawn to play against each other in the foursomes. Mother and Father, together with some other family members and friends, turned up to watch but to this day I do not know which side they were supporting. It was bitterly cold with a fairly strong east wind blowing, so much so that I wore my 'British Warm' from army days and just took it off when it was my turn to play a shot. This caused a certain amount of disapproval in some quarters but I would do it again as it kept me a lot warmer than any of the other players. It was a match I very much wanted to win as I did not want to be beaten by my younger brother. Modesty prevents me from saying who won the match, but the next day's *Scotsman* reported of the two Old Fettesian brothers: 'Elder brother and economics student William was naturally more sparing in his stroke expenditure than agricultural student Donald...' Despite the cold weather, it was a great two days, and for the record, Cambridge won overall by eight matches to seven.

After the Varsity Match, six of us from Oxford went on a Scottish Tour, playing against most of the Scottish universities. We played on some of the great Scottish links courses all for free, not realising how lucky we were as today you can't play a round on any of these courses between 1ˢᵗ April and 31ˢᵗ October for less than £120, and some them cost a lot more than that.

In the fifties, it was also usual for some members of the Oxford and Cambridge teams to make a tour on the continent in the long summer vacation, but in 1958 none of the Cambridge team could make it. The cost of this tour was about £120 and I managed to persuade my father to fund half of the cost, providing I found the other half by working. As it happened I got a job for six weeks, helping to build the new maternity block at Hillingdon hospital for the princely sum of £10 per week. For most of the time I had a fairly cushy job driving a dumper truck but I mucked in and got on pretty well with the men. The talk was of three things only: football, even though it was summer, sex and politics. The six weeks passed quickly and when I left Father was surprised to be told by the site foreman that he would have me back any time I wanted.

On the tour itself, we were royally treated. At that time, not much golf was played on the continent and what was played was only by a small, rich and privileged elite. Six of us travelled out there in three cars, first to St Moritz in Switzerland, where we stayed for free at the renowned Palace Hotel and played in the Engadine Amateur Championship. As, however, there were only eight in the field, of which we were six, being a quarter finalist is not quite as good as it may sound. From St Moritz we broke the journey to Villa d'Este and played at Menaggio where Ted Dexter's father was an influential member. Menaggio is a delightful little course in the foothills of the Alps on the western shores of Lake Como in Northern Italy. Although it measured only 4,370 yards, the course was great fun and had seven short holes, one of which was blind even though it was only seventy-five yards long! After the game, Ted, who had been Captain of the Cambridge side at Rye a few months earlier and was later to become the distinguished England cricket captain, invited us back to his father's house for drinks before we continued our journey south to the famous Villa d'Este Hotel at Cernobbio, which was also on the western shores of Lake Como. The hotel was in a magnificent position on the lakeside and they only charged us a nominal amount to stay but we did have to pay for our food and drinks. We played against the Villa d'Este Club which was a few miles south of Cernobbio, and also at Monza which was close to the famous racing car track. After a wonderful week there, we returned to Switzerland to play in the Swiss Open at Crans-sur-Sierre. It was an event which most of the British and other European tournament professionals played in, and in 1958 it was won by the Ryder Cup player, Ken Bousfield, by one stroke from the Belgian, Flory van Donk. After the first thirty-six holes, I disappointingly failed to make the cut for the final thirty-six holes by one shot.

Following a memorable two weeks, we made the long drive back to reality and England via Paris, where we went to the Folies Bergere, and Ostend.

Golf in my third and final year was pretty much a repeat of the second, culminating in March 1959 with the Varsity Match against Cambridge, this time at Burnham and Berrow in Somerset, where again Cambridge won, this time by eight matches to six with one halved. At The Royal Worlington and Newmarket Golf Club, traditionally the home of Cambridge golf, we had a reunion in April 2009 to celebrate the 1959 match's fiftieth anniversary. There was an enormous feeling of camaraderie, good humour and fellowship and we were instantly able to pick up where we had left off, as if the intervening half century had not happened. After lunch we played an eighteen holes match, though unhappily I was not able to play because of my arthritis, and although temporarily the spirit of rivalry was resumed in that everyone was trying to win, at the end of the day the result of the friendly contest – a draw – did not really matter. It was still serious, yet fun and sometimes very funny!

Talking of reunions, we had a similar one for the slightly different teams in 2008 at the Berkshire, to celebrate the fiftieth anniversary of the 1958 match. Of the two teams in 1958, one from each side had died, both from alcoholism. At lunch I sat next to Nicky Winter who, apart from a fleeting meeting in Putney High Street sometime in the 1990s, I had not seen for fifty years. As the wine was being passed round, I offered some to Nicky but he refused, saying that he was only drinking water. So it was that we discovered that we had more in common than just golf, indeed between us we had well over forty years of sobriety and recovery. So out of the twenty who had played in the 1958 match, four were alcoholics, two of whom had sadly died and two who had survived and were in recovery. Four out of twenty is twenty percent, which is much higher than the norm of around eight percent for the UK as a whole, but for fifty percent to have recovered in AA is simply miles above the norm as overall the estimated recovery rate among alcoholics is only two or three percent! This frightful illness is to be found anywhere and everywhere but as the figures show, recovery is extremely rare.

I have not, thus far, mentioned drinking at Oxford. This is not because I did not drink, I most certainly did, but it never got me into any apparent trouble. Whenever I drank I had more than one, and at golf bars, dinners and parties I always had far more than my fair share, though I never remember getting drunk. Indeed, a few years ago, when I was talking to the 1959 golf captain and good friend John Littlewood about my drinking, he said, 'At Oxford you always drank a lot but you never got drunk.' I must stress, however, that at Oxford I never drank secretly.

On my twenty-first birthday I had a few friends in my room for drinks and although I am sure that I drank at least as much as, if not more than anyone else, I remember Christopher Normand, who was at Oriel, and I putting two of them to bed. *You poor sods*, I thought, *you don't know how to handle your drink. Thank God I don't have your problem!* Alcohol is cunning, baffling and powerful, and was seducing me and fooling me into thinking I did not have a problem. What I did not know then was that for a time (and in my case it was for nearly twenty years) and because of a high tolerance, many alcoholics can generally drink large quantities of alcohol without becoming intoxicated. Nor did I realize that alcohol was beginning to have another effect on me: it was taking away what little ambition I had, so that my interest in my work suffered. It was also affecting my golf in that I was not practising nearly as much as I should have liked, and it certainly was not because I did not have the time. I would have denied it, at the time, but I was very slowly beginning to develop a mild yet undetectable craving for the stuff and an ever so slight obsession with it. It was all very subtle, and far from not being an alcoholic, I was unknowingly already showing the symptoms, but it was to be another twenty five years before I accepted my alcoholism. I did not then believe or know that there is far more pleasure and a much better time to be had when one is completely sober; in 1957 I associated drink with pleasure and having a good time.

In some ways, it would have been better if, instead of doing my National Service straight after leaving Fettes, I had gone straight to Oxford. After being commissioned and serving Queen and Country fighting terrorists in Cyprus, I found Oxford, apart from the golf, a distinct let down and was more than a little irritated by some of its petty restrictions. Having been responsible for the lives of my troop only two or three months earlier, for example, I disliked having to climb into college at night because the gates were locked at midnight. I was unimpressed, too, by the rather immature and even childish attitudes of a number of the dons, some of whom seemed to me to live only in their own cloistered academic worlds; very few were men of the world.

Perhaps I was being unfair because one of my problems, which in retrospect I can see all too clearly, was that I did not know what I wanted to do or what I wanted out of life. Alcoholism apart, knowing what you want is probably the single most important thing you need to know if you are to have a successful and happy life. I also know, now, that if you want something, you really do have to want it enough to do the things which you don't want to do in order to get it. All I most wanted in those days and indeed until I eventually put down the glass, was the immediate but short lived good feelings that alcohol could then give me. In short, that was my biggest problem.

After my second term at Oxford, I so disliked P.P.E., and was consequently not doing enough work, that I switched to a much easier and lesser pass degree in economics. For reasons I have never understood, this involved (in my case) having to study military history (First World War and the American Civil War), which I loved, and French for which I had no natural aptitude or flair at all. At best my French was 'Churchillian' and in the words of the old joke it was good enough when in Paris to get me into trouble but not good enough to get me out of it! My military history tutor was a don at St. Peter's College and he was a lovely genial man in his sixties. He really loved his subject and like the great A.J.P. Taylor at Magdalen, was a wonderful story teller. His enthusiasm and love of his subject were infectious and I always looked forward to my tutorials with him. (I think he also liked and respected me for the fact that I had been commissioned in the Guards and had seen active service.) His main hobby was his boat which he kept on the river at Shillingford, where he was Commodore of the boat club. He invited me on to the river one day with his wife. He wore his Commodore's cap and with his Commodore's ensign fluttering in the breeze, we proudly cruised up and down the river. He was in his element and his childlike enthusiasm was a joy to behold. Today, I take a great interest in politics, which after all is tomorrow's history, and in modern British history, so perhaps if I could have my time again and not be an alcoholic, I might have been a historian.

I cannot conclude my account of Oxford without mentioning Dawn. I met her in the middle of my second year through my flat mate of the time; indeed he always said that I pinched her from him. Apart perhaps from Susie at the Bag of Nails, she was the first girlfriend I ever had. Having only a brother and having been at boys only schools, I previously had had no experience of girls and did not then realize just how different they are from men. I did not understand them and I have to say that in many ways

I still don't! Dawn was a lovely but insecure girl and during my last year I fell in love with her. In those days, couples did not live together as they do now and she naturally wanted to get married. Had I been in a position to, I probably would have done so, but I thought it was premature as I had no job or income and could not possibly have afforded to keep her. Even so, our relationship lasted until I went down, when I had to tell her that I was still not in a position to marry her. Our affair thus came to a sad end, due in part to my father's insistence that if I continued with it or got married, he would no longer support me through chartered accountancy articles, which everybody thought I should do. In retrospect, this was probably how it was meant to be, though I am by no means certain that I acted as honourably as I might have. I later heard that soon after we split up she married someone else. Sadly the marriage was relatively short lived and soon ended in divorce. Even more sadly, I subsequently learned that she had died, though quite how or why I have never found out. I still sometimes think about her and wonder what might have been had I acted differently. We had some great times together.

Chapter 4

A Cunning and Baffling Foe
1959 – 1974

After leaving Oxford I commenced articles with Spicer & Pegler, a medium sized firm of City chartered accountants. Not knowing what I really wanted to do, I opted for accountancy as being the least worst option available to me. It was not, however, a good choice because from the outset I found it tedious almost beyond belief. As an articled clerk, my work consisted of auditing, mostly bank reconciliations, in a number of different firms from City banks to tractor manufacturers in Hatfield. It was mind-blowingly boring and pretty brainless, made worse because one had to stay focused and concentrate for much of the time. On top of all this there was studying at night.

While I was still at Oxford, my parents had moved to a large four bedroom flat in Moor Park near Northwood. (They paid £2,750, cash, for it; today it is probably worth around £700,000!) So it seemed sensible for me to live at home, not only because Mother and Father were pleased to have me, but because it saved money, especially since I earned almost nothing at Spicer & Pegler. I enjoyed living with them and did not in the least envy my friends who shared flats in London and had to look after themselves. The only real disadvantage was not being able to bring girls home, but after my experience with Dawn I was not at all keen to have another relationship. In any event, girls would get in the way of golf. My weekends were spent almost entirely playing golf – four rounds were the norm – and I was not yet ready to give it up.

Until I got married in 1967, much of the golf I played was competitive match-play foursomes, which for me is the best and most enjoyable form of golf. I played county golf for Berks, Bucks and Oxon and for the Oxford and Cambridge Golfing Society (The Society), as well as The Moles Golfing Society; additionally there were two memorable Society tours of Scotland and Ireland in 1960 and 1964 respectively. In the latter I was in my prime as a drinker and probably played some of my best golf. We played on Ireland's best courses and we were hosted every evening at dinner. Being Ireland, the drink flowed like water until late at night. Naturally, I drank with the best of them, yet throughout the week I don't recall appearing inebriated and on the golf course I was certainly one of the Society's leading overall points scorers. Everywhere we went, we seemed to be accompanied by priests, especially at the nineteenth hole. 'Now what will you be havin' Father?' was the oft repeated question, and the answer was never in the negative! In all it was the most marvellous fun and I don't think I have ever enjoyed a week more.

It was not the first time I had played in Ireland. In 1960 I had played in the British Amateur Championship at Royal Portrush and in the first round I was drawn against the Irishman, James Bruen, who had won the Championship just after the war in 1946. Bruen was a hero and a legend in his own country, renowned for his long hitting and his unique and curious loop at the top of his swing, but in 1960 he was suffering from a bad wrist and I was told that it was unlikely he would be able to play. Nevertheless, to be on the safe side, I had to turn up on the first tee to claim a walk over. As our starting time approached there was no sign of him until, at the very last minute, he appeared from behind the sand hills, followed by what seemed to me to be the whole of Ireland, who had turned up to watch us play in the pouring rain. There was no time for nerves and I managed to hit two good shots on to the middle of the first green. Jimmy then told me that he intended to give me the match but we should play on in order not to disappoint the crowd. I protested that he could not do this, but he said that his wrist would not last and it would be unfair to me if he played, knowing that if he won he intended to scratch before the next round. This put me in quite a quandary and a state of some confusion with the result that I three putted the first two greens to go two down. We continued playing but I still did not really know whether it was for real or just an exhibition. Fortunately, we both played pretty well and apart from two minor lapses, both of which lost me the hole, I matched him shot for shot. As we were leaving the thirteenth green, however, at which point I was four down, he walked across and, and to the crowds amazement, shook my hand and conceded the match. It was a strange way to win a match and I would much rather have won or lost playing properly. For the record, it was the last time he appeared in a championship and our match was the lead story in the next day's papers and on Irish television; in the next round I was beaten three and two by a very good Irish international, Bill Macrea.

I had been a pretty good putter in my Oxford days, but in the years following I began to develop an involuntary and uncontrollable twitch when putting. Initially, I could usually 'cure' this with a few drinks at lunchtime, but over the years it slowly got worse. I have no doubt that it was caused by alcohol and that the twitch was an early symptom of my alcoholism.

I cannot talk about my post-Oxford golf without mentioning the Halford Hewitt tournament, which was founded in 1924 by Halford Hewitt and is held in early April each year at the Royal Cinque Ports Golf Club at Deal and the Royal St. George's Golf Club at Sandwich. The foursomes knock out competition played over four days is between teams of ten players of old boys from sixty-four public schools. It is one of the best and most anticipated events in the golfing calendar and it was one in which I played for over ten years. Fettes was definitely one of the leading teams in the early sixties, being runners up in 1960 and 1963 before winning in 1964.

Early in the sixties I was invited to become a member of the Junior Carlton Club in London as they were looking for new younger members. I was flattered to be asked and joined partly because they had a flourishing golfing society. Together with Michael Tilbury, who was a friend and fellow member at Denham, we twice won the Bath Club Cup, a competition held annually between most of the London clubs. Play was by match play foursomes over eighteen holes at Woking Golf Club; the first time we won, we beat the Guards Club in the final and one of our opponents that day was Colonel Tony Duncan, whom I had first met when he was my commanding officer at Pirbright. I had always respected him greatly as a golfer and winning gave me a lot of pleasure.

On another occasion, in one of the early rounds, we beat the legendary Group Captain Douglas Bader and the Sunday Times golf correspondent and doyen of television golf commentators, Henry Longhurst. At the sixth hole, Henry had put Douglas into the stream which runs in front of the green. The ball was lying just below the surface and for most people it would have been a case of deeming the ball unplayable and picking out under the penalty of one stroke. Douglas, however, reckoned it was playable. He walked into the stream and with the water up to the ankles of his tin legs he addressed the ball. As he was about to play, Henry whispered to me, 'It's simply a question of someone cleaning his shoes!' Douglas duly played his shot and miraculously managed to get the ball out of the water.

Of all the people I have met, Douglas Bader was by some distance the one I have most admired. Not only was he a good games player, who would have almost certainly played for England at rugby football had he not lost his legs in his air crash before the war, but he had about him a determination never to give up, the like of which I have not seen in any one else. He suffered and beat tremendous pain to learn to walk on artificial legs, and then, after a long battle, eventually persuaded the R.A.F. to let him fly again. As is well known, he became a fantastic leader of men in the Battle of Britain; and when he was shot down over France and bailed out of his aeroplane, leaving one leg behind (the R.A.F. dropped him another one during a subsequent air raid), he was captured and made a prisoner of war. He made more than one attempt to escape on his artificial legs, until the Germans eventually put him in Colditz Castle from which even he could not escape. But it could never have been easy for him, nor could it have been easy for him to learn to play golf to a very respectable standard. Actually, it must have been almost impossibly difficult. I played golf with him twice: the first at Woking and the second some years later, when, playing for the Moles against the Hittites at Hoylake, he and I were comfortably heading to break eighty when we won. Yet on each occasion, thirty to forty years after he had lost his legs, he fell down on the golf course and we had to help him up. In the bar afterwards, I once remarked that he did not drink. 'No,' he replied, 'I find I fall over if I do!'

Most people would consider it a tragedy that he lost both of his legs. I think differently: losing his legs as he did, enabled him to live a far more worthwhile life than would otherwise have been the case, and he became an inspiration not only to all who knew him, but most particularly to others who had lost one or more limbs. In this regard, he did untold good work over many years. He certainly was not everyone's cup of tea and he did not suffer fools gladly, but what a man! Like Churchill, he was a warrior at heart, who, irrespective of the odds, loved a challenge, whether it was learning to walk on artificial legs, being the great Battle of Britain pilot and leader, or indeed just playing golf. It was one of the great privileges of my life to have known him and to have been inspired by him. Later, at times in my own recovery from alcoholism when the going got tough, I thought to myself, *this is nothing compared with what Douglas Bader had to put up with or go through!*

Before leaving golf, I want to mention the Courage Trophy in from memory 1965 at Calcot Park Golf Club in Reading. The Courage Trophy was a thirty-six holes scratch medal competition for low handicap amateurs in the three counties of Berks, Bucks and Oxon. The event, as the name suggests, was sponsored by the local brewers and they had invited the three times Open Champion, Henry Cotton, to attend and give a clinic at the end of the day. In the morning I shot a sixty-eight which, at lunchtime, led the field. As I teed off for my second round after lunch, there sat the great man in his Mini-Moke; he watched me for my first three holes, which

I played in level par. I duly went round in seventy-three for a total of one hundred and forty-one, with which, as a weekend golfer, I was justifiably pleased. In the bar afterwards, Henry came up to me and said, 'I see it runs in the family.' Thinking he was referring to my brother Donald, whom he knew quite well as a golf writer, I enquired what he meant. He replied, 'Lack of diet!'

Apart from my beloved golf, there were my cars. The Standard Nine I had at Oxford pretty much gave up the ghost and was replaced by a brand new two door Morris Minor 1000. It was grey with red leather upholstery, a heater and a Motorola Radio. After the Standard, it was the "bee's knees" and it gave me a lot of pleasure. But then came the Mini and both my brother and I bought one. As well as being an icon, it really was a fun car but it was poorly made, a bit spartan and shoddy; it was also inclined to rust, was noisy, had a dreadful gear box and, having such small wheels, the tyres needed frequent replacing. After the Mini, came a beautiful but unreliable second hand MGA, and in 1963 a brand new pale blue MGB, which cost the princely sum of £903! As I wrote out the cheque for it I remember thinking that I would never write out such a large cheque again! And as I drove the car home, it gave me more pride and pleasure than any car I have since owned could match by far. With its wind up windows, heater, leather seats and distinctive exhaust note, it really was my pride and joy. Contrary to what most people think about open cars, the MG was at its best on a starlit night, the tonneau cover up and heater on, even if in winter one had to wear an overcoat. With its near two litre engine, it was considered quite fast in 1963 but over the many years it was in production, every time they sought to improve the original, they strangely never succeeded.

On reaching the age of sixty five, my father retired after thirty one years as the first Medical Director of Hillingdon Hospital. Apart from his duties as medical director, he was an active consultant physician and surgeon, holding regular clinics and operating sessions each week. On his first day of retirement I remember him saying that he felt that he could no longer be of help to anybody. It was a remark which was typical of him, as all his working life had been spent in medicine in the service of others and I don't think he knew any other way. For many years prior to his retirement, I used to accompany him on his tour of the wards and departments of the hospital on Christmas mornings. It always surprised me just how popular he was with his staff: they were so genuinely pleased to see him and offer him a Christmas drink. Most of these he refused because he was not a drinker and in any case he could not possibly have accepted them all. But I more than made up for him, for it was almost impossible for me to refuse a drink, even though I knew I would be driving him home for lunch. He was an unfailingly courteous man especially to women and he would never leave home without kissing my mother goodbye or without doffing his trade mark trilby, which he invariably wore, to other women. He taught me a lot about manners and etiquette, something which to this day I try to live up to.

He was about as good a father as any boy could ask for and he always took a great interest in what Donald and I were doing and, when appropriate, always gave his full support. In his last few years I would have long discussions with him about almost every subject under the sun. Sometimes they were arguments but they were always good natured. The older I got, the wiser I thought he became and in discussions with other people, I would often argue his point of view; my mother and others told me that he would sometimes argue mine, as even by my middle twenties, I had had many experiences which he had not. (Today, I love nothing more than doing the same thing with my own son and daughter, and I learn a lot from them and how their generation differs from my own. Hopefully it helps to keep me young!)

When he retired, he had been unwell for some time with a heart condition, although I was then unaware just how serious it was. Early in October 1965, he asked me to drive him up to Harley Street where he was due to consult Lord Brock, a leading heart surgeon of the day. It was a beautiful autumn day and as we drove home afterwards along the north side of Hyde Park I asked him how he had got on. He replied, 'It was like going before the firing squad and being told it had been put off until the following morning.' He was not strong enough to withstand what would now be a routine operation and a week later he died during the night. Mother, who was about to become a widow for the next twenty one years, awakened me and told me he was dying and I watched him draw his last breath. It seemed to me that he just conked out having, as it were, run out of gas. He was only sixty-five.

On the day before his cremation, I went to the funeral directors to see his body and to say good bye. As he lay in his coffin he seemed to have shed twenty years; no longer in any pain, he looked so much younger. But it was just his corpse; his personality was no longer there. I thanked him for everything and kissed him good bye on the forehead which, to my surprise, was ice cold. It was a sad and moving experience, so very different from the first occasion I saw a corpse (the terrorist's, in Cyprus). I am glad now that he never saw the worst of my alcoholism, for while he many times told me never to take "drugs", and I never have, he did not tell me not to drink or smoke. I am, however, very sorry that he did not live long enough to know his grand children or they him.

A short while after his death, Mother arranged for a thanksgiving service for his life to be held at Hillingdon Church. (There was no way she was going to call it a memorial service!) The church was packed to overflowing and afterwards we had drinks and a buffet lunch for relatives and close friends back at Moor Park. It was a really good party and I am sure Father would have loved it. Afterwards I drove his first cousin, who had come down from Edinburgh (when we were at Fettes he had often taken Donald and me to play golf on Sundays at Luffness), up to King's Cross to take the train back to Scotland. On the way he said, 'You know I haven't enjoyed myself so much in years!' – I knew just what he meant and in my book that was exactly as it should be!

I had the greatest admiration for the way my mother took Father's death. Whilst I am sure it had come as no great surprise to her, she must have missed him hugely for they had been lovers and soul mates for well over thirty years. Even so, she remained forever cheerful and told Donald and me that he would have wanted us to remember him with gratitude, but that we should get on with our lives as if his death had not happened. They had both sacrificed a lot for us, something which all too often I had regretfully taken for granted.

Around that time, a Dr J.R.B. Johnstone became a member of Denham Golf Club. John was a Scot from Fife, and a graduate of Edinburgh University who had for many years practised as a general practitioner in Hanwell. He was a good golfer, having won the Middlesex Amateur Championship in the early fifties; he was also very fond of a drink, good company, with a fund of amusing stories and we soon became good drinking partners. At the 1966 Golf Club Summer Dance he introduced me to his stepdaughter, Caroline, who was then at Oxford studying for an external London University degree in history. I began taking her out regularly and we were married in October 1967.

One night, shortly before the wedding, I had run out of cigarettes and asked my mother, who smoked about one cigarette a year, if she had one. I was then smoking thirty to forty a day. She gave me one but at the same time suggested that I give them up as I was about to get married and the money so saved would come in useful for other things. Somewhat to my surprise I agreed with her and stopped smoking the very next day. I cannot honestly say that I wanted to give up cigarettes but equally I had no real desire to continue smoking. In actual fact, stopping smoking was quite easy and within a week I was through the physical withdrawals and not missing them at all. (It may sound obvious, but I think it may be helpful for anyone who wants to give up smoking or drinking to realize that **you cannot give up smoking or drinking without giving up smoking or drinking!** There is no other way.)

Initially, Caroline and I rented a small basement flat in Earls Court before buying an attractive two/three bedroom converted flat in Swiss Cottage. It cost some £7,250, financed from part of my eventual share of Father's estate, and seemed a fortune. Now it is considerably less than half the cost of my car! During that first year Caroline used to drive up to Oxford once a week for her tutorial but otherwise studied from home before obtaining her degree, following which she took up a position in marketing with Unilever in Blackfriars.

One day in 1969, I was sitting at my office desk, thinking how good it was not to have smoked for almost two years and marvelling that I had no desire at all to do so. Shortly thereafter, Caroline and I went for a holiday in Norway, taking the overnight ferry from Newcastle to Bergen. After dinner on the ship, Caroline mentioned how much she would like a cigarette. She hardly ever smoked and as she had none of her own, I went and bought a packet of ten Rothmans. She suggested that I might like to join her and though I declined, saying that I really did not want one, she pressed me, saying it would be nice if I were to accompany her and one would not do any harm. I gave in and somewhat reluctantly lit one up. The first puffs were distinctly unpleasant and made me cough; nevertheless, I continued and finished the packet before going to bed! The following morning I had to buy more and from then on I was to smoke continuously and increasingly for the next seventeen years. I was aware that it had been the first cigarette that had done the damage: having lit up one, I had no defence whatever against lighting up the second. What I did not understand was that I was powerless over nicotine and that for the previous two years I had only been "in recovery" from my nicotine addiction. That first cigarette had immediately re-activated the physical craving and thereafter I was completely hooked.

In those early days money was not a problem, we were happy and we had a lot of fun together. Holidaying abroad was then in its relative infancy but after Norway, which scenically was quite magnificent and beautiful, we

[42]

managed quite a few more holidays, mostly in Europe. Despite or perhaps because of the fact that both her father and step-father were keen golfers, Caroline herself positively disliked the game so I played less frequently, averaging, if I was lucky, maybe one round a week. Often I would play at Denham on a Sunday afternoon with John, having left Caroline to spend the afternoon with her mother, Jeanne.

Drink was still not a problem and in the summer we would often go out for a couple of drinks at local pubs, of which there were many both in Hampstead and by the river in Chiswick, where we moved in 1971. Drink was, however becoming a fairly obvious problem with John who, despite functioning seemingly adequately in his work, was beginning to drink more and more. 'If only you could drink like Billy,' or, 'Why can't you drink like Billy?' my mother-in-law used to say to him. I remember on more than one occasion pleading with him on her behalf to try to control his drinking. 'Don't have a drink until six o'clock, or just have only one or two at lunch time,' I would unwittingly suggest. At that time, that would not have been a problem for me, and I could not understand why, despite his promises, he was quite unable to do it. But then I did not understand the progressive nature of alcoholism and I did not understand what powerlessness was; nor did it occur to me to suggest that he went to AA which I then knew nothing about.

One of the stories he used to tell was how after his usual fill of drink during one day, he was seeing a patient at evening surgery who clearly was not happy with what John was telling him and he muttered something about a getting second opinion. 'Well,' said John, 'if you really want a second opinion, I suggest you come back again tomorrow morning!' Whether or not this was a true story I shall never know, but one that certainly was true, because I witnessed it myself, was the occasion one Sunday at Denham Golf Club when, after a no doubt 'heavy lunch', one of the directors of the club collapsed on the way to getting into his Bentley to go home. Amid a certain amount of panic, John, who was playing at the time, was called off the golf course to examine the patient. After completing his examination, he was asked by some anxious members what was wrong. 'He's drunk!' he replied. Amid general disbelief, the good doctor was then asked how he had reached such a diagnosis. With a wry smile, he said, 'Because I recognise the symptoms!' Sadly, John never came to terms with his alcoholism and died in 1976 from an inoperable cancer of the pancreas which was very likely caused by his alcoholism. He was forced by his doctors to stop drinking, but when I went to visit him in hospital a couple of days before he died, he told me that if had not been for his wife, Jeanne, he would certainly drink again. On his death I lost a very good friend, kindred spirit and ally.

In 1972, United Dominions Trust (UDT), a finance house for whom I had worked for over eleven years, asked me to transfer to its merchant banking subsidiary, Old Broad Street Securities Ltd (OBSS), and open an office in Reading. OBSS was then expanding quite rapidly into financing residential and commercial property developments, and it was clear that the new job would involve selling which I was a little unsure about. What attracted me to it, however, apart from a substantial salary increase and a heavily subsidised mortgage, was that I would have an expense account and a company car. Surprisingly, I discovered that I was a good salesman and from the start I enjoyed my work and was successful. Each day I would reverse commute the thirty-five mile journey, Chiswick to Reading, but as it was almost all on the M4 motorway it took little more than half an hour – considerably less than the commute by train to the City. I did a lot of entertaining, particularly at lunchtimes, and drink continued to pose no problems. I always took good care, however, not to send off any reports or do important work after a business lunch, so perhaps it was beginning to have an effect about which, if I were honest, only I knew!

In November 1973, Caroline gave birth to our daughter Clare in Queen Charlotte's Maternity Hospital in Hammersmith. Because she was born by Caesarean Section, I saw her before Caroline did. She was gorgeous, with big blue eyes and a mass of blonde hair, and when I held her in my arms I experienced a feeling of enormous joy and gratitude. It is a feeling many new parents experience I am sure, but for me it was intensely special and I cherish the memory. The feeling was soon to be replaced by one of, *oh Lord, I'm responsible for her!* and I wondered how I was going to cope. In the event and in the short term, I more than coped; indeed, as she was not being breast fed, I helped Caroline with her feeding, always doing the midnight feed. Changing and washing hundreds of nappies (there were no disposables in those days) made me a real expert but more importantly, it made me a real part of her early years.

In 1974 came the secondary banking crisis and property crash. Much of UDT's deposits were raised short term on the London Inter Bank Market and of course most of its lendings were medium term. Consequently and particularly because of its property lending, there was a run on its deposits and, along with many other financial institutions, it had to go to the Bank of England for help. And so it found itself 'in the lifeboat', having, in effect, gone bust.   Although not totally surprised, it nonetheless it came as a shock when I was summoned to London, one November day, to be told that OBSS was ceasing to trade and that, along with several hundred other UDT and OBSS employees, I was, after twelve years with the company, being made redundant and given my P45.

My drinking had nothing whatsoever to do with my redundancy but it marked the end of a very long beginning. What happened next was an accident waiting to happen and marked the beginning of a comparatively rapid, painful and horrendous end.

Chapter 5

Clouds Gather, Storm Breaks
1974 – 1982

When I arrived home I told Caroline that I had been made redundant and no longer had a job. I then went straight to the drinks cupboard and poured myself a very large pink gin. 'Don't worry,' I told her, 'I am not going to get drunk.' **For the first time, I was deliberately using alcohol to anaesthetise the pain of the terrible shame, guilt and fear I was feeling. I was consciously using drink as a drug – a pain killer. Although I did not get drunk that day, from then on I drank every day in steadily increasing quantities until the day I entered treatment in December 1982. I did not realize it at the time, but my alcoholism had shifted up a gear and I was entering the chronic and final stage of my illness: from that moment, alcohol was more and more to become its own antidote; it had become the killer of the pain which increasingly it was to cause and it was then that wanting to drink suddenly and increasingly became the compulsive need to drink. For the next eight years I always had alcohol inside me. During that time I was never completely sober and was to lose virtually everything that I valued and possessed.**

From 1959 to November 1974, I had drunk heavily. This, however, had been mostly at weekends when I probably consumed up to a dozen or so drinks over the two days. Even so, it is interesting to note that for the most part and even allowing for the fact that most of my drinks were doubles, my weekly total of units drunk had not always exceeded the Health Service's recommended limit of three to four units a day. I had also never drunk alone and only very rarely had I appeared intoxicated.

Now, for first time since university, I was out of work and it presented, to say the least, quite a few problems. Caroline, who was working as a part-time teacher, was expecting our second child the following March and it was clear that the modest amount of money I had received by way of redundancy and severance pay would not last very long. Additionally, I was about to lose the company car and the subsidised mortgage on which OBSS was actively seeking repayment. Getting a new job in my line of business was not going to be easy: unemployment in the finance world was high and there was no shortage of job seekers.

Prior to my transfer to OBSS, I had been in charge of the recovery, where possible, of UDT's corporate loans mainly to motor distributors and dealers. They were then called bad and doubtful debts, a much better and more correct term than 'toxic assets' which has suddenly come into vogue of late. In this post I frequently came into contact with the world of insolvency and consequently knew many of the well known liquidators and receivers of the day, who were about the only people whose businesses were flourishing in the economic downturn. One such was Gerry Weiss of W.H. Cork Gully and Co, Chartered Accountants and Insolvency Specialists and following my approach to him early in 1975, he arranged an interview for me with the staff partner. I duly impressed sufficiently to be offered a job, in effect as senior assistant to Gerry Weiss, albeit at a reduced salary and without a car or subsidised mortgage. I had little option but to accept for in reality I was very lucky to be offered a job at all. Their offices were in Eastcheap barely fifty yards from UDT's offices.

Gerry Weiss was a man for whom, from the moment I met him, I had enormous respect. A Jewish refugee, he was a small man with a speaking defect such that his voice, although clear, was faint and rather weak. So, although he was an intellectual giant when it came to insolvency knowledge and law – no one had a better command of it than he – public speaking was difficult if well nigh impossible for him. One of my functions, therefore, was to become his 'voice' by reading his speeches, reports or lectures for him. I enjoyed this and it enabled me to learn a lot that I might not have otherwise. Gerry was also the partner in charge of the very unusual Section 206 Scheme of Arrangement which Cork Gully was setting up to administer the collapse of the then enormous William Stern property empire. In addition, we were responsible for arranging the creditors' meeting for Willie Stern's subsequent personal bankruptcy which, at that time, was the biggest ever.

Gerry had two other aspects to him which I found interesting. Firstly, he was the right hand man to Sir Kenneth Cork, soon to become Lord Mayor of London, who was the chairman of the Cork Committee set up by the government to make recommendations to improve insolvency law, which eventually culminated in the Insolvency Act of 1986. Secondly, Gerry was the chairman of the London Festival Ballet in which he took a very great interest, both artistically and financially. I was involved in this in a minor way and consequently he gave Caroline and me complimentary tickets for some of the ballets they performed in London. My work for him was varied and interesting and it went very well for a year or so.

We eventually solved the OBSS mortgage problem by selling our house and buying another slightly larger one on the same estate by the Thames, between the end of the boat race and Strand on the Green. The Triumph GT6 which had been a second car also had to be sold, as with two infant children it was much too small; it was replaced by a practical second-hand Volkswagen Estate. Apart from being the dullest to drive of all my cars before and since, it was otherwise near perfect in every way. Having said that, on the way to one holiday in Cornwall, the brakes failed and I had to drive the last fifty miles with no brakes. Shades of my old Riley over twenty years previously when I was in The Blues at Windsor!

Charlie was born on 24th March 1975, also at Queen Charlotte's in Hammersmith and also by Caesarean section. I am sure he won't mind my saying, he was nothing like as pretty as his sister and he was a bit jaundiced, but still he was my son and, like Clare, I loved him to bits from the very start. Despite money being much tighter and the work harder at the office and at home with the children, we enjoyed life, often visiting the grannies either in Hanwell or Windsor, where my mother had bought a flat. I was beginning to drink more heavily in that I was then drinking every day and at lunch times, but my tolerance was still high and I generally could still hold it pretty well.

The weekends were thus pretty domesticated and my golf was much reduced. However, for many years in the summer I had played for the Moles in their annual match against Hunstanton Golf Club on the Norfolk coast. The match consisted of two rounds of foursomes on the Saturday and two more on the Sunday with a fairly heavy evening of partying and drinking in between. I am not sure of the exact year but it was probably 1975, I arrived at the club on the Sunday morning feeling very much the worse for wear and not at all looking forward to playing golf. As I entered the bar, the barman looked at me and said, 'I have just the thing for you.' With that he poured me a large brandy and milk. I drank it down and had another for good measure and I definitely felt better. On reflection, this was a significant moment: it was the first time I knowingly used alcohol as its own antidote. It is one of the reasons why chronic alcoholics drink first thing in the morning: they need it to get rid of the withdrawals and get going.

After a couple of years at Cork Gully, my work became more administrative and much less intellectually interesting or challenging. Whether or not because of this, I am not sure, but I began to drink more and more at lunch time and made quite a few 'drinking friends' both inside and outside of

[48]

Cork Gully who were doing the same. Then one morning at about eleven o'clock, I was feeling a bit below par when suddenly the thought struck me that a drink would be the answer. Accordingly I popped out to a nearby pub and had a large whisky. I promptly felt better, and so began the practice, whenever I could, of having a drink around eleven o'clock, quickly to be followed by earlier and longer lunch hours. On one occasion, I went in to see Gerry Weiss after my eleven o'clock whisky.

'Have you been drinking?' he asked.

'No. Why do you ask?' I replied, somewhat taken aback.

'Because,' he said, 'I can smell it on your breath!'

'No' was of course my instinctive answer whenever I was asked if I had been drinking and in a sense I believed it to be true because I did not regard having one or even two drinks as drinking – it had to be a lot more than two before the word 'no' became a lie. Nonetheless, I was genuinely surprised that Gerry should have noticed anything, and it was the first time anyone outside of the family had confronted me about drinking. It did not stop me drinking in the mornings but it did make me try to be a lot more careful, at least for a while.

Shortly after this incident, I was playing golf at Royal Worlington and Donald was going to give me a lift home. Just as Donald said it was time to leave, I ordered another drink. 'You're drinking like an f...ing alcoholic!' he remonstrated. I was angry and hurt, and it seemed that I was not as good as I thought at concealing the extent of my drinking. I slept most of the way home, but I distinctly remember the occasion because Donald had touched such a sore point.

My lunches became longer and longer and I started to take drink into the office in my briefcase or coat pocket. I would then conceal it in my desk drawer and sneak drinks when I was alone or when no one was looking. I got away with it to the extent that no one ever actually caught me in the act, but people were beginning to notice in other ways. Although I could not see it, my drinking was beginning to affect my work: a lot of papers went into the waste paper basket or into a drawer which I mentally marked as 'too difficult', and my in-tray was growing larger and larger simply because I could not be bothered to deal with it.

At home, too, Caroline began challenging me on the amount of my drinking. Whenever she did so I would deny it in the same way that I denied it to Gerry Weiss. I resented this hugely because I really did not think she had any justification for it. She became increasingly obsessed with trying to control the situation, for example, by marking the level in the whisky bottle, which I would initially counter by replacing the alcohol I drank with water, until eventually the bottle was all water and no whisky! She then took to hiding bottles, so I did the same and often discovered drink which she had hidden from me! Getting rid of my empty bottles was often a problem. I overcame this by, under the cover of darkness, placing them in neighbours' dustbins or shamefully throwing them into the Thames. Looking back on all this, I can see just how crazy it was. But then, what neither Caroline nor I knew was that I was powerless over alcohol: if I could not control my drinking, nobody else could control it either.

In 1978 I decided to change jobs before I was given the sack by Cork Gully; I switched to a rival insolvency firm, Stoy Hayward & Partners, who had offices in Baker Street. After spending a short time in the office, I was given charge of a receivership in Dalston in North London, which was continuing to trade pending the sale of its constituent parts. Because Thursday was their half day, I was alone every Thursday afternoon with the inevitable result that I would drink solidly from noon until five thirty. On one such afternoon, I found myself waking up on the floor of my office with no recollection of having passed out or, as you might more correctly say, having over-dosed on whisky. This gave me a fright but I quickly recovered and thought no more of it. It happened only the once but, subsequently, I found myself regularly going to sleep on the train home and waking up at the terminus in Richmond, two stops after I should have got off. It was all very embarrassing and difficult to explain away to Caroline, who often used to meet me off the train.

We were having more and more rows about my worsening drinking and money. She decided that she should take control of the family finances and demanded that she become a mandatory joint signature on my bank account. Very reluctantly I agreed but it was nonetheless very humiliating to be given pocket money every day, sufficient only to buy lunch and cigarettes. In order to get more 'drink money', I started to fiddle my expenses at work and to pinch money from the children's piggy banks. This was not all. By this time, my mother, who was then in her early eighties, had sold her Windsor flat and was living near to us in Chiswick in an Abbeyfield home. I regularly went to see her, often taking the children, but I have to confess these visits were nothing like as altruistic as it might appear. The real purpose was to take money from her handbag, which was easily done when she went to have her tea. She always kept a lot of money in her purse so that I reckoned she would not miss the odd ten or twenty quid. Although she never mentioned it to me, she surely must have noticed. I felt terribly guilty about all this and although I would never admit it, it showed just how low I was sinking. To this day, the theft of money from her piggy bank is the single thing Clare most remembers about my alcoholism.

Caroline had a younger sister who lived in Vienna and each summer she would take a week's holiday to visit her. I used to look forward to her trip to Vienna far more than I think she did as it meant that, although I had to look after the children, I was still free to drink pretty much all that I could. Having said good bye to her at Luton Airport, the first thing I would do before driving home was buy a large whisky at the bar. Much as I would deny it, alcohol was inexorably taking more and more control over me.

In 1980, the Royal and Ancient Golf Club of St. Andrews, of which I was a member, advertised in one of the papers for a Secretary of the Rules of Golf Committee. This was a job which, under normal circumstances, I would have been very interested in, especially as I knew the rules almost by heart. Although Caroline was adamant that she would not move to St. Andrews, I applied for the post, attended an interview in London and was subsequently short-listed for a final interview at the Caledonian Hotel in Edinburgh. The afternoon before the interview, armed with a bottle of whisky in my bag, I caught the shuttle from London Airport to Edinburgh. Having checked in at the Roxborough Hotel, where Father and I had stayed the night before I first went to Fettes, I decided to have a couple of whiskies in my room before dinner and taking a nostalgic stroll around Edinburgh. Several whiskies later, I decided to have sandwiches sent up to my room instead of having dinner. Before the evening was out I had finished the bottle of scotch and ordered one or two more from the bar before going to sleep.

I had wanted to do well at the interview, even though, if successful, I was pretty sure I would have to turn it down unless of course I was prepared to leave Caroline. However, I awoke the next morning feeling pretty rough and sensing that I had already blown my chances. What the hell! I thought, I would still have a go, anyway. I was probably reeking of whisky when I entered the room to be confronted by three members of the club, all wearing their R & A blazers and all strangers to me. The chairman was the club secretary Keith MacKenzie, a man who seemed completely devoid of charm and to whom I took an instant dislike. The interview did not go well and when asked if there was anything that I would like to ask them, I played what I thought might be my trump card. I asked why Greg Norman had not been disqualified when he holed in one at the first hole in the first round of the 1979 Open Championship at Royal Lytham and St Anne's. Clearly irritated they asked me what I meant. I explained that by holing in one he was in breach of Rule One of the Rules of Golf, which stated: 'The game of golf shall be played between tee and hole by successive strokes.' Norman had holed by a single stroke and not successive strokes and therefore, according to the letter of the law, should have been disqualified. I suggested that the rule, which had stood for years, should be altered to: The game shall be played between tee and hole by, a single or successive strokes. They clearly were not amused by what they may well have considered impertinence and, as I expected, I was not offered the job. Nevertheless, the rule was subsequently amended in the way I had suggested. I felt that this at least made me 'all square' with them!

Around this time, Caroline and her mother persuaded me to see the consultant psychiatrist and top man specialising in alcoholism at St Thomas' Hospital in London. As an alcoholic in denial, I did not tell him everything about my drinking but I nevertheless conceded quite a bit about the extent of it and Caroline for her part filled in most of the gaps. (You can often learn a very great deal by what a spouse or partner has to say about the other half's drinking!) To my surprise and great joy, however, he told her I did not have a drinking problem but we did have a marriage problem! Caroline was justifiably furious as it was, in retrospect, an astonishing and in my view quite disgraceful diagnosis to have made. Anyone who knew anything about alcoholism would have diagnosed otherwise, and as Caroline angrily remarked on the way home, 'We might just as well have gone to see a chimpanzee!' I sometimes wonder what would have happened if, as he should have done, he had told me I was a chronic alcoholic.

Our home life was getting worse and worse and always the arguments were about my drinking and money. At work, having completed the receivership in Dalston, I returned to the office in Baker Street. Verbally, I was often complimented on my work and though I had been confronted about my drinking and told that they thought I might have 'a bit of a drinking problem', I was not offered any help; on the contrary, I was to receive two warning letters about it, both of which I put straight into the waste paper basket. I was eventually sacked because of my continued drinking yet, strangely, they made me work my month's notice. In fact, when the month was up and in the absence of any contrary instructions, I continued to work as usual for nearly two weeks. It was only when the partner for whom I worked looked at me one day and said, 'You shouldn't be here should you?' that in May 1981 I was finally given my P45.

Telling Caroline I had been sacked was not something I was looking forward to and when I did she was, to say the least, not best pleased. The next day, in the presence of her mother, I was told in no uncertain and irate terms that she wanted an immediate divorce whereupon they both started laying down stringent financial terms. Slightly in shock at the sudden, angry and indeed brutal nature of these demands, I was not at that point prepared to agree to anything other than, because of the children, an equitable divorce settlement; to my surprise, even this was not at the time considered nearly good enough; nor was there, either then or subsequently, any suggestion whatever made that I needed and should perhaps seek help.

I was in two minds about the divorce because although I was very resentful that Caroline should want to leave me and in effect take my children away from me, I was also looking forward to being a bachelor again, getting a new job and having some fun.

It only took about three months to complete the sale of the house, but living together in the interim was very difficult. Although I was not in a position to do anything about it, my heart nonetheless went out to the children, who were most upset at the prospect of their parents splitting up. I always feel so sorry for the children in any alcoholic marriage for, unlike the non-alcoholic spouse or partner, they have no choice in the matter. Additionally, as mine subsequently told me was true of them, they often feel guilty and (wrongly, of course) responsible for the break-up. Caroline and I eventually parted company in August 1981 and this was the last time that my children were to live under the same roof as me. Out of the equity after paying off the mortgage, Caroline took the half share to which she was legally entitled plus an undocumented loan from me that was sufficient to enable her to buy an unencumbered three bedroom house in Chiswick for herself and the children.

Initially, I went to live in a flat in Dolphin Square in Pimlico, owned by my former next door neighbour who kindly offered me the use of it on a short term basis, albeit sharing with his nephew. After paying Caroline, I had about £13,000 and out of this money I had to pay alimony and a maintenance allowance for the children. Instead, however, of trying to get a new job, on most days I found myself, full of varying degrees of fear, shame, guilt, self-pity, resentment and remorse, sitting in the flat drinking whisky. In fact, I had quickly reached the stage of being unemployable and incapable of working, and although I said to myself I would start looking for a job 'next Monday', I did nothing; always when next Monday came, I would put it off until the following Monday. In the meantime, I was telling

[53]

everybody that I had got a new job with a small insolvency firm with whom I had had previous dealings. Amazingly, this was a lie and a pretence that I managed to keep up for a whole year.

Almost immediately I had a brief affair with a woman I knew, which was good while it lasted but we soon ended it by mutual agreement. By that time I had been invited to dinner with another old neighbour and reintroduced to Mary, whom I knew slightly as one of his old girl friends. I asked her out and soon we were meeting regularly.

By this time I was beginning to really experience and be aware of alcoholic blackouts which are a form of amnesia, such as, an inability to remember what happened the previous evening when, as far as others were concerned, the alcoholic appeared to be functioning normally. I probably would have remained unaware of them had it not been for the fact that on many mornings when I wanted to use my car, I had no recollection of where or in which street I had parked it the night before. On other occasions, and this had also happened to me when I was still working, I would speak to someone, usually on the telephone, who would refer to our conversation of the previous day, and I would have absolutely no recollection of any such conversation - this could be very embarrassing!

Despite my heavy drinking, Caroline was more than happy for me to have the children at the weekends as it gave her time off. I always enjoyed the time with my children and always tried to make sure they had fun. Mary was also very kind when they came to visit. Even so, these weekends were both happy and sad for as Sunday evenings approached the children would go quiet, and in the early days they would sometimes end in tears as I took them home to their mother. Of course, this was a little unfair on Caroline as whilst they were associating me with having a good time at the weekends, they probably associated her with the weekday normality of school. On one occasion, when I told Clare that for some reason I would not be seeing her the following weekend, she looked at me with tears in her eyes and said, 'That means I am going to have to miss you for a whole two weeks.' The lives of children whose parents have divorced are certainly not easy and they should never be used as footballs between warring parents. In this I think that Caroline and I were largely successful.

Within weeks of starting to see Mary, I was invited up to Newton-by-the Sea in Northumberland to meet her mother and other members of her family. When I was then asked to spend Christmas there with my children, I began to think that Mary might have had designs on me, not least because I had a readymade family.

[54]

Shortly before Christmas, I left Dolphin Square and stayed in a small hotel in Pimlico. Usually, I spent evenings with Mary and she suggested that, instead of spending money staying in the hotel, it would be much better if I were to move in with her in her flat in Battersea. The trouble was, she thought I had job: in order to maintain the deception, I would have to leave the flat during the day. As, however, that seemed a price worth paying, I moved in with her and each week day morning I would put on a suit, pick up my brief case and get in the car to go to work. Generally, I would go to the hotel in Pimlico and spend the day 'top up' drinking, watching television, talking to hotel guests, most of whom were tourists, and advising them where to go and the best sights and shows to see. At half past five I would then get in the car, go home to Mary and tell her, over a drink, what sort of day I had had at the office.

For reasons which I did not then understand, Caroline seemed delighted at the prospect of the children spending Christmas with me. In Northumberland that year, it was a white one and it snowed quite heavily as we went to mid-night Mass on Christmas Eve at the floodlit local church in Embleton; it was absolutely beautiful. The children enjoyed that Christmas for, despite the sometimes bitterly cold winds, there was a variety of things to do, be it snowballing, walking the dogs in the snow or on the beach, feeding the horses or going to the Boxing Day meet of the Percy Hunt. As for me … every day there seemed to be one or two drinks parties somewhere in the county, and wherever we went the drink flowed like water.

On a later occasion, when Mary and I were staying with her mother, the elder of Mary's two younger sisters was also staying. Sue loved her drink and one morning when I was raiding the drinks cabinet at eleven o'clock, she walked into the room and caught me in the act of pouring myself a large sherry. With a wry smile on her face she asked me to pour one for her as well and as I handed it to her she winked and said, 'It takes one to know one.' Coming from her I did not mind the comment; indeed, I think I was probably relieved to have found an ally.

Early in January 1982, I had a call from Caroline to tell me that she wanted our decree absolute expedited as quickly as possible as she wanted to get married before the end of March, which was when her fiancé was due to retire from the Navy. For pension reasons, it was important for him to retire as a married officer. It turned out that I had met her fiancé the previous summer when she had moved into her new house; he was a near neighbour and had helped with moving her belongings into her new home.

He had given us lunch and remarked that he could not understand why we were getting divorced as we seemed to get on so well! I was genuinely pleased that Caroline was to wed again, not least because I liked him and because it would mean that I did not have to pay her alimony from my ever dwindling funds. More important, however, was that he would become my childrens' stepfather, a job he was to do supremely well. For this I shall always be grateful to him

As time went by, Mary began talking more and more about marriage, which, if I had been honest, I should have told her I did not want. To have done so, however, would have exposed the facts that, firstly, I was not working and hence would quite soon run out of money and secondly, though I would never admit it, I had a drink problem. Perhaps the most pernicious aspect of alcoholism is that of denial, which clouds the alcoholic's capacity for choice. My reality was that the only thing that really mattered was the drink, which was completely taking control of me. The very last thing I could do was voluntarily admit the truth, despite feeling the most awful fraud, as indeed I was: not only was I telling lies but, far worse, I was living a lie. If not being kidnapped, certainly I felt I was being trapped, much like a bank robber must feel knowing he was about to be found out and caught. In his book, *I'll Quit Tomorrow,* Vernon Johnson says: 'Alcoholism cannot exist unless there is a conflict between the values and behaviour of the drinker.' This explains perfectly the situation I was in. In my heart I knew that what I was doing was wrong; as such, it was in conflict with my real values; yet I was completely helpless or powerless to do anything about it. This was a fact and it is what alcoholics do. It is not an excuse, but rather an explanation, and only a tiny minority of alcoholics ever achieve recovery. Until recovery is achieved or death first intervenes, always the drink will win out. Alcoholism is cunning, baffling and powerful and, in my case, very patient for it had taken some thirty odd years for me to reach this point.

'An alcoholic in his cups is an unlovely sight.' This is a quotation from the book *Alcoholics Anonymous,* and although I was not a fall down drunk or on a park bench, I think that it was nevertheless an apt description of me at that time. What is it about chronic alkies and/or other lame ducks that make them attractive to some people? Why do so many non-alcoholics leave one alcoholic only to jump into bed with another? At thirty five, Mary had a history of failed, lame-duck relationships – I was the lamest of them all! She may not have known that I did not then have a job but she certainly knew that, to say the least, I drank very heavily. It was also obvious that drinking had been the cause of my divorce. I was later to learn in recovery that someone who needs to be needed will usually choose someone who needs to be saved. It was clear that I needed saving and I believe that there was evidence that Mary needed to be needed. It is the only reason I can think of to explain why she should think I was worth bothering with.

And so it was that with a heavy heart I agreed to marry her; the wedding was arranged for 17th September 1982. Because I was divorced, Mary and I were unable to find a priest who was prepared to marry us either in London or Northumberland, so we had to settle for Wandsworth registry office, surely one of the most unromantic places in the world. Saying my vows amid the plastic flowers, I wondered what on earth I was doing. This was followed by a reception in London and a blessing service and reception a week later in Northumberland. I thought it was all unnecessarily extravagant but I had no option other than to go along with it, nor indeed had I any right to criticise it in any way. Drink-wise, I managed to get through it all without making a fool of myself, although it took an enormous effort.

We had a short, unmemorable honeymoon in very wet weather in Scotland and frankly I was glad when we eventually got back to London and I resumed my fictitious work. By that time my alcoholism had reached the stage where I was drinking an average of one and two bottles of scotch a day so that I would be awakened very early every morning by the pains of withdrawals, sweating, shaking and retching, as I was unable to keep the first drink down. I had terrible feelings of fear, despair, loneliness, guilt and shame about the person I had become. I could not start the day without a drink but as soon as I succeeded in getting one down, I was off again on the same ghastly merry go round of drinking until I went to bed and passed out. I was no longer drinking to feel good, only to feel less ill; I could no longer live with drink yet even though it was no longer 'working', I still could not live without it. It was hell on earth! My greatest fears were those of being found out, as I knew I soon would be, and also of finding out myself. I was terrified of being put under the spotlight as I knew it would expose me for the complete fraud I had become and of which I was so ashamed.

Mary was a moderate church goer and we used to go to the local church by the river in Battersea on most Sundays. The vicar, Canon John Morris was a lovely charismatic man and partly at Mary's suggestion I approached him with a view to receiving confirmation classes. Earlier that summer we had spent a few days in Cornwall and one day we went to Tintagel Castle on the north coast. As I looked down at the sea crashing against the rocks far below, I thought how small and powerless I felt, yet even if I was no more than a tiny pebble on the beach, somehow there must be a way out of all my problems. It was a very humbling moment and fleetingly it gave me a little hope that perhaps if I could somehow find help, all might yet be well. It was also a defining moment and I am sure that this incident had much to do with my seeking confirmation and subsequently finding recovery.

At the age of sixteen I had turned my back on God; perhaps if I were to turn to him at age forty-six, he would help me. It was a covert cry for help, made the more attractive by the fact that John always offered me a whisky when I went for my weekly classes. I can remember nothing of what he taught me as it went in one ear and straight out of the other, but I was duly confirmed sometime in October, some two months before I entered treatment.

In AA's words: *The unhappiest person in the world is the chronic alcoholic who has an insistent yearning to enjoy life as they once knew it, but cannot picture life without alcohol. They have a **heartbreaking obsession** that by some miracle of control, they would be able to do so.*[3] Because of my chronic addiction to alcohol this is what I had become. But although alcoholic drinking had almost run its course with me, I was still not ready to admit that I was beaten. Nevertheless, within a few short weeks, a miracle did happen, though not in the way I was expecting. (I think it worth pointing out that anyone who doesn't believe in miracles is not being realistic!)

As many of our wedding presents consisted of money, Mary and I opened a separate joint wedding bank account and the amount paid in to it was about £400. By the time we returned to London my money had almost run out and in desperation I was forced to raid this account. When she found out, Mary was justifiably furious. Her suspicions were aroused and to make matters worse, she accidentally drank from my cup of coffee one morning; of course, it was heavily laced with whisky. Unbeknownst to me, she had rung the company I said I was working for and discovered that I was not employed there. My worst fear was of being found out but Mary simply sat me down that morning.

'I know you haven't a job and I think you need help,' she said.

'Yes,' I replied, 'I think I probably do.'

It was the first time in years that I had been half honest with myself, and to my surprise Mary did not berate me or get annoyed. Even more to my surprise, I felt quite relieved that she knew and that my deception was now out in the open: I no longer had to lie. I told her a little of what was going on with me but I was in no way ready to tell her all.

She insisted that I go and see her doctor just off Sloane Square and fortunately for me he knew a lot more about alcoholism and drug addiction than most doctors. I was with him for about an hour during which time I confessed to most of what I had been drinking and to some of what I had been up to. Cleverly he did a deal with me: he said that he would give me some pills to take for a week and if I could refrain from drinking during that time, I might be all right; if, on the other hand, I was to drink at all during that week, I would have to enter treatment. I agreed, but immediately upon leaving his surgery, I repaired to the nearest pub where I ordered a couple of large whiskies and reflected upon my situation. Needless to say, I drank every day that week and completely failed his test. When I saw him again and told him what had happened, he told me the results of the liver test he had taken the previous week, which indicated that if I were to continue drinking I had less than two years to live. He also told me in no uncertain terms that **I was a straight up chronic alcoholic.** He then picked up the telephone and booked me into Broadway Lodge, a treatment centre in Weston-super-Mare and told me that I had to attend there that afternoon. I protested that I had the children coming that weekend, but to no avail, as he would have none of it. He also told me that a friend who wished to remain anonymous had agreed to pay my treatment fees which were substantial. Reluctantly I agreed. I was beaten and I could see that I really had no choice. Mary would not have me and there was nowhere else to go.

On the way home I stopped at the bank, drew out my last remaining £50 and went to the pub for a 'farewell' drink. Once home, I packed a bag and before leaving had one final drink with Mary. Ironically it was a gin as we had run out of whisky and I remember thinking that I might not be having another drink for quite some time. Over twenty seven years later, it remains my last drink. We got in the car and driving down to Weston I told Mary that she was not to worry as it would be all right and that I was not an alcoholic! It was 17th December 1982, three months to the day since we were married.

PART TWO
The Solution

Chapter 6

Broadway Lodge, Weston-super-Mare
Conditional liberation from the shackles of illness
1982 – 1983

'We believe that addiction to alcohol and drugs (chemical dependency) is a chronic, progressive, primary and incurable disease, not a problem of morals or willpower. The disease, if left unchecked, will prove terminal either directly through the effect of the drugs on the organs of the body, or indirectly through causing accidents, etc. The disease is tripartite: mental, physical and spiritual and is characterised by loss of control over alcohol and other mood-altering substances. That is to say, the inability of the patient to predict what will happen when they take a drink or use drugs. If the patient receives the correct treatment there is a good chance that the disease will be arrested and the patient able to lead a normal, fulfilled life. Our goal is to help the patient live without chemical support.'[4]

Broadway Lodge opened in 1974 (since when it has admitted over 7,000 patients into treatment) and was the first treatment centre in the United Kingdom to operate what has become known as the Minnesota model of treatment for alcoholism and drug addiction. Such centres were pioneered in America and were based on complete abstinence and the first five steps of the recovery programme of Alcoholics Anonymous (AA). At the time I was there it was one of only a very few such treatment centres in Britain.

Having said goodbye to Mary with some relief, I began to wonder just what I had let myself in for. I was soon to find out and it all began when I was interviewed by one of the night nurses and put on a short course of detoxification lasting six days. This was designed to minimise the effects of withdrawal from alcohol, which otherwise could be extremely dangerous and on occasions fatal. She also took my photograph to remind me what I looked like on the day I entered treatment. I have it still! Also during the first week I saw the doctor who gave me a physical check up. Since my initial detox, I have never been medically treated for my alcoholism.

I was then taken to the main smoke-filled sitting room to be introduced to some of the other patients. Despite the stunning view of the lights of Cardiff across the Severn Estuary, my eyes lit upon a large scroll hanging on the wall upon which were written The Twelve Steps of the recovery programme of Alcoholics Anonymous (AA), the first one of which read:

1. We admitted we were powerless over alcohol – that our lives had become unmanageable.

I got stuck on the word powerless and as you will see I was to be unable to get past it for nearly eight weeks. Although I was unaware of it at the time, acceptance without reservation of this simple step is the foundation on which the whole of the recovery programme is built. Without such acceptance one simply does not begin.

The other patients comprised a total of about thirty alcoholics and, to my astonishment, drug addicts, of both sexes and varying ages. They came from a wide variety of backgrounds, from rich and poor, and from nobility to the streetwise East End cockney. All of us had ended up in the same place – alcoholism, drug and other addictions are no respecters of race, colour, class, wealth, sex, religion or academic ability. In addition there was one person with an eating disorder (Bulimia Nervosa and Anorexia Nervosa) and one or two who were additionally addicted to prescribed medication such as Valium, Atavan and other sedatives and anti-depressants. In short, my peers were addicted to a number of different mood altering drugs and all were receiving precisely the same treatment. Almost all were addicted to nicotine. We referred to ourselves as being alcoholic and chemically dependent.

The treatment mainly consisted of:
- regular one-to-one sessions with our allotted personal counsellor (most of the counsellors were themselves alcoholics and/or addicts in recovery)
- two group sessions a day, in many of which patients would each share examples of powerlessness and damage and, where necessary, group members would confront any denial in those who were silent
- lectures on the illness and on the first five steps of the AA programme
- specific written assignments and some other activities such as meditation and relaxation.

In addition we were each given some daily domestic task to carry out, such as cleaning, gardening, washing up and even cooking breakfast on Sundays.

On my first morning I attended a group session at the start of which we went round the room introducing ourselves, stating our names and the fact that we were alcoholic and chemically dependent. When it came to my turn, without giving it any thought and because I did not want to appear the odd man out, I said, '**My name is Billy and I am an alcoholic and chemically dependent.**' Although I was miles away from complete acceptance of my powerlessness, it was the first time I had ever uttered such words and the first time that I had begun to confront my denial. I have been saying those words ever since.

Later that morning, I was introduced to my counsellor, Ed Lindsey, who said, 'Hello, my name is Ed and I am an alcoholic. I have been sober for five years and have never felt happier.' He then briefly explained what the treatment was about and went through some of the house rules, the most important of which was that drink and drugs were completely forbidden and if any of us was found drinking, using or in possession of alcohol or drugs, we would be asked to leave immediately.

He concluded by saying, '**You may find Billy that during your stay in treatment you will experience a strong desire to walk out and leave. If you do, you should remember that if you do walk out, you will be going back out with the same chap you came in with to leave behind.**'

I took this to mean that I had to commit myself to recovery no matter how I felt or how much I might want to pick up a drink. Reluctantly and without fully understanding what I was doing, I voluntarily made the commitment. Without having done that and sticking to it, I would not be alive today. As it happened, I did not experience any overwhelming desire to walk out, but I subsequently took the same message with me into AA and to this day it remains indelibly in my memory. This session with Ed had a profound effect on me because he was the first sober alcoholic and AA member to whom I had ever spoken: he was telling me about alcoholism and recovery from personal experience. Although at that stage, I did not by any means fully comprehend what he was saying or accept that I myself was an alcoholic, I instinctively knew he was being honest and he was talking in a language I could understand. He gave me hope: if he could recover, then perhaps I could too. In fact, the only counsellors who had any effect on me were those who were themselves alcoholics or addicts. They were the ones to whom I could relate and they were only ones I trusted.

In the afternoon group session which followed this interview, Ed, who was taking the group, told us: '**You have a chronic, primary illness called** alcoholism and it is not your fault. The illness is mental, physical and spiritual. If you continue drinking, always it will get worse, never will it get better, and further, you have the illness that tells you that you have not got it - denial. It is progressive, incurable and fatal if not arrested. But although incurable, you can arrest the illness and recover through complete abstinence from alcohol and all other mood altering chemicals, and by practising the Twelve Step recovery programme of Alcoholics Anonymous, one day at a time.'

(During the course of recovery, I have come to realize that it is an illness of low self-worth, fear and loneliness as well).

Later Ed added, '**The only difference between an alcoholic and a lunatic is that an alcoholic feels guilt.**' (And in my case, shame)

As if to underline the fatal and incurable nature of the illness, Ed told us in 'group', a day or two later, that Broadway Lodge had a pretty good recovery success rate of about seventy-five percent. That meant that out of the twelve of us sitting in group that day, *three* of us would die. I looked around the room trying to assess who might recover and who might die, almost forgetting that I too was one of the twelve! For me, however, the point was well made or I would not be here. It is absolutely essential that any alcoholic or other drug addict understands the exact nature and seriousness of his illness for it is something we forget at our peril.

It was also explained that we were chemically dependent. Chemical dependency includes both drug addiction and alcoholism (addiction to the narcotic drug alcohol), and refers to a primary illness or disease characterised by addiction to a mood-altering chemical.

When people are chemically dependent, they have lost the power of choice over using mood altering chemicals. They may be able to stop for a while but they will return to its use again and again, despite their best intentions, logic and will-power. The illness is characterised by continuous or periodic impaired control over drinking and/or drug use – either prescribed or illegal –, preoccupation or obsession with the mood altering drug(s) of choice together with a sometimes overwhelming compulsion to drink and/or use. A sufferer's thinking also becomes increasingly distorted particularly by denial, which is a defence mechanism to protect an over-inflated ego from accepting the truth. It includes rationalisations (using your intelligence to deny the truth) designed increasingly to reduce awareness of the fact that alcohol/drug use is the cause of their problems and not the solution to those problems. (Certainly in my own case I was, whilst drinking, incapable of seeing that all my problems were the consequence of my drinking. Throughout the final stages of my drinking, I always thought that I drank because of my problems.) Typically, alcoholics or addicts are the last to admit that they may have a drinking or drug using addiction. Denial becomes an integral part of the chemical dependency disease process, a major obstacle to recovery and a major factor in or the cause of relapse. In the words of AA it is the 'cunning, baffling and powerful' part of chemical dependency that tells the addicted person that they do not have a problem. If a person is in denial, he cannot start the recovery process.

But it was not just my powerlessness that I was in denial of: I was also in denial of the fact that alcoholism and chemical dependency are progressive diseases. Whilst from the beginning I associated drinking with pleasure, as time went by it became associated more and more with the avoidance of pain. The useful formula, therefore, which should be indelibly imprinted in all of our minds, alcoholics and non-alcoholics alike, is:

PAIN + ALCOHOL (OR A DRUG) = TEMPORARY RELIEF + **INCREASED PAIN.**

I further learned that alcohol is a sedative, hypnotic drug C2 H5 OH. Take away the colour, the taste and the water and you have ether. When a person is drinking, the brain and the body have no idea whether they are in an operating theatre under anaesthetic or in the pub having a few beers. The brain also receives the same message from alcohol as it does from sleeping pills and tranquillisers. All mood altering drugs act on the brain and if an alcoholic is in recovery, he cannot risk taking any other drug which would alter the mood, as such mood alteration would cause him to lose control of the mind and would probably lead back to the drug of choice, namely alcohol. Similarly, a heroin addict must refrain from taking alcohol, which in any event is very often a 'gateway' drug to heroin, or he will revert to heroin. This phenomenon is known as cross addiction and can be very difficult for some to accept, especially me, as the only drugs I ever took were alcohol and nicotine. Even though I have never taken for example heroin or cocaine, were I to do so, I would be running a very great risk that it would quickly take me back to alcohol.

This was the first time I had been told what alcoholism, chemical dependency and cross addiction were and I was in a state of some shock for these were cold hard facts that I was being asked to digest; they were entirely new to me and quite contrary to what I had always thought. I was being asked to unlearn nearly all my previous thinking. If I did not stop drinking or using other mood altering chemicals, I was going to die, and the first thing I had to do in order to recover was to accept that I was powerless over alcohol/mood altering chemicals. Bad news though this was, I was nevertheless slightly encouraged by the fact that it was possible to get well if I were to do what was being suggested and practised the AA programme as a way of life. Even so, I was appalled by the prospect of abstinence - I had no desire whatever to stop drinking, nor had I any real idea what the AA programme entailed. Why, I wondered, had nobody ever told me about this before? To put it mildly, I was very confused and bewildered. Yet paradoxically, I was also intrigued and wanted to know more.

We were also told of Williams Glasser's theory that we are ill because we were irresponsible; get responsible and we will get well.[5] Bearing in mind that chemical dependency is a primary illness, I have some difficulty in accepting the first part of this statement but I have absolutely no quarrel with the second half. Indeed, I am profoundly grateful that I alone have the responsibility of staying away from the first drink and of practising the AA Twelve Step programme of recovery in order to arrest my otherwise fatal illness and hence become well. What would someone with cancer, Parkinson's or Motor Neurone Disease give to know that all they had to do to recover was not to pick a drink and follow a few simple instructions? Even so, and mainly because of ignorance and denial, it remains a fact that only about two or three percent of alcoholics recover from their illness.

As I have mentioned, at most of the daily group sessions we would share examples of powerlessness and damage and though I had little difficulty in identifying with others in the group, I was not prepared to share myself. I was in a state of denial and was to remain so all the time I was resident in Broadway Lodge. On one of the rare occasions when I did open my mouth, I happened to say that I had never hit either of my two wives. (As a boy, I had been taught by my father never to hit a woman.) To my astonishment, my peers did not believe me. We had been told we had to be honest and here I was telling the truth yet I was not being believed. I was very upset about this until a week or so later when Ed told the group that he had received letters from both Caroline and Mary, confirming that I had never hit either of them. The group is not always right!

Nor are some of the counsellors always right. About three weeks after I arrived, I happened to be talking to one of the new lady counsellors. I thought her grasp on her own sobriety was somewhat tenuous as she was quite tense, nervous and unsure of herself. Certainly she did not have the kind of sobriety that I wanted. Much to my amazement, she asked me if I realized that I would never be able to play golf again. When I asked why, she said that as there are bars at golf clubs I could never go near a golf course again. I did not believe her and on remonstrating I did manage to get her to concede that it might be all right, provided I changed in the car park and did not go into the club house. I was so taken aback that I went to Ed, who fortunately told me that it was a lot of nonsense and that certainly I would be able to go into clubhouses and play again – and play better than I did when I was drinking. This taught me that there are people who, even in recovery, are still quite sick and I realized that the people I should take most notice of were those who were well and had what I wanted.

The first passage of the Big Book that I can recall reading gave me comfort and some reassurance. I vividly remember one occasion when it was read to us.

If we are painstaking about this phase of our development, we will be amazed before we are half way through. We are going to know a new freedom and a new happiness. We will not regret the past nor wish to shut the door on it. We will comprehend the word serenity and we will know peace. No matter how far down the scale we have gone, we see how our experience can benefit others. That feeling of uselessness and self-pity will disappear. We will lose interest in selfish things and gain interest in our fellows. Self-seeking will slip away. Our whole attitude and outlook upon life will change. Fear of people and economic insecurity will leave us. We will intuitively know how to handle things which used to baffle us. We will suddenly realize that God is doing for us what we could not do for ourselves.

Are these extravagant promises? We think not. They are being fulfilled among us – sometimes quickly, sometimes slowly. They will always materialize if we work for them.[6]

I had entered Broadway Lodge a week before Christmas. During the first week whilst I was being de-toxified (incidentally I experienced no withdrawal symptoms whatever during this time), I was not allowed any contact with my wife, relatives or friends and I was wondering what Christmas would be like without a drink and where Mary would be spending it. Christmas Day turned out to be happy for me for three main reasons. The first was something one of the counsellors, who had come in to wish us a Happy

Christmas, said to me. He was telling me how he had been reduced to drinking the anti-freeze from his car radiator, and how he had recovered and been sober for a number of years. Then he said: **'If I can do it, then you can do it. The good news is that you can get well if you want to and the bad news is that nobody else is going to do it for you. If you don't pick up the first drink you can't get drunk. It is the first drink that does the damage – one drink is too many, one hundred not enough.'** Perhaps because it was so obvious, I had never thought of it like this before and it made a strong impression. It was a powerful message, which I have never forgotten.

The second reason was being allowed to watch, on television, the Agatha Christie film, *Death on the Nile* with Peter Ustinov and David Niven. It was the first time in years that I had not gone to sleep in a film but had been able to concentrate on it and enjoy it throughout. It was also the first time I had heard of Monsieur Hercule Poirot!

The third and most important reason it was a happy day was because I was sober. It was the first of my twenty eight consecutive sober Christmases.

Just after Christmas, I was told of the unexpected death in Northumberland of Mary's sister Sue, who had been killed in a car crash on her way home from Kelso races. Apparently the Mini she had been driving had gone straight into the back of a stationary lorry and burst into flames. I was very sorry to learn of her death as I felt, remembering morning drinks at Newton, that she was a kindred spirit. This was later confirmed in my own mind when the post mortem revealed that she was way, way over the legal drinking limit. And so she had become yet another young victim of this awful disease. I was sorry, too, for Mary as it was a sad loss for her, coming on top of the problems she was having with me. All I could do was to write her a letter of sympathy, as I also did to her mother.

Another letter I later had to write to Mary was one of apology. I was summoned to Ed's office one day and he asked me if I had had a vasectomy. I was astonished and replied in the negative. 'Well,' he said, 'Mary believes you have and she is very angry about it.' She had apparently been told this by our former next door neighbour. It was true that in the late seventies, after the births of my two children, I had considered having a vasectomy and had discussed it with Caroline and my G.P, but in the end I had decided against it. I did remember discussing the general topic of vasectomy with my former neighbour, one evening. But I was sure that I had never told him I had actually had the operation and that he had got the wrong end of the stick. I was forced, however, to concede that **in drink I could have**

told him otherwise and so I duly had to write a letter of apology to Mary, explaining what had happened.

Amongst the tasks we were required to do at the commencement of treatment was to write down fifty examples of powerlessness and damage and this was followed by the writing of a life story, particularly as it had been affected by alcohol. This had to be read out to a small group of a dozen or so peers and it was, without doubt, the scariest thing I have ever had to do. It took me some forty minutes to read and at the end of it I was asked, 'How do you feel?' My reply was, 'Numb,' though on reflection I think a more accurate answer would have been, 'Naked and vulnerable.' Each member of the group, including me, had to write a confrontation letter back to me saying what they thought. Some were sensible and helpful whist others were quite vicious and abusive. The best, though, was the one I wrote to myself:

8th January 1983

Dear Billy,

Thank you for reading me your life story.

It makes the most shocking reading – the story of a reasonably intelligent person who was selfish, idle, deceitful beyond belief, and completely untrustworthy. A person who, for the last ten years or so, has left a trail of destruction and damage behind him without, it would seem, caring or giving a damn.

From 1975 onwards you systematically set about destroying your marriage notwithstanding the fact that you had two young children whom you say you adore and whose upbringing, unfortunately for them, was fifty per cent entrusted to you. How lucky for them it was not one hundred per cent.

On finding yourself redundant in 1974 you chose drink in order to escape your inadequacies when to anyone else the obvious thing would have been to act responsibly and to fight for the super family which you did not deserve. From then on you thought only of yourself and your wretched whisky. You were little concerned for the welfare of your then wife and your children. You were financially irresponsible and must have been hell to live with. You made life unmanageable for your wife and because, inter alia, of the constant rows must have damaged your children. To what extent I suspect even you do not know. All I hope, for their sakes, is that it was not too much. In future you had better try as hard as you can to make amends to them. You caused your marriage to end in divorce and your children a broken home. Fortunately your ex-wife has remarried and I hope has now found the happiness which she never could have found with you.

Following the breakup of your marriage, you then set about spending the capital you received from the sale of your home and were too bloody idle and selfish to find yourself a job.

Not content with that you perpetrated a deceit on Mary which was so gross that I cannot find any words adequate to describe it. How could you possibly do such a thing to the girl you say you love? Billy you are a complete and utter fraud who appears to have no sense of shame or guilt. If you go on like this, I no longer want to know you.

You are lucky that you now have the opportunity to get well if you really want to. Take it for your own sake and in order that you may make amends to Mary (how do you think she must be feeling?) and the rest of your respective families. Get rid of your pride, arrogance, selfishness, untrustworthiness, dishonesty and above all your irresponsibility and there maybe something worthwhile left. For God's sake don't blow it now.

Your alcoholic and chemically dependent friend,

Billy.

What I now find particularly interesting is how it was written from 'the other me' and only from the points of view of those I had harmed or damaged. Although the letter shows that I was not in denial of the damage I had done to others, it takes no account whatever of the damage I did to myself or of my powerlessness over alcohol, which at that time I had not accepted. The letter does not recognise that, given my powerlessness, drink was increasingly controlling me and that accordingly there was an inevitability about everything that happened to me and what I did. Drink was more and more taking me to places I did not want to go to and making me do things I did not want to do, and I was powerless to do anything about it. In his book, *I'll Quit Tomorrow,* Dr Vernon E. Johnson says: *Our most striking observation has been that alcoholism cannot exist unless there is a conflict between the values and the behaviour of the drinker.*[7] I believe that this is the reason why alcoholics feel guilt and shame. Certainly my behaviour was driving a coach and horses through my own value system as is shown so vividly in the letter.

I very much enjoyed the lectures we were given, made copious notes, and became quite fascinated with the disease concept of alcoholism. In spite of all that I was learning, however, I still found it impossible to concede that I was powerless over alcohol, not least because I did not understand powerlessness. I answered a thirty-one point questionnaire as to whether or not I was an alcoholic and scored thirty affirmatively. The one question I answered in the negative asked whether I had noticed a decline in my tolerance. The questionnaire helped me to understand I was an alcoholic but still I had problems about powerlessness. In desperation I went to Ed and asked him to explain exactly what it meant. He explained, **'If one is an alcoholic and picks up a drink, one cannot predict with certainty how many one will have, when one will put the glass down, or indeed *if* one will put the glass down - or what one's behaviour will be.'** It was the words 'predict with certainty' that I picked up on and I began to realize that even with me – the great controlled drinker – there had been occasions, even in the early days, when I had drunk more than I meant to and times when my behaviour had definitely been out of order.

Yet still I was in denial and could not accept I was completely beaten by alcohol. To help me with this I was given a verbal which I had to say out loud at the start of every group for a week: **My name is Billy and I'm an alcoholic and chemically dependent. I am not a gentleman drunk but a sick person trying to get well. If I don't get honest, my pride will kill me.** I felt a complete idiot having to say this, but the point is that it was true.

After reading our life stories, we were taken to evening AA meetings in Weston-super-Mare which I found interesting. I did not, as yet, feel a member of AA because I had not accepted my powerlessness and did not want to stop drinking. (Tradition 3 of AA states: 'The only qualification for AA membership is a desire to stop drinking.'[8]) I noticed, however, that there was a lot of laughter in the rooms and that one or two people seemed very relaxed, contented and happy - and not drinking. They were sober and they were helping others!

Also after reading our life stories, we were required to attend at least one of the family group sessions held on Sunday afternoons when spouses and other family members attended. I hope not to sound insensitive, considering what they may have had to put up with, but I was astonished at just how angry and dysfunctional most of them were, and I began to realize why, unlike other sick people, chronic alcoholics in early recovery are very rarely given grapes or bunches of flowers! In my case, I did receive a number of letters of support, however, two of which particularly stand out in my memory. The first was from John Sheridan who reminded me of some of the things of which I was still capable, if only I could find the resolve to accept my problem and recover from it. The second was from Donald, who I think would agree that we have never been the greatest of communicators, but his letter was inspiring and I am very grateful for all the help he has given me in the years since.

While I was at Broadway Lodge, I was told of the death of my old Uncle John at his home in Norwich. Uncle John, who was the second eldest and only remaining survivor of father's three bachelor brothers, was a doctor and dental surgeon whom we used to go and visit every summer with my mother and my children. A lifelong bachelor, in his mid-eighties when he died, he had had a lady companion, also a dentist, of many years standing called Joan who lived next door to him. They never married, and when my mother later asked Joan why, she said that it was because he had never asked her! Having been born in the nineteenth century, he was very much of the old school and apparently had been very upset by my divorce from Caroline. 'We have never had a divorce before in my family,' he once told Joan, to which she replied, 'But none of you ever got married!' As one of his only three living relatives, I had expected to inherit a part of his estate but I was glad that he had survived until after I entered treatment; otherwise, I would have drunk the not inconsiderable legacy which I received a few months into sobriety.

Six weeks into treatment, it was becoming clear even to me that I was stuck at Step One of the AA programme and hence was not making any progress. I had learnt a lot but my denial was still intact, despite having taken a pounding and being weakened. I still could not accept my powerlessness over alcohol. I was beginning to realize that I might be asked to leave and so it did not come as a complete surprise when I was summoned to see Ed in his office. He said to me in the nicest possible way, **'Billy, we are very sorry but we don't think there is anything more we can do for you. We think you may have to drink again. You may have to have a second divorce or you might make it in AA.'** (I did get a second divorce, but I have not, thus far, drunk again and I have, thus far, made it in AA.) He explained that they wanted me to go and stay in Weston-super-Mare for eight weeks, go to at least four AA meetings a week there and stay sober. If I could do that I could come back and complete treatment. In much the same way that Carl Jung had admitted his powerless over Rowland H. and Dr Silkworth had admitted his over Bill W.[1] (See Overture), this was an admittance of my counsellors' powerlessness over me, to whom it was ego deflation at some depth. They were not, however, cutting me off completely and I was not totally without hope and a goal. I did not protest but said 'OK' and packed my bag.

On my last night at Broadway Lodge I was talking to the night nurse and I happened to say, 'You know I have been telling lies all of my life.'

'That's the first honest thing I have heard you say!' she replied.

As I was getting into my taxi the next day, one of the other counsellors said as a parting shot, '**Remember your powerlessness Billy, always remember your powerlessness.**' And up until today, I always have.

The taxi driver duly deposited me at one of the hundreds of guest houses in Weston. After checking in and unpacking, I went downstairs and found myself in the bar! I had not realized it was licensed. For the first time in six weeks I was exposed to alcohol, and as I looked at the inverted bottles of whisky and my favourite malts behind the bar, I realized that a part of me wanted a drink very badly. 'THINK, THINK, THINK!' is an AA slogan displayed at most AA meetings and it is intended mainly for those sorts of occasion in which I then found myself. The part of me that wrote the confrontation letter to myself, and maybe pride, came to my rescue for I found myself thinking, f... all those counsellors; I'll bloody well show them; I don't have to pick up a drink. And so, for the first time in my life, I refused a drink voluntarily. This and to a slightly lesser extent my experience the following day at Tintern, were the closest by some distance that I have been to yielding, but I thank God that on both occasions I had the good sense to think before picking up that drink.

Following this I rang Mary to tell her what had happened and where I was. She was not best pleased to hear that I had been therapeutically discharged – the posh name for being kicked out – but she asked me how I felt. To my surprise I told her that I was scared. It was the first time that I can recall ever admitting I was frightened but, again to my surprise, I found that in sharing it with her a lot of the fear went away. It demonstrated to me clearly that **a problem shared is a problem halved and a problem bottled is a problem doubled**.

Mary explained that the following day she was due to go to Tintern on the river Wye for the weekend, to fish with a couple of friends whom I knew quite well, and I was welcome to join them. I was a bit hesitant as salmon fishing is not my sport and I wondered how much I would enjoy just watching it, but I nevertheless arranged to meet them the following morning at Temple Meads railway station in Bristol. Tintern is a lovely spot and it seemed better than staying in Weston. We checked into a small hotel close to the famous abbey ruins and then went fishing. Being a rather bored spectator, I volunteered to go back to the car to fetch some bit of fishing tackle which had been left behind. As I opened the car boot, there staring me in the face was a half filled bottle of Teachers whisky. I experienced the same feelings as I had the day before: half of me really wanted to take a swig. It would have been so easy and no one would have known. But no, I was not going to be beaten that easily; so for the same reasons as the day before, I refused a drink.

At dinner that evening, the wine and the brandy flowed steadily but I was not in the least tempted. Curiously, I felt a strange feeling of neutrality about it as, for the first time, I found myself regarding liquor as poison, the more so as the others gradually became a bit the worse for wear. I had never looked at it like this before, and I also realized that people even partially under the influence of drink become sillier and sillier and the conversation more and more boring and repetitive. For the first time ever, I was both glad and grateful that I did not want or have to be in the same state. An added bonus was that the next morning I felt much better than they did! The First Step was beginning to sink in and make a bit more sense, but I still was not completely convinced that I was powerless over alcohol.

That first week I was very conscious that I had to attend my minimum four AA meetings a week as I naively thought that Broadway Lodge would somehow be checking up on me. On one evening, I arrived at the Y.M.C.A. at seven o'clock for the seven thirty meeting and was slightly puzzled that I did not recognise anybody. There were a couple of ladies making tea and some old men in flat caps talking amongst themselves. I approached one of the ladies and asked tentatively if this was the AA meeting. 'Yea love,' she replied. Time went on and still I could see nobody I knew so I asked the lady again, 'Is this the AA meeting - Alcoholics Anonymous?' 'No, love,' she replied, 'this is the Allotment Association!' In a state of near panic, I realized I had got the dates wrong and had to hastily find the correct venue for that night's meeting.

I went to all the required AA meetings and I stayed dry but I did not enjoy the meetings because I still did not really want to stop drinking. I was 'white knuckling' it. What I can now see clearly is that I was in a state of grief at the prospect of losing what I thought was my oldest and best friend – alcohol. Even so, I was beginning to realize that, in fact, alcohol was treacherous and far from being a friend, it was my deadliest enemy. I felt betrayed. But still I could not accept having to live the rest of my life without having a drink and having to go to AA. It seemed to be all doom, gloom, ginger ale and Jesus.

I had very little money at this time but having signed on at the Labour Exchange, I had enough money to pay for my lodgings and to live frugally. My mother, God bless her, gave me money for my cigarettes, then about forty a day.

On the first Sunday evening in February 1983 and the second after my therapeutic discharge, I went to a meeting of Narcotics Anonymous at Corpus Christi Church as there were no AA meetings on in Weston that night. I figured that since alcohol was a narcotic drug, I was qualified to attend. So doing was the turning point in my life for as I sat down and collected my thoughts, my eyes focused on a slogan in front of me which said:

INSANITY IS MAKING THE SAME MISTAKE TWICE AND EXPECTING A DIFFERENT RESULT.

It was the convincer that I needed and it hit me straight between the eyes; in an instant its message went from my head to my heart, sometimes the longest journey in the world. *That's it*! I thought. My mind flashed back to that occasion in 1969 when, on the boat on the way to Bergen, one cigarette had led to thirteen years of smoking like a chimney. It was the first cigarette that had done the damage then, and I understood and knew exactly what would happen if I were to pick up a first drink: it would be the same as that first cigarette and I would soon be back in the state I was in eight weeks earlier – and as with the cigarettes, I might well be unable to stop. As I reflected on what had happened, I saw that I had stopped complying because I had fully conceded to my innermost self that I was a chronic alcoholic. I had accepted without any reservation whatever and surrendered to that which I had denied for so long: I was utterly powerless over alcohol which had for years been controlling me. I not only knew it but I could feel it deep inside. At last my grieving was over and I said goodbye to alcohol. (To be free you have to say goodbye.)

And ye shall know the truth and the truth will set you free. (John 8:32, Darby Bible) Surrendering to the truth, accepting that I am and always will be an alcoholic, and saying goodbye to alcohol were the liberating forces I had been seeking for so long. And the obsession and compulsion to drink was lifted right out of me. I knew then that I wanted to live more than I wanted to die, that I wanted to be sober more that I wanted to drink. I saw that for the first time in years I had a choice: I could either do it my way, and I knew for sure where that would take me, or I could do it the AA way, God's way. I had had a spiritual experience or awakening which was very intense. I felt humble yet strangely elated, grateful and at peace with myself. I was an alcoholic and it was OK to be an alcoholic. Miraculously and in the words of the Big Book, I had stopped living in the problem and started to live in the answer – and the problem went away. With my denial broken, the civil war that had raged within me for so long was over and at last I knew and understood why we have to surrender to win and why alcoholism cannot be beaten if you refuse to admit complete defeat. Though I did not realise it at the time, I had experienced what I now call the power of powerlessness and it was this gift which gave me back the power of choice. It may be paradoxical but for me it was, nonetheless, what activated the switch from the negative to the positive, from wanting to drink, indeed needing to drink, to wanting to be sober; it was and remains the key to my recovery. At the beginning of chapter 5 I described how wanting to drink had manifestly become needing to drink and one of the great paradoxes of alcoholism, at any rate for me, is that with the total acceptance of and surrender to Step 1, I changed from needing recovery to wanting it and to being sober – and twenty seven years later, I still want above all else to be sober.

I knew that there were certain people in AA who had what I wanted and all of them were working the Twelve Step programme of recovery. I could see that the programme worked only if you worked it, for it is a programme of action. Accordingly, I committed myself to AA and recovery with enthusiasm, and, literally, with a new lease of life. I accepted and trusted The Twelve Step programme without reservation. It was something I knew I could do and that if I did, I would get well.

It is a sobering thought that had it not been for what I had learned about chemical dependency and the nature of multi and cross addiction in Broadway Lodge, I almost certainly would never have gone to an NA meeting and hence would never have seen the slogan/statement, originally attributed to Albert Einstein, that brought about and clinched my acceptance of and surrender to my powerlessness, which saved my life. Sometimes life hangs on very slender threads for I have never since seen that slogan in any of the thousands of AA meetings I have gone to.

I read a great deal about the illness and recovery and was fascinated by what I was learning. Apart from AA literature, there were two books which made a big impression on me. The first was *Why Am I Afraid to Tell You Who I Am?* by John Powell. The answer it gave to that question was: *'But if I tell you who I am, you may not like who I am, and it is all that I have … If I expose my nakedness as a person to you, do not make me feel shame … I can only know that much of myself which I have had the courage to confide in you.'* It also went on to say: *'To live fully, we must learn to use things and love people, not to love things and use people.'* As I have said, when I was at Broadway Lodge I had the greatest difficulty in sharing, in talking about myself. This book helped me to see why and, as it was important to discover who I was, I resolved henceforth to share in all the meetings I went to. At first it was difficult and daunting but with time and practice it became easier and indeed fun. Sharing is the catalyst by which we recover and, paradoxically, as we became ill by using our mouths so too we become well by using our mouths! I believe it is true that we are as sick as the secrets we keep.

The second was a pamphlet, *A Rational Counselling Primer* by Howard S. Young. In it he explained that it is not an event that makes us angry but the view we take of it. Therefore, thinking produces feelings which in turn usually produce actions. Almost all misery-producing ideas have one characteristic in common: they contain one or both of the words 'awful' and 'should'. Always, therefore, we would be well advised to question why we think something is really so awful or why something should or shouldn't have happened. We all exaggerate, often to impress, by using phrases like 'it was a complete and utter nightmare' or 'it was absolutely fantastic', and I have learned that nothing is ever as bad as it seems or as good as it seems. In my own case, some of my worst disasters have turned out to be blessings in disguise, and what appeared to be an end was really a new beginning. When we change the way we look at things, the things we are looking at change. I also learned in the early eighties from a legendary and wise old timer who died sober shortly afterwards that 'very little matters and most things don't matter at all'! For an alcoholic, I would now say that the only things that really matter are staying away from a drink and working the Twelve Step programme to the best of our ability. If we do that, everything else will work out OK or as it is meant to. In reality there are few other, if any, really big deals.

During my first six weeks at Broadway Lodge I was in denial of my anger but the more I thought about it, the more I realized that actually my anger should properly have been directed against alcohol, which had been well on the way to killing me and had caused me so much pain and so many problems. As by this time I had accepted and surrendered to my powerlessness, I was grateful to be in recovery and no longer alcohol's compulsive slave. I was no longer angry – my anger had all gone.

The time went by quite quickly and I faithfully attended my minimum four AA meetings per week. On most weekends I went up to London to see Mary, which by and large I found quite difficult. It was clear to me that I was a very long way from regaining her trust or forgiveness which, considering how much I had deceived her was not at all surprising. I felt very much, as I am sure was the reality, that I was on trial and not to be trusted.

After the eight weeks were up and as I was still sober, I resumed treatment at Broadway Lodge as they had promised but, to my relief, as an outpatient. The treatment consisted of weekly half-hour sessions with the aftercare counsellor Eric E. who was himself in recovery. At these he gave me work to do and showed me how to take the first five Steps of the AA programme. As such he was acting as my sponsor and it was pure AA. (My detailed experience of how I did the Steps is described in Chapter 9.)

I completed exactly eighteen weeks of treatment the day after doing my Fifth Step. As I said goodbye to Ed, to whom I shall always be grateful, he said, 'Billy you have a lot to offer.' I did not deny this but replied, 'Yes, I think maybe I have.' His final words to me that day were, 'Good luck. Remember that we make no guarantees here but if you don't go to AA and work the programme, you won't make it.' The inference behind this was that I, and I alone, am responsible for my recovery and that if I did not accept this and go to AA, I would not recover. It was a responsibility that I was, and still am, very happy to accept.

My earliest memory. Father's MG 10 years on in 1949

Mother and Father, North Queensferry 1949

Newly commissioned, May 1955

A 1933 Riley Stelvio identical to the first car I owned in 1955

Self in Ferret scout car, Cyprus 1956

The 1958 Oxford Golf side and below a few grey hairs and 50 years on in 2008

[82]

McTavish after his 50th Christmas – December 2009

Father in 1964, a year before he died

Billy Steel, watched by son Charlie, demonstrates to readers of the front page of the *Daily Telegraph* of the 22nd June 1987, where this photograph appeared, the correct address position for hitting a solid mid-iron to the heart of the 18th green.

In the background is the wreckage of what had been the only Bristol Blenheim IV Second World War bomber still flying. After spending several years in mothballs it had recently been restored at great expense, and was on only its second flight since restoration. As part of an Air Show, it was intended merely to fly over Denham Airfield, but the pilot decided to "touch and go", landing but immediately taking off again. The Blenheim duly touched down, but it failed to take off as intended, and crashed on the 9th fairway (narrowly missing Iain and Maureen MacCaskill, who were playing that hole) and ended up near the 18th fairway. Fortunately, nobody was hurt, apart from minor injuries to two of the crew. The pilot was subsequently prosecuted, and Iain MacCaskill gave evidence at the trial.

This photograph and text appear in Denham Golf Club, A Centenary Portrait published by the club in 2010 to celebrate its centenary.

Views from our flat. The Thames Flood Barrier and varied traffic on London's river

My son Charles at Turnberry, October 2007

Self at Turnberry, October 2007

My grandchildren James and Pippa, June 2010

Chapter 7

The Early Years of Sobriety
Resolving some of life's problems proved far from easy
1983 – 1990

As I drove back to London, somewhat elated at having at last successfully completed treatment, I wondered what the future might hold for me for I was very aware that sobriety – recovery – was a lifelong process. I might perhaps have solved the problem of my drinking but I still had to solve the many problems which it had created and, above all, I had to solve the problem of *staying* sober – *staying* recovered. In this, I was taking the first tentative steps along the road travelled by only a comparative few – there is far more to recovery than just stopping drinking. Early in sobriety we reap what we sowed while we were drinking and the problems we face have to be dealt with without picking up a drink and this can be very daunting and frightening, so much so that often it seems easier to pick up a drink – and many do. Picking up a drink, however, will never solve anything. There were two tasks, neither of which I thought would be easy, which required my immediate attention: first, to find a job; second, to make amends to Mary, on an ongoing basis.

Initially, Mary and I both went to Broadway Lodge once a fortnight for aftercare treatment. When, at the second session, I had to admit that I did not yet have a job, I was asked to make a commitment, not to them but to myself, that by our next visit I would have found one. And so, on returning to London, I set about writing my C.V., which was easy until I got to the last two years when I was unemployed. How was I to explain that one away?

As soon as I had entered treatment, Mary had had no hesitation in telling the whole world that I was an alcoholic, so I have never had any trouble over breaking my anonymity; but to put it on a C.V. was a very different matter. It seemed to be asking for trouble as the general ignorance and misconception of alcoholism was (and still is) such that any reference to it would ensure that the C.V. would go straight into the waste paper basket. I contacted an employment agency in Holborn who specialised in insolvency; they agreed that it would be a mistake to mention my alcoholism on my C.V. and, in the end I simply said that I had been ill. Even so, it did not go down well with the firms it was sent to. When I went into the agency again, however, a very helpful junior, barely out of school, suggested I telephone Howard Tilly, also in Holborn, whom he knew were looking for insolvency administrators/managers. He gave me the name of the managing partner, John Cox, so I rang and arranged an appointment to see him.

As soon as I was sitting with him, I felt I could be myself. I handed him my C.V. and explained that I was an alcoholic in recovery, by then some six months sober. We seemed to hit it off straight away and had a long discussion about alcoholism and all its ramifications. He had clearly come across alcoholic employees before! Having done my Fourth and Fifth Steps in treatment proved of enormous benefit in this situation as I had rid myself of all the guilt and shame I had hitherto felt about my alcoholism and I could talk about it without embarrassment. I doubt I would have felt nearly as free or confident in speaking about myself and my illness had I not done those steps beforehand.

Although I did not know him, it transpired that we had been contemporaries at Oxford and further, that the partner for whom I would be working had been a Cambridge golf blue whom I knew slightly and who was then the secretary of the Oxford and Cambridge Golfing Society. I was given the job immediately, on the proviso that a clause would be inserted in my contract to the effect that if I were to drink again they would have the right to terminate it forthwith. In actuality, no such clause was ever included. I duly started work on 1st July 1983, very pleased to have fulfilled the commitment I had made to myself in aftercare.

My existing Alfa Romeo Alfasud was clapped out and rusting and now that I had a job I felt fully justified in buying a new car with some of the money I was due to inherit from my late Uncle John. I ordered a new Vauxhall Astra GTI and went to see my bank manager to arrange a bridging loan, pending the receipt of Uncle John's money. When I told him I was an alcoholic in recovery, he told me that he could see I was better as he had noticed a distinct improvement in my hand writing! In some ways this car was a bit of a luxury as Mary had a VW Camper van called 'Brunhilde' which, with its sleeping accommodation, fridge, cooker and sink, was splendid for picnics and camping with the children. (We had even taken it to Royal Ascot the previous year when I was still drinking. I very much doubt, however, that I will ever go there again as the cheque I had written for our tickets to the Royal Enclosure subsequently bounced!) The VW was, however, very slow and not much fun to drive, whereas the Astra was the opposite. Besides, I did not want to be dependent on the use of Mary's car, or beholden to her, especially as I intended to play some golf.

Things were not so good at home. Looking back, I confused gratitude with love. I was extremely grateful to Mary, and I still am, for when I most needed help she was the one who was instrumental in arranging for me to go into treatment. I was determined to make amends to her for the wrongs I had done her but, try as I did, nothing seemed to work: instead of getting better, our relationship got steadily worse. Thinking I must do everything to regain her trust in me, and not realising she was incapable of trusting, I said yes to practically everything and then became resentful when I had to do things that I did not want to do. I was a people pleaser and a doormat with 'Welcome' written all over it! I was saying yes not because I wanted to but because I wanted Mary to think well of me; in the process I was letting her walk all over me. Eventually I did learn to say 'no' – which incidentally can be a very positive act – and matters became worse still.

As stated in Chapter 5, I think Mary was attracted to me because I needed to be saved. The reality, however, had now changed and I was a very different person from the one she had married. I was sober, had a job and was quite capable of looking after myself: I no longer needed saving. And the spotlight was now on her, as, interestingly, during aftercare at Broadway Lodge, as much if not more attention was paid to Mary as to me. I remember the mantra 'accept the defects you cannot change in the other, and work on those you can change in yourself'. It was excellent advice but it takes two to tango and I increasingly felt that all the changes were being made by me. What I wanted was a harmonious, intimate relationship with a wife who was my best friend and lover and to be honest, Mary ticked none of these boxes. I didn't know what she wanted but whatever it was, I certainly did not seem to be giving it to her. She was going to Al-Anon, the sister fellowship of AA for the relatives of alcoholics, but she remained angry and unforgiving and seemed to be deriving nothing like the benefit from it that I was receiving from AA. One of the ways she expressed her anger and insecurity was belittling me whenever she could. On one occasion when we had some friends to supper and a bottle of champagne was produced, she grabbed the bottle from me and gave it to one of the guests, saying, 'Michael would you open it? Billy is so hopeless.' There are many things I don't do well but one thing I certainly could do after years of practice was open a bottle of champagne!

Despite all this, the children were with us at least every other weekend and we often had fun together. I loved having the children and I desperately wanted to make what amends I could to them more than I did to anyone else. Many of those weekends were spent with Mary's mother in Northumberland or with her other relatives around the country. One weekend, I tried to make amends to my mother-in-law. She was, to put it mildly, a rather eccentric woman and when I had finished saying my piece she exclaimed that I was the first alcoholic she had ever met! Not only had her daughter Sue, so recently killed in a car crash, been manifestly an alcoholic, but there were a number of old soaks at most of the drinks parties which we had gone to all over the county. I let her remark go as I had no desire to argue with her or hurt her further, but the ignorance and denial surrounding alcoholism is astonishing.

Towards the end of my drinking, golf had given me up as I had become almost incapable of hitting the ball without a lot of alcohol inside me. In one Moles match at Worplesdon I had had to play without having a drink as I had arrived early at the golf club only to find that the bar was shut. Having the morning shakes, I could hardly hit the ball at all, which was embarrassing beyond belief and I vowed then and there that for the time being I would not play again. By lunchtime we were nine down and the thirty-six holes match was effectively over. I did play better after a fairly liquid lunch but by then the damage had been done and it was too late.

Now that I was sober, I went back to Denham and after hitting a few shots and having a couple of lessons from John Sheridan, I realized that I could still hit the ball pretty well. I did not, however, have a handicap as my old one had lapsed. To get a new one, I had to return three medal cards and I duly put in scores of ninety-three, eighty-four and seventy-three. The difference of twenty shots between the worst and the best must have confused the handicap committee but in the end they gave me a handicap of nine. As the seventy-three indicated, I knew I could play better than that and duly entered the Rudd Foursomes knock out competition with John Henderson, who was then one of the longest serving members of the club. We won the event which gave me special pleasure as it was the sixth time I had won it in four different decades. The following year, playing with a different partner, we were runners up. As a player in my late forties I had definitely passed my best but I enjoyed taking part and still had it in me to play a good round.

I had returned to working in insolvency as a duck returns to water: as if I had never been away. Although I did not broadcast the fact that I was an alcoholic, most people knew I did not drink and did not seem any more bothered about it than I was, which was not at all. From the day I sobered up, we always had drink in the house and still do; far more, in fact, than when I was drinking. I have always felt comfortable about this as if I wanted a drink I could get one easily enough anywhere. Thankfully, I have no more desire to drink the stuff that Carl Jung described in his letter to Bill W. as 'the most depraving poison'[9], than I have to drink arsenic. For me every bottle or glass of booze has the word POISON written all over it.

Throughout this early period I attended an average of three or four AA meetings a week and did regular service with the local groups, and later with the Chelsea Intergroup and London Region. I did it because I wanted to be an active, contributing member of the Fellowship and because I wanted, above all else, to be sober, for without my sobriety I would be no use to myself or anybody else. My primary purpose in life was to stay sober and help other alcoholics to achieve sobriety – and it still is. I had soon gone from being unable to imagine life without a drink and with having to go to AA for the rest of my life, to being unable to imagine life **with** a drink and **without** going to AA. It was a change brought about by going to meetings and practising the Twelve Steps to the best of my ability. I still go to meetings on a fairly regular weekly or twice weekly basis and I just love it.

Towards the end of 1983 Mary sold her flat in Battersea and together we bought a four bedroom terraced house a couple of streets away in Lavender Sweep. The purchase was financed by money from the sale of the flat, money from Uncle John's legacy and a mortgage, for which I was responsible. This move was against my better judgement and my gut feelings but I was still at the stage of thinking that part of making amends was letting Mary have her own way. It was quite a nice house but it needed a lot of work, not all of which we could afford, especially as Mary, who was a qualified physiotherapist, was showing no sign of seeking a job as a physiotherapist or anything else, and in fact had not worked, and did not work, in all the time we were together.

After about two years it was becoming increasingly clear to both of us that our relationship was going nowhere. We had nothing in common, we were travelling in opposite directions, and our life together seemed to have become a series of disagreements, arguments and occasional rows over just about everything. In short it was a very sick, dysfunctional and destructive relationship with little or no harmony, affection, gentleness, love or love making. We seemed to be destroying each other. Mary went to see a counsellor with the Drug and Alcohol Foundation in Victoria who had been recommended to her by someone she knew in Al-Anon. After a couple of sessions her counsellor asked to see me as well, so I went along and told them both how I saw our relationship. Mary had heard it all before but was visibly shocked on hearing me say it to another person. We had one more session together before Mary gave up seeing him altogether and I continued on my own. These sessions had nothing to do with my alcoholism but everything to do with my deteriorating marriage. I had changed enormously from the very sick chronic alky that I had been but Mary did not appear to have changed at all; neither of us was benefiting in any way from being together. In a meeting with the counsellor, which happened to be on my fiftieth birthday, it became clear to me that perhaps the only hope for our sanity would be a trial separation to see if, apart, we could become mature enough to be able to live together. (I did not realize it at the time but today I am certain that until people learn to live on their own, they are not mature enough to be entitled live with another. It is, I believe, one of the reasons so many marriages or relationships break down.)

'When are you going to tell her?' the counsellor asked. 'Tonight,' I replied, and so I did. I remember practically nothing of the talk with her but I made it clear that I wanted a trial separation of about three months to see if we could each make sufficient changes to make our marriage work. I could not leave immediately as I had nowhere to go and during the short period that we continued to live under the same roof, I was reminded of the similar situation with Caroline before our home was sold. As it turned out, almost unbelievably, Caroline's mother offered to put me up temporarily and I was grateful to accept. She had always had a soft spot for me, and I for her, despite her many eccentricities, general unmanageability and the unpleasantness surrounding my divorce from Caroline. I got along very well with her and I think she was impressed that I had then been sober for over three years. She was happy for me to come and go as I pleased, and when I had the children and brought them to the house, it was a sort of double whammy for them all in that grandmother and grandchildren were able to see each other as well.

For a couple of months I had little or no contact with Mary but when I did talk to her after three months it was clear that little had changed apart from the fact that she had taken in a lodger and changed the locks, something that I thought was quite unjustified in view of the fact that I was part owner of the house, was paying the mortgage and posed absolutely no physical threat to her. I was prepared to continue the separation but was slightly surprised when I received a letter from her solicitors saying that they thought there should be a divorce on a clean break basis.

Accordingly, I pre-empted them and instructed my solicitors to petition for divorce, which infuriated Mary as she felt she should be the petitioner, not the respondent. As it did not bother me which way it was done, I allowed the proceedings to go forward on the basis of her counter petition.

I made her what I thought was a generous financial offer. Although she turned it down, it was more than she was eventually awarded when the final amount was determined by the Court some years later. The decree nisi went through relatively quickly and it was agreed that the house should be sold. Mary, however, stalled for as long as possible until I finally tried to hasten the matter by stopping payment of the mortgage. I explained the position to Abbey National and more or less invited them to start repossession proceedings. Nevertheless, and in spite of innumerable excuses and delays, it took until January 1989, three years after we first separated, before the sale was eventually completed. The only good news in all this was that we made a very handsome profit on the sale.

It took another two or three years to obtain the decree absolute and the last time I saw Mary was in Court when unfortunately she was taut with disapproval and refused even to look at me. The decision to end that marriage was one of the most agonising I have ever taken but I am sure that it was the correct one. I had tried my best to make amends to her but in the end I decided that the best amends I could make was to leave her. I remain, however, very grateful for the help and support she gave me when I most needed it. Without this I help I doubt very much if I would still be alive today and I really do hope that she has since been able to find happiness.

By the time the decree absolute came through, much water had flowed under the bridge. After leaving Mary, I had a wonderful sense of relief and freedom, as if a great weight had been lifted from my shoulders. I felt uncluttered and I could even fit all of the few possessions I had into my car! I was also free to play more golf again. For the first time in years, I was able to have fun, a very important ingredient in a happy sobriety as well as life in general, and one which is almost entirely about attitude. I formed a close friendship with a very attractive girl called Liz, whom I met in AA and who was in the process of divorcing for the second time. We were good companions for a year or so and spent a number of very good weekends in Le Touquet just across the channel in France. We helped each other in recovery a lot but we never became lovers.

In November 1986 we both decided to give up smoking. I was smoking over fifty a day and try as I did I could not cut down, despite the fact that by this time I was becoming increasingly conscious of the fact that my smoking was chronic and was causing more and more bronchitic breathing and coughing. I was becoming tired of wanting to want to give them up and knowing I was addicted, I knew that stopping altogether was the only way out. Realising that it would be much easier if we sought help, we enrolled in a course at the Middlesex Hospital, consisting of one and a half hour sessions on five consecutive evenings. Before the first session I went into a pub opposite the hospital and had what I felt might well be my last cigarette. As I drew on the cigarette, I thought about how unpleasant smoking really is and it reminded me of the occasion nearly four years previously when I had what was to prove my penultimate drink in the pub just before going into Broadway Lodge.

Once the course started, I somewhat reluctantly volunteered to blow into a device similar to a breathalyser. My blow registered a figure of forty-four on the scale which the doctor in charge told me was a record and it meant that my blood comprised 44/1000ths or 4.4% carbon monoxide. We were shown some films of the effect of smoking and how it could lead to acute bronchitis, lung cancer and emphysema. It was the effect of emphysema which horrified me the most and it suddenly occurred to me just how insane it was to stop drinking simply to kill myself smoking. In exactly the same way as I had suddenly wanted to be sober more than I wanted to drink when I saw the slogan 'Insanity is making the same mistake twice and expecting a different result', I knew in an instant that I wanted *not* to smoke more than I wanted *to* smoke. In both cases I wanted to live more than I wanted to die. I already knew from my experience with Caroline on the boat to Norway in 1969 that I had no defence against the first cigarette and that all I had to do was to avoid lighting one. The course itself was very helpful and educative and the withdrawal symptoms and cravings disappeared surprisingly quickly. Furthermore, it was not that difficult because I really wanted to stop and I had accepted my powerlessness over nicotine. I soon stopped coughing and I stopped using asthmatic inhalers without realising it. I felt so much better and I even began to whistle again, something I had not done for years. An added and unexpected bonus at the time was a distinct improvement in my self-worth.

As an ex-smoker I can now honestly say that I never really enjoyed smoking. People who smoke may tell you otherwise but therein lies their denial. Apart from the feeling in the early days of being grown up, itself an illusion, the only enjoyment I believed I had was not enjoyment at all, merely relief from the withdrawals that smoking was forever perpetuating.

Withdrawals are stressful and far from relieving stress, which many people believe smoking does, smoking actually increases stress in the same way chronic alcoholic drinking creates stress. As a smoker I was continually seeking the peace of mind which, as an ex-smoker, I have now found and which all non smokers have all the time. There are absolutely no benefits to be obtained from smoking yet it still probably contributes to more premature deaths in Great Britain, every year, than anything else. According to the Central Office of Information, on average each cigarette is said to reduce the life of a regular smoker by five and a half minutes.

The hold tobacco had on me for so many years, and why I could not give it up earlier, never ceases to amaze me. Nevertheless, as with drinking, I am very grateful that eventually I was able to stop. My experience of smoking again on the way to Norway helped me to stop drinking and, paradoxically, stopping drinking helped me to stop smoking. In reality it was the same thing, just a different drug! 'C'est la vie' – if one lives to tell the tale!

In February 1987 my mother who was then 86 and who had been quite badly arthritic for some years, fell and broke her hip. She was admitted to the West Middlesex Hospital in Isleworth and the following day was operated upon. On hearing the news of her fall I immediately went to see her in hospital and tried to comfort her. Prior to the operation she told me how pleased she was to have had a good life and that whatever was to happen to her she was very grateful for that. She also told me, which brought a tear to my eye, that I was her best friend. It was as if she knew that she did not have long to live and it occurred to me then, looking at her in her calmness, that she fully accepted that the end might be nigh and that she was ready to move on. This was the last lucid conversation that I had with her because after the operation, which was not a success, she lost and never recovered her mind; for a month or so she was little more than a vegetable. I went to see her every day but one, and it was very painful to see this person, who had hitherto been such a bundle of life, in that state. I was very glad, however, that I had been sober for the last four years of her life and that I had been able to visit her regularly, often with Clare and Charles, and talk to her one to one. For her part she asked but little and she really was delighted that I was sober and recovering from my illness. She had been a fabulous mother to Donald and me, always encouraging us and supporting us in all that we did. If she had a fault it was that she spoiled us too much for she was very self-sacrificing, almost always putting the interests of her husband and sons before her own.

As I visited her in hospital day after day it became obvious that she was not improving and I found myself praying that she might be spared any more suffering and be allowed to die. Even so, when she did die it still came as a bit of a shock. I remember thinking *oh God!* when I realized that I had become the oldest member of the family and would no longer have her wise counsel to turn to. But she had been a widow for over twenty years and I was genuinely pleased at the thought that she and my father might be again having dinner together that night. It thus occurred to me that I had accepted her death straight away and that I did not have to grieve for her. I had done my grieving when I gave up alcohol and, today, I believe that acute and lasting grief arises out of non-acceptance and has more to do with dependence than with love; with love the pain is less severe and the acceptance comes more quickly. I still miss the company of both my parents but from the start I accepted their deaths; rather than feeling pain, I am grateful for having known them and my memories of them are happy ones.

In the summer of 1987 I renewed acquaintance with a girl I had met socially three years earlier when neither of us was free. The first time I took her out was on her fortieth birthday and it was the beginning of a love affair which continues to this day. One lovely autumn evening in late October, we found ourselves walking along the Thames embankment as they switched on the flood lights on the other side of the river; it was incredibly beautiful, peaceful and romantic as we held hands for the first time. I had never before realized that hands could talk and when they did I knew that this was going to be special. Sarah has forbidden me to write about her or us here, as she says this book is about me and not her. I respect her wishes except to say that twenty two years later I have long since grown accustomed to her face as I suspect she has grown accustomed to mine.

I left Baker Tilly (as it had become known) in January 1989 and went to train as a chemical dependency counsellor at Western Counselling Services in Weston-super-Mare. Western Counselling was then run by Eric E. the ex Broadway Lodge aftercare counsellor who had taken me through the first five Steps in 1983. Like many recovering alcoholics, I had for some time wanted to become a counsellor and having sold the house which Mary and I had bought, I had sufficient funds to be able to do so. Training, for the most part, initially consisted of going through treatment again and since I had already done it sincerely and in depth six years previously, I found myself just going through the motions. Being six years sober and, dare I say it, being well, it was impossible to repeat the process because

I always knew what to expect next. The rest of the training consisted of doing the same work as the other counsellors and was for the most part unsupervised. I really enjoyed taking groups and passing on much of what I had learned at Broadway Lodge and since.

I lived in one of the patients' residential houses and apart from being in general charge there, my only specific duty was to administer the nightly detox medication at ten PM. From five o'clock, the evenings were my own and when it was fine I would drive to the nearby Burnham and Berrow Golf Club, where I had played in the 1959 University Golf match over thirty years previously. I usually had the course pretty much to myself and it was an absolute delight playing on those long, hot summer evenings.

A little over six months later, I had completed my training and duly received my certificate to that effect. It had previously been agreed with Eric that I would run a Western Counselling office in London for out-patients. It opened in September 1989, but from the start, the venture was not a success as I was not given the support which had been previously agreed and Eric refused to pay me more than the nominal amount (which had included full board) that he had paid me when I was training. I had not foreseen this and I had no option but to resign. Unfortunately I did not part company from Eric on anything like the best of terms but I was nonetheless genuinely sorry that it had not worked out. I tried to get other work as a counsellor but always money was the problem – everyone expected me to do it for nothing. As a result I reluctantly had to return to insolvency, this time with a small but busy practice in north London.

Throughout the period since completing treatment at Broadway Lodge in April 1983, I stayed sober only because I attended AA on a regular basis and practised its recovery programme as best I could. In the chapters that follow are insights into what AA really is and a précis of how I personally practised and continue to practise its Twelve Step recovery programme.

Chapter 8

Alcoholics Anonymous
Spiritus contra Spiritum

Alcoholics Anonymous is a fellowship of men and women who share their experience, strength and hope with each other that they may solve their common problem and help others to recover from alcoholism.

The only requirement for membership is a desire to stop drinking. There are no dues or fees for AA membership; we are self supporting through our own contributions.

AA is not allied with any sect, denomination, politics, organisation or institution; does not wish to engage in any controversy; neither endorses nor opposes any causes.

Our primary purpose is to stay sober and help other alcoholics to achieve sobriety.[10]

This definition, known as 'The Preamble', is read at the start of almost every Alcoholics Anonymous (AA) meeting in Britain, and is the only definition of the Fellowship I have been able to find in all of its literature. As such it is almost as much about what the fellowship is not, as about what it is. There can be no doubt, however, even amongst sceptics, that many millions of alcoholics have recovered from alcoholism in AA and that the method used by AA remains hugely more successful than any other. How then did it start, how has it developed over the years and why is it so successful?

In the spring of 1935, a New York stockbroker, William G. Wilson (Bill W), who had been sober for about six months and was having the greatest difficulty in staying sober, sought out another alcoholic, not to drink with, but in order to stay sober. He reasoned that only by helping another alcoholic would he achieve this. As a result, on 12th May 1935, he met with a well-known surgeon, Dr Robert Smith, in Akron, Ohio, to talk about his alcoholism in the hope that through the sharing of their drinking experiences they might help each other to stay sober. Although Dr Bob, as he was affectionately to become known, did not stop drinking for some weeks, on the 10th June he had what was to be his last drink. Thus it was that on this date, 10th June 1935, AA came into being, Bill W and Dr Bob being its two founding members. (As co-founders and partners, Bill and Bob were very much the driving force behind the development of AA, right up to the time of Dr. Bob's death in 1950.) They in turn sought out other alcoholics; one by one they stayed sober and AA grew, 'chain style'. By March 1936 there were ten members staying sober and by the end of 1936 the number had grown to fifteen. It was from this tiny beginning that the Fellowship of AA has grown to having well over an estimated two million members worldwide today.

After three years of largely trial and error in determining the principles on which the society should be based, and after much failure in getting alcoholics to recover, three groups emerged – the first in Akron, the second in New York and the third in Cleveland. The total membership then amounted to some sixty sober alcoholics. At that time it was decided that the experiences of the early members should be set down in a book, which was duly published on the first of April 1939, when the membership numbered about one hundred. The book was called *Alcoholics Anonymous* and from it the fledgling fellowship took its name. In essence the book is the story of how the early members found a way to stay sober and recover from alcoholism. In Part 1, alcoholism from the alcoholic's point of view is described and The Twelve Steps of AA are set down. To this day, these remain AA's simple programme for recovery. Part 2 of the first edition of the book consisted of thirty stories in which individual alcoholics describe their drinking experiences and recoveries. Affectionately known as the Big Book, it is the basic text of the fellowship.

Following the publication of the book, a huge chain reaction set in as more and more recovering alcoholics carried their message to others. Alcoholics flocked to AA in their thousands due largely to the Big Book and to good publicity in magazines and newspapers mainly in America but also throughout the world. Much support and endorsement were also given to the movement by doctors and clergymen. However, this rapid growth in membership brought about many problems as to how large numbers of recovering alcoholics, all of whom were ex-drunks, could work and live together in harmony and to good effect. The main problems, to name but a few, related to money, personal relations, public relations, organization and management both of the groups and head office. Mostly as a result of trial and error, AA's Twelve Traditions took shape and were first published in 1946, later to be confirmed at the first International Convention held in Cleveland, Ohio, in 1950. The Twelve Traditions (see Appendix 1) are really guidelines as to how an international organization with no bosses can function and operate effectively.

Sixteen years after the first printing, the second edition of the Big Book was published in 1955. By then one hundred and fifty thousand copies had been distributed and the fellowship had mushroomed to nearly six thousand groups with a total membership of well over one hundred and fifty thousand recovered alcoholics. Groups were to be found in each of the United States and all of the provinces of Canada. AA also had flourishing communities in Great Britain (the first meeting in Britain was held in room 202 of the Dorchester Hotel, London, on 30th March 1947), Scandinavia, South Africa, South America, Mexico, Alaska, Australia and Hawaii. All told, promising beginnings had been made in some fifty countries and US possessions.

In March 1976, the third edition was printed when the total worldwide membership was conservatively estimated at over one million with almost twenty-eight thousand groups meeting in over ninety countries. Between 1955 and 1976, over 1,150,000 copies of the second edition had been sold. The second and third editions both retained the basic text of the first edition; only the sections containing the stories of recovered alcoholics (parts 11 and 111) were altered and added to.

The fourth edition, in which still more stories were added and some others omitted, came off the press at the start of the new millennium in March 2001. During the twenty-five years since the third edition had been published, the worldwide membership of AA had doubled to an estimated two million or more, of which approximately half were now women, with nearly one hundred and eighty thousand groups meeting in approximately one hundred and fifty countries around the world. Quite apart from the huge numbers of lives which have been not only saved but also enhanced, it is remarkable to think that all of this started with one alcoholic talking to another in order to stay sober.

AA literature undoubtedly played a major role in the fellowship's growth in the last quarter of the twentieth century and *Alcoholics Anonymous* has been translated into forty-three languages. Twenty-one million copies of the first three editions of the book were distributed and as at 31st December 2008 the overall sales had risen to 29,467,709. Since then, further sales of the fourth edition will have taken total sales well past thirty million. It is, therefore, one of the best selling non-fiction books ever written; yet comparatively few people have ever heard of it or know of its existence!

By 2009 there were some four thousand groups meeting each week in the United Kingdom with an estimated total membership of almost forty thousand – roughly double the number in 1983 when I joined.

It is not generally known that the great psychiatrist Dr Carl Jung played a vital role prior to the founding of AA, though he himself was unaware of it until Bill W. wrote a letter of appreciation to him in January 1961. In it he told Jung how AA had come into being and of the part which he himself had played. Jung, who was then an old man and soon to die, replied to the letter a week later. Not only does this exchange of letters reveal, in one of the co-founders own words, some of the historical ancestry of AA, it also shows how Jung, who was deeply involved with scientists, felt the necessity in the nineteen thirties to be cautious in revealing his profoundly held belief that the ultimate sources of recovery from alcoholism are spiritual.

My dear Dr Jung:
This letter of great appreciation has been long overdue.

May I first introduce myself as Bill W., a co-founder of the Society of Alcoholics Anonymous. Though you have surely heard of us, I doubt if you are aware that a certain conversation you once had with one of your patients, a Mr Rowland H., back in the early 1930s, did play a critical role in the founding of our Fellowship.

Though Rowland H. has long since passed away, the recollections of his remarkable experience while under treatment by you has definitely become a part of AA history. Our remembrance of Rowland H.'s statements about his experience with you is as follows:

Having exhausted other means of recovery from his alcoholism, it was about 1931 that he became your patient. I believe he remained under your care for perhaps a year. His admiration for you was boundless, and he left you with a feeling of much confidence.

To his great consternation, he soon relapsed into intoxication. Certain that you were his "court of last resort," he again returned to your care. There followed the conversation between you that was to become the first link in the chain of events that led to the founding of Alcoholics Anonymous.

My recollection of his account of that conversation is this; First of all, you frankly told him of his hopelessness, so far as any further medical or psychiatric treatment might be concerned. This candid and humble statement was beyond doubt the first foundation stone upon which our Society has since been built.

Coming from you, one so trusted and admired, the impact upon him was immense.

When he then asked you if there was any hope, you told him that there might be, provided he could become the subject of a spiritual or religious experience – in short, a genuine conversion. You pointed out how such an experience, if brought about, might remotivate him when nothing else could. But you did caution, though, that while such experiences had sometimes brought recovery to alcoholics, they were, nevertheless, comparatively rare. You recommended that he place himself in a religious atmosphere and hope for the best. This I believe was the substance of your advice.

Shortly thereafter, Mr H. joined the Oxford Groups, an evangelical movement then at the height of its success in Europe, and one with which you doubtless are familiar. You will remember their large emphasis upon the principles of self-survey, confession, restitution and the giving of oneself in the service of others. They strongly stressed meditation and prayer. In these surroundings, Rowland H. did find a conversion experience that released him for the time being from his compulsion to drink.

Returning to New York, he became very active with the "O.G." here, then led by the Episcopal clergyman, Dr Samuel Shoemaker. Dr Shoemaker had been one of the founders of that movement, and his was a powerful personality that carried immense sincerity and conviction.

At this time (1932-34), the Oxford Groups had already sobered a number of alcoholics, and Rowland, feeling that he could especially identify with these sufferers, addressed himself to the help of still others. One of these chanced to be an old schoolmate of mine, named Edwin T. ["Ebby"]. He had been threatened with commitment to an institution, but Mr H. and another ex-alcoholic "O.G." member procured his parole and helped to bring about his sobriety.

Meanwhile I had run the course of alcoholism and was then threatened with commitment myself. Fortunately I had fallen under the wonderful care of a physician – a Dr William D. Silkworth – who was wonderfully capable of understanding alcoholics. But just as you had given up on Rowland, so he had given up on me. It was his theory that alcoholism had two components – an obsession that compelled the sufferer to drink against his will and interest, and some sort of metabolism difficulty which he then called an allergy. The alcoholic's compulsion guaranteed that the alcoholic's drinking would go on, and the allergy made sure that the sufferer would finally deteriorate, go insane or die. Though I had been one of the few he had thought it possible to help, he was finally obliged to tell me of my hopelessness; I too, would have to be locked up. To me, this was a shattering blow. Just as Rowland had been made ready for his conversion experience by you, so had my wonderful friend, Dr Silkworth, prepared me.

Hearing of my plight, my friend Edwin T. came to see me at my home where I was drinking. By then, it was November 1934. I had long marked my friend Edwin for a hopeless case. Yet here he was in a very evident state of "release" which could by no means be accounted for by his mere association for a very short time with the Oxford Groups. Yet this obvious state of release, as distinguished from the usual depression, was tremendously convincing. Because he was a kindred sufferer, he could unquestionably communicate with me at great depth. I knew at once I must find an experience like his, or die.

Again I returned to Dr Silkworth's care where I could be once more sobered and so gain a clearer view of my friend's experience of release, and of Rowland H.'s approach to him.

Clear once more of alcohol, I found myself terribly depressed. This seemed to be caused by my inability to gain the slightest faith. Edwin T. again visited me and repeated the simple Oxford Groups' formulas. Soon after he left me I became even more depressed. In utter despair I cried out, "If there is a God, will he show himself." There immediately came to me an illumination of enormous impact and dimension, something which I have since tried to describe in the book Alcoholics Anonymous *and also in* AA Comes of Age, *basic texts which I am sending to you.*

My release from alcohol obsession was immediate. At once I knew I was a free man.

Shortly following my experience, my Friend Edwin came to the hospital, bringing me a copy of William James's Varieties of Religious Experience. *This book gave me the realization that most conversion experiences, whatever their variety, do have a common denominator of ego collapse at depth. The individual faces an impossible dilemma. In my case the dilemma had been created by my compulsive drinking and the deep feeling of hopelessness had been vastly deepened by my doctor. It was deepened still more by my alcoholic friend when he acquainted me with your verdict of hopelessness regarding Rowland H.*

In the wake of my spiritual experience there came a vision of a society of alcoholics, each identifying with and transmitting his experience to the next – chain style. If each sufferer were to carry the news of the scientific hopelessness of alcoholism to each new prospect, he might be able to lay every newcomer wide open to a transforming spiritual experience. This concept proved to be the foundation of such success as Alcoholics Anonymous has since achieved. This has made conversion experience – nearly every variety reported by James – available on almost wholesale basis. Our sustained recoveries over the last quarter century number about 300,000. In America and through the world there are today 8,000 AA groups.

So to you, to Dr Shoemaker of the Oxford Groups, to William James, and to my own physician, Dr Silkworth, we of AA owe this tremendous benefaction. As you will now clearly see, this astonishing chain of events actually started long ago in your consulting room, and it was directly founded upon your own humility and deep perception.

Very many thoughtful AAs are students of your writings. Because of your conviction that man is something more than intellect, emotion and two dollar's worth of chemicals, you have especially endeared yourself to us.

How our society grew, developed its Traditions for unity, and structured its functioning will be seen in the texts and pamphlet material that I am sending you.

You will also be interested to learn that in addition to the "spiritual experience," many AAs report a great variety of psychic phenomena, the cumulative weight of which is very considerable. Other members have – following their recovery in AA – been helped by your practitioners. A few have been intrigued by the "I Ching" and your remarkable introduction to that work.

Please be certain that your place in the affection, and in the history of our Fellowship, is like no other.

Gratefully yours
William G. W.
Co-founder
Alcoholics Anonymous

January 30, 1961

Dear Mr W.
Your letter has been very welcome indeed.
I had no news from Roland H. anymore and often wondered what has

been his fate. Our conversation which he has adequately reported to you had an aspect of which he did not know. The reason I could not tell him everything was that those days I had to be exceedingly careful of what I said. I had found that I was misunderstood in every way possible. Thus I was very careful when I talked to Rowland H. but what I really thought about, was the result of many experiences with men of his kind.

His craving for alcohol was the equivalent, on a low level, of the spiritual thirst of our being for wholeness, expressed in medieval language: the union with God.

How could one formulate such an insight in a language that is not misunderstood in our days?

The only right and legitimate way to such an experience is, that it happens to you in reality and it can only happen to you when you walk on a path which leads you to higher understanding. You might be led to that goal by an act of grace or through a personal and honest contact with friends, or through a higher education of the mind beyond the confines of mere rationalism. I see from your letter that Rowland H. has chosen the second way, which was, under the circumstances, obviously the best one.

I am strongly convinced that the evil principle prevailing in this world leads the unrecognized spiritual need into perdition, if it is not counteracted either by real religious insight or by the protective wall of human community. An ordinary man, not protected by an action from above and isolated in society, cannot resist the power of evil, which is called very aptly the Devil. But the use of such words arouses so many mistakes that one can only keep aloof from them as much as possible.

These are the reasons why I could not give a full and sufficient explanation to Rowland H. But I am risking it with you because I conclude from your very decent and honest letter that you have acquired a point of view above the misleading platitudes one usually hears about alcoholism.

You see, alcohol in Latin is "spiritus" and you use the same word for the highest religious experience as well as the most depraving poison. The helpful formula therefore is: spiritus contra spiritum.

Thanking you again for you kind letter.

I remain

Yours sincerely

C.G. Jung[11]

So there we have it from the great doctor himself. *Spiritus contra spiritum – spirituality versus alcohol(ism).* This to me is the very essence of AA for I am convinced that any alcoholic who thoroughly follows AA's spiritual path will always overcome his alcoholism and/or other addictions.

Bill wrote very extensively about AA and recovery and was responsible for almost all AA literature during his lifetime. (Much has also been written since and some of the more important books are listed in Appendix 5.)

What is it about AA that makes it the most successful form of treatment? To a large extent the answer is in the above correspondence, in which it is clearly recognized that although alcoholism is an incurable, threefold illness, the ultimate sources of recovery are spiritual. I would suggest, therefore, that there are five main factors which taken together, in my opinion, make AA and its recovery programme unique. (There are other much younger anonymous fellowships for addictions other than alcoholism, but they are effectively AA's offspring.)

1.   In a letter dated 1940, Bill W. says: *It has been said of AA that we are only interested in alcoholism. That is not true. We have to get over drinking in order to stay alive. But anyone who knows the alcoholic personality by first hand contact knows that no true alky ever stops drinking permanently without undergoing a profound personality change.*[12] The purpose of the Twelve Steps is to bring about this personality change, conversion experience or spiritual awakening. (See Appendix 2 for exactly what AA means by this spiritual change). As such it is the only treatment that fully recognizes the spiritual nature of the disease and provides the suffering alcoholic with a spiritual Twelve Step programme of recovery based on complete abstinence. **Science and medicine do not and cannot do this.**
AA's Twelve Steps are a group of principles, spiritual in their nature, which, if practised as a way of life, can expel the obsession to drink and enable the sufferer to become happily and usefully whole.[13] If followed to the best of one's ability, they are not only a promise but a guarantee that one will become well. When I entered Broadway Lodge in December 1982, I was very depressed, very unhappy and in a million little pieces; a near broken man. But as a result of practising the Steps, I have become, over the years, for the most part happy and contented; and, moreover, I have been patched up and put together again so that hopefully I am

a worthwhile and useful member of society. Speaking purely for myself and as I have already said, the most marvellous and miraculous thing about the Steps is that they have changed me from being someone who needed to drink, who could not live without it even as it was killing me, **into someone who does not want to drink; indeed, the very last thing I want is, by taking a drink, to hand back control of my life to a toxic chemical! I want above everything else to be sober.**

I would like to stress that I am not using the words 'spiritual' and 'spirituality' in the context of established, doctrinal religion, but in relation to how we feel. Members of AA can be of any religious denomination or none at all, as AA caters every bit as much for atheists and agnostics and makes no attempt to convert them to any religion. During the last days of my drinking I was what can only be described as spiritually bankrupt: I felt bloody awful, depressed, full of negativity and near suicidal; I could see no way out of my problems. Then came the moment when I saw the slogan in the NA meeting: Insanity is making the same mistake twice and expecting a different result. It was then that I took the First Step, accepting and surrendering to my powerlessness over alcohol. And it was at that moment that I started my spiritual growth through my commitment to sobriety, AA and, although I was not fully aware of it at the time, to a spirituality comprised for the most part of love, honesty, gratitude, joy, patience, kindness, goodness, faithfulness, responsibility, self-control and humility.

'Real sobriety', as opposed to being 'dry drunk' which is Twelve Steps away from being sober, is a state of surrender that, if maintained, will bring about positive changes in thoughts, feelings and actions that will ensure recovery. Negativity and pessimism are self-defeating and it is impossible to get out of depression, which I believe is almost invariably a symptom of an addiction of one kind or another, unless one has hope and hence becomes optimistic. Self-centredness, dishonesty, resentment, fear and other negatives are all barriers to spiritual growth and will, if allowed to become dominant, block the spiritual growth which, for us, is a lifelong process achieved by practising the AA recovery programme. For my money, it is the act of surrender which initiates the switch from negative to positive, from pessimism to optimism, from wanting to die to wanting to live, from wanting to drink to wanting to be sober, from darkness to light.

Spirituality is also the ability to get our minds off ourselves for we are always at our best when we are self-forgetting. In my experience spirituality always and only shows up in the doing – in helping others. As Leonardo da Vinci reputedly remarked over five hundred years ago, 'I am impressed with the urgency of doing. Knowing is not enough; we must apply. Being willing is not enough; we must do.' In the final analysis spirituality is love.

I do not believe that it is possible to recover fully from alcoholism without help. I could not have done so on my own as, apart from anything else, I would not have known what to do – I needed the help of a power greater than myself – and I still do. In AA this greater power is often referred to as *God as we understand Him*: we are all free to believe in whatever greater or higher power we like. We can perceive God however we choose – even if it is only 'two heads are better than one'! **Whenever and wherever the word God appears in this book, it is referring to a higher power or power greater than myself/yourself in whatever way I/you choose to understand or perceive that power to be.**

How we achieve recovery is outlined in the most succinct way in chapter 5 of the Big Book. In my view, it is the most important section of the whole book:

Rarely have we seen a person fail who has thoroughly followed our path. Those who do not recover are people who cannot or will not completely give themselves to this simple program, usually men and women who are constitutionally incapable of being honest with themselves. There are such unfortunates. They are not at fault; they seem to have been born that way. They are naturally incapable of grasping and developing a manner of living which demands rigorous honesty. Their chances are less than average. There are those, too, who suffer from grave emotional and mental disorders, but many of them do recover if they have the capacity to be honest.

Our stories disclose in a general way what we used to be like, what happened, and what we are like now. If you have decided you want what we have and are willing to go to any length to get it - then you are ready to take certain steps.

At some of these we baulked. We thought we could find an easier, softer way. But we could not. With all the earnestness at our command, we beg of you to be fearless and thorough from the very start. Some of us have tried to hold on to our old ideas and the result was nil until we let go absolutely.

Remember that we deal with alcohol – cunning, baffling, powerful! Without help it is too much for us. But there is One who has all power – that One is God. May you find Him now!

Half measures availed us nothing. We stood at the turning point. We asked His protection and care with complete abandon.

Here are the steps we took, which are suggested as a means of recovery:

1. We admitted we were powerless over alcohol – that our lives had become unmanageable.
2. Came to believe that a Power greater than ourselves could restore us to sanity.
3. Made a decision to turn our will and our lives over to the care of God as we understood Him.
4. Made a searching and fearless moral inventory of ourselves.
5. Admitted to God, to ourselves, and to another human being the exact nature of our wrongs.
6. Were entirely ready to have God remove all these defects of character.
7. Humbly asked Him to remove our shortcomings.
8. Made a list of all persons we had harmed, and became willing to make amends to them all.
9. Made direct amends to such people wherever possible, except when to do so would injure them or others.
10. Continued to take personal inventory and when we were wrong promptly admitted it.
11. Sought through prayer and meditation to improve our conscious contact with God as we understood Him, praying only for knowledge of His will for us and the power to carry that out.
12. Having had a spiritual awakening as the result of the steps, we tried to carry this message to alcoholics and to practise these principles in all our affairs.

Many of us exclaimed, "What an order! I can't go through with it." Do not be discouraged. No one among us has been able to maintain anything like perfect adherence to these principles. We are not saints. The point is, that we are willing to grow along spiritual lines. The principles we have set down are guides to progress. We claim spiritual progress rather than spiritual perfection.

Our description of the alcoholic, the chapter to the agnostic, and our personal adventures before and after make clear three pertinent ideas:

(a)   That we were alcoholic and could not manage our own lives.
(b)   That probably no human power could have relieved our alcoholism.
(c)   That God could and would if He were sought."[14]

This passage embodies the famed Twelve Steps of recovery, the basic AA treatment which, if followed thoroughly, guarantees continued and lasting recovery from alcoholism. The practising of the Steps will always work their magic. Seventy five years of AA experience has proved that the question is not whether the practising of the Steps will work but rather will the alcoholic practise or work the Steps. Any alcoholic who commits (doing the thing you said you would do long after the mood you said it in has left you) himself to this simple process will recover and it is tragic that so many either are not given the opportunity or, given the opportunity, fail to take it.

There are many who turn down the opportunity that AA provides, which begs the question: why? In the profoundly true words of Herbert Spencer: *There is a principle which is a bar against all information, which is proof against all arguments and which cannot fail to keep a man in everlasting ignorance – that principle is contempt prior to investigation.*[15] I would suggest that the main reason why so many people turn down AA is because of ignorance and contempt born out of intoxication, denial, prejudice and fear. The only essentials for recovery, and these are indispensable, are honesty, open-mindedness and willingness.

2.   The second factor making AA unique lies in the significance of who is delivering the message that recovery is possible. All his drinking life the alcoholic is subjected to the authority of so called non-alcoholic 'experts', be they doctors, priests, counsellors employers, judges, spouses and so on, and told, 'this is what you should do' or 'this is what you must do.' But when the alcoholic arrives in AA he is told 'this is what I did.' Suddenly he is listening to a completely different singer, singing an altogether different song in a language he can identify with. This singer does not judge or condemn, but understands; does not berate, but empathises. The newcomer is told 'if I can do it, you can do it.' He is given hope and is no longer alone. This new singer is of course the real

expert because his expertise is the consequence of experiences that no non-alcoholic can ever have. Because of this, a non-alcoholic cannot help an alcoholic in anything like the same way a sober alcoholic can. When I was in treatment I would not listen to non-alcoholic counsellors or other members of staff because I did not think they knew what they were talking about, as indeed was usually the case, but I was prepared to listen to those who were in recovery. I can best sum up what I mean by quoting the words of AA's co-founder Dr Bob. Speaking of his first encounter with Bill W in May 1935 he said:

*The question which might naturally come into your mind might be: "What did this man do or say that was different from what others had done or said?" It must be remembered that I had read a great deal and talked to everyone who knew, or thought they knew anything about the subject of alcoholism. But this was a man who had experienced many years of frightful drinking, who had had most all the drunkard's experiences known to man, but who had been cured by the very means I had been trying to employ, that is to say the spiritual approach. He gave me information about the subject of alcoholism which was undoubtedly helpful. **Of far more importance was the fact that he was the first living human with whom I had ever talked, who knew what he was talking about in regard to alcoholism from actual experience. In other words he talked my language.** He knew all the answers, and certainly not because he had picked them up in his reading.* [16]

3.   AA gives us a primary purpose in life, something which most of us, myself included, never had before. In AA, one has to want sobriety more than anything else: *Our primary purpose is to stay sober and help other alcoholics achieve sobriety.* [10] It is not enough to need it. It is, however, the most wonderful thing to have a primary purpose, for one can then also have secondary and tertiary purposes outside of AA, which I believe are so necessary if we are to fully turn our lives around and be happy. But without our primary purpose, we have nothing, and it is my belief that we stay sober by helping other alcoholics to achieve sobriety as this, more than anything else, is what keeps us well. When one alcoholic reaches out to help another alcoholic, the former will always benefit irrespective of what happens to the latter. Like 'Surrender to Win', this is one of the great paradoxes of AA: 'To Keep It You Have to Give It Away'!

[113]

4.   AA is a community in the truest sense and of the type to which Carl Jung referred in his letter to Bill W.: a community in which everyone helps themselves by helping another. The sense of community I felt as a child during the Second World War disappeared when the war ended and there was no longer a common enemy and a common purpose – the community as such no longer existed. In many ways the feelings I experience in AA are similar because when newcomers enter AA they are in great crisis and they then begin, as we all do, the struggle against our common enemy: alcohol. Together we help each other to travel the spiritual journey of recovery and because we are not cured and are all but one drink away from a 'drunk', the journey lasts until death. (As sober alcoholics we only ever cross the finishing line on the day the lid goes on the box!) As a result the community of AA is ongoing and hence will assuredly continue to grow and flourish.

5.   Finally, AA is financially self-supporting through voluntary contributions from its own members and the sale of its AA approved literature. Because of this, it declines all donations from non-alcoholics – we are each responsible for our own recovery. In Britain, AA is a registered charity and in 1985 a bill was passed in Parliament giving it the legal right, which it did not previously have, specifically to decline donations from non-members. This is in accordance with Tradition Seven of AA's Twelve Traditions (see Appendix 1). The Big Book says: *The A.A. groups themselves ought to be fully self-supported by the voluntary contributions from their own members. We think that each group should soon achieve this ideal; that any public solicitation of funds using the name Alcoholics Anonymous is highly dangerous, whether by groups, clubs, hospitals, or other outside agencies; that acceptance of large gifts from any source, or of contributions carrying any obligation whatever, is unwise. Then too, we view with much concern those A.A. treasuries which continue, beyond prudent reserves, to accumulate funds for no stated A.A. purpose. Experience has often warned us that nothing can so surely destroy our spiritual heritage as futile disputes over property, money and authority.* [17]

Quite apart from the fact that I owe my deliverance and life to AA, it is the most wonderful, extraordinary and fascinating organisation I have ever known. The early history of AA and the 'story' of how over seventy five years it has grown and developed simply by one alcoholic carrying its message to another is truly remarkable and awe-inspiring; it is a fellowship that I am very proud to be a member of and an AA meeting is the only place in the world where I can walk into a room full of strangers and reminisce! Earlier I referred to the nature of University and Society golf as being serious, yet fun and occasionally very funny. I would say the same of AA but I would add one important word, *deadly* serious, yet fun, and occasionally very funny.

Quite early in my recovery I remember seeing Henry Kissinger, the eminent former American Secretary of State, being asked on TV what he thought was the most important event to have happened in his life. His reply: 'The founding of Alcoholics Anonymous.'

In its relatively short life of seventy five years and from the smallest of beginnings, AA has grown at an astonishing rate and will continue to do so in the years to come. Even so, it has barely scratched the surface; the problem of alcoholism both here in the U.K. and worldwide is incalculable and there is more work than ever still to be done.

Chapter 9

The Twelve Steps to Recovery

Unless each AA member follows to the best of his ability our suggested Twelve Steps to recovery, he almost certainly signs his own death warrant. His drunkenness and dissolution are not penalties inflicted by people in authority; they result from his personal disobedience to spiritual principles.

The same stern threat applies to the group itself. Unless there is approximate conformity to A.A.'s Twelve Traditions, the group too can deteriorate and die. So we of A.A. do obey spiritual principles, first because we must, and ultimately because we love the kind of life such obedience brings. Great suffering and great love are A.A.'s disciplinarians; we need no others.[18]

The Twelve Steps are AA's basic programme of recovery and, as I have said, if practised as a way of life, they will expel the obsession to drink and enable the sufferer to achieve sobriety and become well. They have since been adopted in their entirety by all the other younger anonymous fellowships and have been found equally effective in enabling addicts other than alcoholics to recover from their addictions.

First published in the Big Book in 1939, the Twelve Steps originated from the Oxford Groups and in particular the Episcopal clergyman Dr. Sam Shoemaker who died in 1963. Bill W., who wrote them, said:

It was from him that Dr. Bob and I in the beginning absorbed most of the principles embodied in the Twelve Steps of Alcoholics Anonymous, steps that express the heart of A.A's way of life. Dr Silkworth gave us the needed knowledge of our illness, but Sam Shoemaker had given us the concrete knowledge of what we could do about it. One showed us the mysteries of the lock that held us in prison; and the other passed on the spiritual keys by which we were liberated.

....But the important thing is this: the early A.A. got its ideas of self-examination, acknowledgement of character defects, restitution for harm done, and working with others straight from the Oxford Groups and directly from Sam Shoemaker, their former leader in America and from nowhere

else. He will always be found in our annals as the one whose inspired example and teaching did most to show us how to create the spiritual climate in which we alcoholics may survive and then proceed to grow. A.A. owes a debt of timeless gratitude for all that God sent us through Sam and his friends in the days of A.A's infancy.[19]

Bill W. also wrote *Twelve Steps and Twelve Traditions* ('12 x 12'), a series of essays designed to help the alcoholic to better understand the Steps and Traditions and suggest how he might best approach the Steps. I never really understood any of them until I had taken each of them, one by one. An account follows of how I approached them, what they mean to me and the effect which they have had and continue to have in my own recovery and life. I stress, however, that it represents my own personal view and experience and is not necessarily the view of other members of AA or of AA itself.

1. We admitted we were powerless over alcohol – that our lives had become unmanageable.

*The unhappiest person in the world is the chronic alcoholic who has an insistent yearning to enjoy life as once he knew it, but cannot picture life without alcohol. They have a **heartbreaking obsession** that by some miracle of control they will be able to do so.*[3]

This step is the very foundation of recovery and, like any sound foundation, it must be solid. Without a thorough understanding and complete acceptance of powerlessness, the addiction will not be arrested and there will be no recovery. Without this step, those remaining are of little or no value. The following extract from The Big Book emphasises the importance of powerlessness and how denial must be broken:

Most of us have been unwilling to admit we were real alcoholics. No person likes to think he is bodily and mentally different from his fellows. Therefore, it is not surprising that our drinking careers have been characterized by countless vain attempts to prove that we could drink like other people. The idea that somehow, someday he will control and enjoy his drinking is the great obsession of every abnormal drinker. The persistence of this illusion is astonishing. Many pursue it into the gates of insanity or death.
We learned that we had to fully concede to our innermost selves that we

were alcoholics. This is the first step in recovery. The delusion that we are like other people, or presently maybe, has to be smashed.

*We alcoholics are men and women who have lost the ability to control our drinking. We know that no real alcoholic **ever** recovers control. All of us felt at times that we were regaining control, but such intervals - usually brief – were inevitably followed by still less control, which led in time to pitiful and incomprehensible demoralization. We are convinced to a man that alcoholics of our type are in the grip of a progressive disease. Over any considerable period we get worse, never better.*[20]

This extract later helped me to see why I had had so much trouble with the First Step. For twenty years I did not drink every day but whenever I did drink, I drank heavily. It was only very rarely, however, that I was ever seen to be drunk. Because I had a high tolerance for alcohol and could drink large amounts without showing signs of intoxication (one of the symptoms of alcoholism), and because I had held down responsible jobs for many years I believed I could control the amount I drank and I denied that I was powerless over it when, in fact, I was a functioning alcoholic. Despite the fact that during the last eight years of my drinking I was losing everything, I held on to the belief that I was in control. I even believed that if at times I wasn't in control, I would be able to regain control. This belief persisted right up until the day when I finally took the first Step. Only then did I admit that I was powerless and accepted it without any reservation whatsoever. For me one of the most important sentences in The Big Book is: *Some of us have tried to hold on to our old ideas and the result was nil until we let go absolutely.*[14] My belief that I could control my drinking, despite all the evidence to the contrary, was probably the oldest of my old ideas and I was not able to let go of it until I accepted that it was untrue.

It is a well known saying in AA that you have to **surrender to win.** Not until complete defeat is accepted can any progress be made. What I did not realize for quite some time after I sobered up is that it is our over inflated egos – the King Baby in us – that have to be deflated at least to the extent where we can be sufficiently honest with ourselves to accept that alcohol has beaten us – our denial has to be broken. We must then surrender for good. Without such surrender, no 'rock bottom' is ever effective.

Throughout my time in Broadway Lodge I had difficulty in accepting my own powerlessness; I was, however, 'complying'. Compliance can best be described as partial acceptance or partial surrender and whilst it may for a time prevent the alcoholic from drinking, it will often act as a block to total acceptance and surrender. It is partly conscious and partly sub-conscious. It is, as it were, going along without taking a drink but begrudgingly so and without conviction or enthusiasm. Sometimes it is not too difficult but at other times not picking up a drink can be very hard and contrary to what we want to do. At such times it is what we call 'white-knuckling it'. It was only when I saw the slogan, 'Insanity is making the same mistake twice and expecting a different result' that I truly surrendered and gave up my reliance on my own omnipotence and defiance and was really ready to accept help and begin to recover. At last I could then feel my powerlessness in my gut, in my very bones. I had stopped complying. I accepted that I could **never again drink safely** and I knew the truth of the saying 'once an alcoholic, always an alcoholic'.

Compliance can often last a long time and it is during this period when we are most at risk from that most subtle and dangerous foe called **'euphoric recall'**, which is when we cling on to the idea that drinking was always fun, quite forgetting the dreadful states we were in when we last had a drink. It has its origin in 'the insistent yearning to enjoy life as once he knew it'[3] and it is the very cunning aspect of denial which, particularly prior to complete acceptance, causes the thought to come into our minds that 'a drink would be nice' or worse 'I can handle just one drink' or 'one drink won't do me any harm'. To yield to such thoughts can prove fatal and they must be immediately banished should they come into our minds. The following extract from The Big Book illustrates how relapse can so easily happen if we are not always on guard:

What sort of thinking dominates an alcoholic who repeats time after time the desperate experiment of the first drink? Friends who have reasoned with him after a spree which has brought him to the point of divorce or bankruptcy are mystified when he walks directly into a saloon. Why does he? Of what is he thinking?

Our first example is a friend we shall call Jim...he got drunk again. We asked him to tell us exactly how it happened. This is his story: 'I came to work on Tuesday morning. I remember I felt irritated that I had to be a salesman for a concern I once owned. I had a few words with the boss, but nothing serious. Then I decided to drive into the country and see one of my prospects for a car. On the way I felt hungry so I stopped at a roadside place where they have a bar. I had no intention of drinking. I just thought I would get a sandwich. I also had the notion that I might have a customer for a car at this place, which was familiar for I had been going to it for years.

I had eaten there many times during the months I was sober. I sat down at a table and ordered a sandwich and a glass of milk. Still no thought of drinking. I ordered another sandwich and decided to have another glass of milk.

Suddenly the thought crossed my mind that if I were to put an ounce of whiskey in my milk it couldn't hurt me on a full stomach. I ordered a whiskey and poured it into the milk. I vaguely sensed I was not being any too smart, but felt reassured that I was taking the whiskey on a full stomach. *The experiment went well so I ordered another whiskey and poured it into more milk. That didn't bother me so I tried another'.*

Thus started one more journey to the asylum for Jim. Here was the threat of commitment, the loss of family and position, to say nothing of that intense mental and physical suffering which drinking always caused him. ***He had much knowledge about himself as an alcoholic. Yet all reasons for not drinking were easily pushed aside in favour of the foolish idea that he could take whiskey if only he mixed it with milk!***

Whatever the precise definition of the word may be, we call this plain insanity. How can such a lack of proportion, of the ability to think straight, be called anything else?

You may think that this is an extreme case. To us it is not far-fetched, for this kind of thinking has been characteristic of every single one of us. We have sometimes reflected more than Jim did upon the consequences. But there was always the curious mental phenomenon that parallel with our sound reasoning there inevitably ran some insanely trivial excuse for taking the first drink. Our sound reasoning failed to hold us in check. The insane idea won out. The next day we would ask ourselves, in all earnestness and sincerity, how could it have happened.[21]

The theory of powerlessness is not difficult to grasp but to accept it totally is quite another matter. Despite all the evidence to the contrary (which they deny), many alcoholics continue to delude themselves that they are the masters of drink. Bottom line, however, they must either break their denial and accept and surrender to their powerlessness or die. It is that simple – yet very, very few accept. Most die simply because paradoxically **you cannot experience victory if you refuse to surrender and admit defeat.**

Denial can run very deep: alcoholics may have to lose families, marriages, homes, jobs, money, and fall far before they can admit defeat and surrender. Only when this happens is 'rock bottom' reached. I believe, however, that rock bottoms can be raised. There is certainly evidence that many people are now joining AA much younger than even a few years ago. This is due, in part, to the fact that many are now starting to drink while still children with immature bodies, but it is also due to the fact that most are also taking other drugs in far greater numbers and quantities. But rock bottoms could be raised more if the general public was much more aware of what a serious and deadly disease alcoholism is; and if the alcoholic was much more frequently made to face the consequences of his drinking. Far too often he is 'enabled' to continue drinking because members of the family, friends, employers, colleagues, and others with whom he comes into contact either deny his alcoholism or cover up for his drunkenness for understandable but nevertheless mistaken reasons. As a result the disease continues to flourish – the exact opposite of what is wanted.

Perhaps the greatest enabler of all is money. I am sure that the best thing that happened to me in the end was completely running out of money. Had I still had money in the bank, I would undoubtedly have gone on drinking and blaming my problems on everything except drink. Rich people relatively rarely seem to make it into recovery simply because their money enables them to carry on drinking until one way or another it kills them.

Enabling does nothing to raise a rock bottom because it allows the alcoholic to evade rather than face the consequences of his drinking so that he gets sicker and sicker, ultimately to death. Raising a rock bottom can also sometimes be done by way of an intervention, preferably in a treatment centre where success is more likely because the intervener would most likely be an alcoholic in recovery and hence more able to gain the confidence and trust of the alcoholic and persuade him that at least recovery is possible.

In theory, a rock bottom can occur at any point on the downward path of the Jellinek Chart (see Introduction) which illustrates graphically and clearly the progressive nature of both active disease and recovery. Unfortunately most alcoholics end up at the bottom of the chart, very frightened, lonely, suffering greatly and going in vicious and ever decreasing circles without hitting rock bottom before drinking themselves to death. As one alcoholic said to another at the funeral of a third, 'It's a pity Fred never got to AA.' 'Yes,' replied the other, 'but he wasn't bad enough for that.'

As with powerlessness, unmanageability also has to be accepted before the foundation that Step One is becomes solid. Unmanageability is related to and a direct consequence of alcoholic drinking. Anyone who is drunk is temporarily unmanageable but a drinking alcoholic is unmanageable all the time. His whole life becomes completely chaotic. Yet the alcoholic will almost always use this unmanageability as an excuse for drinking and not see it as the inevitable consequence – a consequence that brings with it a whole host of problems with which the newly sober alcoholic has to deal. Reaping what he has sown, he will have some or all of marriage/relationship problems, money problems, job problems, legal problems – in some cases the prospect of prison – and many more. As I have already described, my own life had become so unmanageable that there was no life left to manage. It had all gone.

Having laid this vital foundation, the practising of the remaining Steps becomes essential if a fulfilled and contented sobriety is to be achieved.

2. Came to believe that a Power greater that ourselves could restore us to sanity.

For me, Step One was the most difficult to take; Step Two, on the other hand, was by far the easiest. I took it without realising it; in fact, you could say that it took me. When I looked at the Step in some depth, I was forcibly struck by the word 'sanity'. It had been suggested to me that if I were to have any doubts about my sanity, I should write down some of the things I had done while I was drinking. I had written only a few when I realized that what I was writing down were the acts of a complete lunatic. They also made me realize just how unmanageable my life had become, thus confirming and cementing my acceptance of this aspect of Step One. To me, the word insanity implies a complete lack of awareness or recognition of the insane condition by the insane person. By the time I took Step Two formally, I had been sober for about three months, by which time my mind was clear enough for me to recognise my previous insanity, and it was only then that I really began to appreciate that alcoholism is a mental illness, as well as a physical and spiritual one.

In recovery, I never suffered from the delusion that I had done it all alone. I was only too conscious of all the help I had received from Mary, her doctor, the counsellors and my peers in Broadway Lodge and of course from members in AA. God apart, to whom I had turned when I was confirmed, all of these certainly constituted a Power greater than myself and it was blindingly obvious that such a Power could not only restore me to sanity but was already restoring me to sanity. I was a hell of a lot saner that I had been.

Not everyone has the same experience of this Step as me. Over the years

[122]

I have observed that there is a tendency for the majority of AA members to fall into one of two main categories. There are those who, like me, find Step One very difficult to accept and Step Two quite easy, and there are those who find Step One quite easy and Step Two very difficult. Many of the latter are agnostics or atheists and are, to say the least, antagonistic toward recognising any power greater than themselves. To them I always say that two heads are better than one and ask them if they really think they can sober up on their own. I add that anyone walking into AA asking for help subconsciously acknowledges a power greater than themselves as no one ever asks for help from a power inferior to themselves!

All we are asked to do in taking the first two steps is to accept them without reservation. They are about acceptance and nothing else and, unlike the remainder of the steps, no further action is required.

3. Made a decision to turn our will and our lives over to the care of God *as we understood Him.*

The following '...three pertinent ideas...'[22] are the very cornerstone on which AA philosophy is based and they dispel completely the notion popularly held by many non-alcoholics that alcoholics are weak-willed people who simply need to pull themselves together. They show that it is virtually impossible to recover on one's own and are closely related to the first three steps which are sometimes thought of as 'I can't, He can, let Him'.

(a) That we were alcoholic and could not manage our own lives.

(b) That probably no human power could have relieved our alcoholism.

(c) That God could and would if He were sought.[22]

The third idea requires us to trust and to risk and it is only when we are convinced 'that God could and would [relieve our alcoholism] if He were sought', and not before, that we can move on to Step Three. This strongly implies that if one is not convinced, one should go back to the beginning and start again until one is convinced. Either that or put the Big Book in the waste paper basket and try some more controlled drinking!

'God as we understood Him'
A large number of alcoholics, if not the majority, enter AA saying that they are agnostics or atheists who want nothing whatever to do with God. Either that or they blame Him for their woes and certainly do not trust Him. The early members of the Fellowship who wrote the Twelve Steps appreciated this and the fact that there would be varying perceptions of

God as future members would comprise not only atheists and agnostics but people of all religious denominations. The all-encompassing concept of *'God as we understood Him'* was therefore introduced, allowing for any perception of God and making the Twelve Step Programme spiritual as opposed to religious.

I perceive God as the Christian God, though I am by no means certain and becoming increasingly less certain with the passing of the years. Perhaps, however, it matters not that I know Him, only that He knows me. I dislike much of the cant, dogma and ritual of doctrinal religion and I rarely go to church because although I love church music, sermons that come from the heart and the sense of stillness and calm to be found in so many cathedrals and churches, I simply have never sensed the presence and power of God in church in anything approaching the same way as I do in an AA meeting. Christ, however, I regard as being the best spiritual teacher who has ever lived and it is from his teachings that AA's spiritual programme is derived.

The first words of the Step, 'Made a decision ...' mean, in this context, making a firm commitment (doing it even after the initial desire to do so may have passed) to turning '...our will and our lives over to the care of God *as we understood Him'*. The word 'care' was perhaps the most important to me because I was conscious that from the moment when I had decided not to be confirmed, I had turned my back on God and lived my whole adult life according to my own set of addictive rules, with disastrous results. With my back to God, I could not see Him. Early in my recovery I came across the writing of an unknown author which seemed to reflect in the clearest way my own story and how I was feeling.

FOOTPRINTS

One night a man had a dream. He dreamed
He was walking along the beach with the LORD.
Across the sky flashed scenes from his life. For each scene
He noticed two sets of footprints in the sand:
One belonged to him and the other to the LORD.
When the last scene of his life flashed before him,
He looked back at the footprints in the sand.
He noticed that many times along the path of his life
There was only one set of footprints in the sand.
He also noticed that it only happened
at the very lowest and saddest times in his life.
This really bothered him and he questioned the LORD about it.

[124]

"LORD you said that once I decided to follow you,
You'd walk with me all the way.
But I have noticed that during the most troublesome times in my life,
There is only one set of footprints.
I don't understand why when I needed you most
you would leave me."
The LORD replied "My precious, precious child,
I love you and I would never leave you.
During your times of trial and suffering
When you see only one set of footprints,
It was then that I carried you."

I had survived when by all normal standards I should have died, and very often someone had been carrying me.

When I consciously made my decision to turn my will and my life over to the care of God, I realized that I had, in fact, unconsciously made the decision when I took the First Step and decided to commit myself to AA and its Twelve Step Programme. In turning my will and my life over to the care of God, I was re-affirming my commitment to being sober and taking the necessary steps to that end. It is what I wanted and still want to do, and I believe it is what my God also wants me to do – it is His will for me. I committed myself to the Steps and left the result to God. 'I can't, He can, let Him.' It was the best decision I ever made and the only commitment I have ever completely stuck to.

Having taken Step Three, it is advisable to get on with Step Four and the remaining eight Steps immediately as, in my opinion, any procrastination at this stage may threaten a full and lasting recovery. Before attempting Step Four, however, it is essential to ensure that a firm foundation is in place to base it on. In other words, the first three Steps must be strong and accepted without reservation. They are sometimes likened to the legs of a three legged stool upon which the Fourth and Fifth Steps are placed to form the seat: if any of the three legs is weak, the stool will break and give way – Step Four will be neither searching nor fearless, and hence of little or no value.

4. Made a searching and fearless moral inventory of ourselves.

This Step requires effort and often much courage. It is also, together with the Fifth Step, the one at which many of us baulk and procrastinate, putting off doing them for as long as possible or even indefinitely. Many never attempt to take them at all and sadly relapse and die.

Despite being told that alcoholism is an illness which is not our fault, we still feel guilt and shame, and, for me, Steps Four and Five have most to do with getting rid of that guilt and shame, letting go of the burden of baggage from the past, getting to know, accept and like myself, and feeling forgiven. With regard to guilt, I can do no better than to quote from my favourite AA pamphlet, *A Member's Eye View of Alcoholics Anonymous*. This pamphlet contains the text of a paper read some fifty years ago to a class of alcoholism counsellors at one of the large American universities by an AA member with sixteen years sobriety.

It may also appear to some of you that in the Fourth and Fifth of its Twelve Steps, A.A. might very well be accused of talking out of both sides of its mouth at once. If you will recall these Steps are:

4. *Made a fearless and searching inventory of ourselves.*
5. *Admitted to God, to ourselves and another human being the exact nature of our wrongs.*

*Here it would appear, is an organization that on the one hand claims that there is no moral culpability involved in the disease of alcoholism, and on the other suggests to its members that recovery entails a searching and fearless accounting of this culpability to God and to another human being. I personally feel that this apparent paradox results from the empirical knowledge gained by the founders of A.A. I believe they found, as we all have since, that no matter what you tell the newcomer about the disease of alcoholism, he still **feels** guilty. He cannot blind himself to the moral **consequences** of his drinking: the blight he has visited upon those around him and the shame and degradation he has inflicted upon himself. This load of conventional guilt – and I use the word "conventional" advisedly – as well as the alcoholic's stubborn and perverse wish to cling to it, is the oldest of his "old ideas." It is the oldest because it started first, and in most cases it will be the last to go. But go it must if the alcoholic's attitude toward himself and hence the world around him is to undergo any basic change. That's why I believe the founders of A.A. learned in their own experimentation that the alcoholic must be given a **conventional** means of unloading this burden of **conventional** guilt. Hence the Fourth and the Fifth Steps.*

Initially, I was largely unaware of these reasons for the Fourth and Fifth

Steps, so I took them pretty much on blind trust and found that there was nothing to fear. It is not changing that hurts, it is our reluctance to change that hurts. That which we resist, persists!

There is no set way of taking inventory but it does require guidance, almost invariably from someone in recovery who has taken all Twelve Steps. Under the guidance of the aftercare counsellor at Broadway Lodge (himself an alcoholic), and after reading the relevant sections on Step Four in both the Big Book and *Twelve Steps and Twelve Traditions* (which guide many through this Step), I took inventory based on a Hazelden model which includes personality defects, the seven cardinal sins, the ten commandments, and virtues, attitudes and responsibilities and is thus much more comprehensive than either of the AA ones. (See Appendix 4) It had been just over four months since my last drink when I did this Step and even in that short time there had been profound changes in my thinking, attitudes and behaviour, so that once I started, I found that I was doing it with great enthusiasm. There were moments when I could not stop writing, so intrigued was I by what I was discovering and learning, and I completed it over two or three days in a total of about thirty hours.

When drinking, I had practised all the character defects in spades, so much so that they were increasingly, and ultimately entirely dominating my life. I had become completely overrun by fear and all the other negative emotions, so much so that any virtues that I still possessed were swamped to such an extent, that they might just as well not have existed at all. All that mattered was where the next drink was coming from. In doing my Fourth Step I began to see that the extent and dominance of all these character defects were the consequences of years of drinking and in the final and chronic stages of my illness I was using drink to temporarily anaesthetise the pain of the fear, guilt and shame that I was feeling. I could not live with drink, nor could I live without it. I could also see that after four months without a drink my character defects were nothing like as dominant or overwhelming as they had been and I was beginning to feel quite good about myself. This alone was a remarkable change.

When I looked at the seven cardinal sins I found that I had committed them all and similarly I had broken all of the ten of the commandments. Although I never actually killed anyone there had been moments when I had wished people dead, including myself, and I certainly now believe that whilst under the influence of alcohol anybody, again including myself, is capable of doing anything and 'there but for the Grace of God go I'.

Sobriety above all else is about change and while it is necessary to know about our defects, it is also necessary to know what we are going to replace them with. The inventory I followed also required me to look at the asset side of the balance sheet and the small virtues which are important but so often overlooked. In going through them, I was relieved to find that I had practised them all; even, in the chronic stages of my drinking. I had for example occasionally been kind, considerate, punctual and even honest. These little virtues, to name a few, were things on which I could build: I could work on being more kind, being less dishonest by being more honest, being less angry by being grateful. In much the same way, I could change my attitudes and take more responsibility. Responsibility is a word hated by alcoholics for they and drug addicts of all kinds are amongst the most irresponsible people on earth. Yet if we are to recover, we have to become responsible, not only for our recovery but also for the other responsibilities considered in the inventory and this we do by practising all the Twelve Steps as a way of life.

This is the Step which requires the most effort, written work and courage. It is vital that it is done as fearlessly and thoroughly as possible, though there is really nothing to fear. All the Steps are tools which help us to get well and are for our benefit. I found the prospect of doing the Fourth Step far more daunting than the actual doing of it. As I wrote and the more I wrote, the more I began to know myself and realize that I was not all bad and that I did possess, as I believe everyone does, the attributes which, if worked on, would make me into a loving and worthwhile human being. My Fourth Step was as thorough and fearless as I knew how and nothing was left out which should have been included. I have never felt the need to do another.

5. **Admitted to God, to ourselves and to another human being the exact nature of our wrongs.**

Why am I afraid to tell you who I am?
But if I tell you who I am, you might not like who I am, and it is all that
I have.
If I expose my nakedness to you – do not make me feel shame.
I can only know that much of myself which I have had the courage to
confide in you.

These and other insights from *Why am I afraid to tell you who I am?* by

[128]

John Powell clarify for me why the Fifth Step is necessary: without it I would never have discovered or accepted who I was or received forgiveness for the many sins I had committed.

Writing my life story and reading it to a dozen or so of my peers in Broadway Lodge was the scariest thing I have ever had to do but whilst it was undoubtedly beneficial to me, it was neither a Fourth nor a Fifth Step. The day after completing my Fourth Step I took the Fifth one, reading it with Brian, a trainee counsellor at Broadway Lodge who was himself an alcoholic and an addict. We were not complete strangers, but we knew little about each other. The important thing to me was that he was an alcoholic. I believe it is enormously helpful if the human listener is a fellow alcoholic as only he or she will have the necessary empathy and is unlikely to judge as we reveal the exact nature of our wrongs. Although I approached this Step with some trepidation, I needn't have worried as I was immediately put at my ease. At the beginning, Brian drew my attention to the empty chair signifying the presence of my God in the room. Strangely, I felt that somehow He was also inside of me. I talked without interruption for the whole of the morning on the negative side of my inventory. As we broke for lunch, Brian told me that he had observed from my body language that my children meant a very great deal to me and I had certainly been feeling that as I talked about them. After lunch I talked for two or more hours mostly on the asset side of the balance sheet and concluded with the Serenity Prayer.

I found this step a very moving and spiritual experience, though it is not necessarily so for everyone. When I had entered treatment, I was very frightened, bewildered, lonely, and full of denial, guilt, shame and self-hatred. During the eighteen weeks since then, I had been loved back to quite a high degree of spiritual and mental health and at the end of my Fifth Step I felt very humble yet at the same time strangely elated. The great weight of guilt and shame had been lifted from my shoulders and were gone. It was good to be Billy and I was really aware of the person I was and could become. Above all I felt forgiven, not least because I had forgiven myself. At last I was free of the shackles of my illness and my predominant negative emotions. I had found the love of God in me and I was no longer alone.

In some ways Step Five can only be as good as the Step Four on which it is based. Done well, however, it can be a wonderfully healing Step which strengthens the feelings of powerlessness and surrender so necessary for ongoing recovery. Since taking my own Fifth Step, I have been privileged to listen to a number of others over the years and the interesting thing is that, whilst each had their individual differences, essentially they were all the same – and they were all mine!

Step Five marks the end of the drinking past to which we need never return. We have identified our defects of character, defects which must be dispensed with if we are to achieve a happy and useful sobriety in the future. In Steps Six and Seven, therefore, we let go of the past and look to the future.

6. Were entirely ready to have God remove all the defects of character.
7. Humbly asked Him to remove our shortcomings.

These two Steps are simple and very much a pair. They are sometimes called the 'forgotten Steps' and certainly I did not initially give them due diligence. It was not until I read the appropriate passage on them in the Big Book that I sat down and really thought about them. It says that having read our Fifth Step, we should, on returning home, carefully review the previous ones to ensure that we have done them as thoroughly and as well as possible; that our work to date was a solid foundation on which to build further. If that is the case then we should be ready to let God remove all our defects of character. By ready, and speaking only for myself, I mean that I genuinely wanted Him to remove them, even though some of my defects were 'old friends' which in some ways had enabled me to survive. But go they had to, as they certainly were not going to equip me to live soberly in the future.

It is not until we come to Step Seven that we actually ask God to do anything for us and it is suggested that we do so humbly. In my experience the words humble, humbly and humility are much misunderstood and are often confused with humiliation or being humiliated. One of the best definitions of humility I have seen is: *To those who have made progress in A.A., it amounts to a clear recognition of what and who we really are, followed by a sincere attempt to become what we could be.*[23] To do this honestly, one's ego has to be deflated or what might be called 'right-sized'. It is interesting to note that one cannot feel humiliated if one is humble. In other words humility is essentially about being honest, so I believe that only if we sincerely or honestly ask God to remove our short comings is He likely to take much notice of us. Even then, we must play our part too, and put in our own effort and work. I am reminded of an old gramophone record I heard as a child: the late Sir Bernard Miles was playing an old

Hertfordshire character who was lovingly attending to his governor's beautiful garden, one day, when he was hailed by the passing vicar. 'It's wonderful what God can do in a garden with a bit of help,' he said. 'Ahh, yea,' replied the gardener in his rich brogue, 'but you should have seen it when He had it to His-self!' And so it is with Step Seven, I believe: if we simply ask God to do it all for us, nothing very much will happen because God requires genuine assistance from us. This I believe we give to Him by, in effect, forming a partnership with Him, in which we are the junior partner, completing the rest of the Twelve Step programme and always trying to adopt its principles as a way of life.

8. Made a list of all the people we had harmed, and became willing to make amends to them all.

The order in which the Twelve Steps are written is no accident and accordingly they should be taken in that same order. Steps Four and Five are the consequence of the first three Steps being properly taken and, following the experience of self-awareness and acceptance gained from doing them, they lead into the taking of the Sixth and Seventh quite naturally. But Steps Eight and Nine are different in that they require us to consider other people as well as ourselves. Because of this there can be a definite temptation to skip them. In the short term, it may seem easier to avoid even thinking about them but in the long term, recovery and personal growth will be impeded unless these steps are addressed and due amends made where appropriate. So it's best to just get on with it, sooner rather than later, if progress is to be made. While other people may benefit from the making of amends, the person who will benefit by far the most is the alcoholic and it was this that helped me to become willing to 'get on with it and do it now'. I wanted to make these acts of reconciliation and restore relationships because by so doing we would all benefit.

As I have said, when I was in Broadway Lodge I was told that I had an illness which was not my fault; that my powerlessness over alcohol meant that alcohol was controlling me and I was not responsible for my actions or behaviour when I was drinking; that I was, however, accountable for them, and it is for this reason that we have to make amends. Further I was told that in sobriety I, and no one else, am responsible for my recovery and not picking up the first drink. Thus the Eighth and Ninth Steps are essentially about restoring relationships which have been damaged, sometimes irretrievably, by years of drinking. Like the Fourth and Fifth Steps they are the ones at which we are inclined to baulk, although, paradoxically, they are also the steps on which many make a start from the very beginning of recovery. I myself wrote letters from a very early stage to nearly all those closest and dearest to me, telling them of my alcoholism, how sorry I was for all I had done, and how I hoped all would be well in the future. In retrospect they were probably all a bit naïve and over the top, but they were all well received and almost everyone seemed to be pleased that I had stopped drinking. In those days of early recovery that probably was enough for them.

The first requirement of this step is a list and without it no start can be made. In listing the people we have harmed, it is necessary to keep a sense of perspective – something some of us are not always very good at – and include on the list only people who should properly be there. At the same time it is sensible to list all those people against whom we hold or have held resentments, or who we think should be making amends to us as we will invariably find, if we look closely enough, that they are the same people we have harmed the most. People who have died or whom we may never meet again should be included on the list because even if in a physical sense it may not be possible to make amends to them, we must still be willing to do so were it possible. Finally, do not what I initially did and forget to include yourself, for without any doubt, we had also harmed ourselves.

9. Made direct amends to such people wherever possible, except when to do so would injure them or others.

In the early days of my sobriety I thought that making amends amounted to little more than saying sorry and in a very few cases this may well be true. But I did not fully appreciate what making amends meant or involved. The verb to amend means to correct, to improve and to change for the better. The only three things over which I have control and can change for the better are my thinking, my attitude and my actions or behaviour. So in making direct amends to people I had harmed and hence to improve my relationships with them, I had to amend or change my behaviour. It was not enough to say that I loved my children, I had to behave lovingly towards them, not just once, but on a permanent basis and similarly so with everyone else. This was and is not always easy but there is no doubt that to the extent that I have been able to do it, so the quality of nearly all my relationships has improved beyond all recognition.

Sometimes amends will be rejected by the person to whom they are offered and if this does happen, we should try not to feel angry, rejected or discouraged. Unfortunately not everyone is capable of forgiveness and in such circumstances we should remember that we have done our best and that another's rejection is not our problem. In my own case, by far the most difficult amends I had to make were to my second wife Mary, and, as recounted earlier, I was unable to regain her trust and have a mutually loving relationship with her.

Many people to whom we are making amends may not want to be reminded too much of the pain they have undergone and when this happens, it is often wise not to go into too much detail. My mother was a case in point: being eighty two years old when I sobered up, for her it was more than enough that I was sober and could visit her, and during her last few years we became very close friends which was of enormous value and joy to me. I cherish her memory as I do that of my father. In making amends to my mother, I believe that I also made them to my father.

The last part of this step, '...except when to do so would injure them or others' requires forethought and consideration for others. For example, inviting the sack by confessing past actions or omissions to an employer would clearly not benefit a spouse or children. Marital infidelity is another area where confession could do more harm than good. In such cases it is best to use common sense and discretion while taking care not to use phoney discretion as a cop out for not making amends. Sometimes it can be difficult to know when to make amends and when not to, but the most important thing is to be willing to do so and then acting on this willingness by changing past behaviours and acting responsibly and lovingly.

There may be some wrongs we can never fully right. We don't worry about them if we can honestly say to ourselves that we would right them if we could. Some people cannot be seen – we write them an honest letter. And there may be a valid reason for postponement in some cases. But we don't delay if it can be avoided. We should be sensible, tactful, considerate and humble without being servile or scraping. As God's people we stand on our feet: we don't crawl before anyone.[24]

Making amends to oneself is also important. It is astonishing how often alcoholics will continue to do themselves harm long after they have put down the glass. Of course no one is perfect and we all make mistakes but the simplest and easiest way to make amends to oneself is to stay sober, go to meetings, practise the Twelve Step Programme in its entirety and come to terms with and deal with any other substance and behavioural addictions we may have. The AA programme is often described as being a selfish programme. Today I am quite clear that the most important person in my life is me, as you are in yours. Unless I put my sobriety and general well being first, I am no use to myself, and just as importantly, I am no use to anyone else. This may seem paradoxical, but it is true.

If we are painstaking about this phase of our development, we will be amazed before we are half way through. We are going to know a new freedom and a new happiness. We will not regret the past nor wish to shut the door on it. We will comprehend the word serenity and we will know peace. No matter how far down the scale we have gone, we will see how our experience can benefit others. That feeling of uselessness and self-pity will disappear. We will lose interest in selfish things and gain interest in our fellows. Self-seeking will slip away. Our whole attitude and outlook upon life will change. Fear of people and economic insecurity will leave us. We will intuitively know how to handle situations which used to baffle us. We will suddenly realize that God is doing for us what we could not do for ourselves.

Are these extravagant promises? We think not. They are being fulfilled among us – sometimes quickly, sometimes slowly. They will always materialize if we work for them.[25]

10. Continued to take personal inventory and when we were wrong promptly admitted it.

Step Ten is the first of the three maintenance steps which are taken on a daily or continuing basis. At least once a day, I try to remember to re-affirm my powerlessness and unmanageability, which are the foundation of the programme; and most evenings I try to review my day, taking stock of the good things I have done as well as recognising my errors and omissions.

Everyone makes mistakes and whenever they are made by somebody else we at least expect them to make an apology. When they don't, as is often the case, we can get argumentative, angry and resentful to the extent that even a trivial error can harm a relationship, sometimes permanently. And often the need to be always right prevents the correction of a mistake by a simple apology. As a late friend of mine used to say of his wife, 'She is not always right, but she is never wrong!' This need to be right is usually the consequence of an inflated ego and low self-worth, made worse over a period by the unwillingness to apologise. Surprisingly few people realize that the words 'I am sorry', said sincerely, put an end to an argument. However, if someone does not apologise there is no need for me to continue to play the arguing game, as the lack of an apology is the other person's problem, not mine. If the mistake is mine, by apologising promptly I have done what I can to correct it. Of course, in situations where material damage has been done, it may be necessary to repair or replace the damaged property. But it is well to remember: never ruin an apology with an excuse!

*It is a spiritual axiom that every time we are disturbed, no matter what the cause, there is something wrong **with us**. If somebody hurts us and we are sore, we are in the wrong also.*[26] Even if there is justification for our soreness or anger, we are also in the wrong because of the wrong attitude we are taking, which is almost certainly making the matter worse. As Eleanor Roosevelt once said, 'Nobody can hurt me without my permission.' And so when taking inventory we should recognize when we are disturbed, take a good look at what we have done or are doing wrong and then take the necessary steps to correct it.

I always think of Step Ten as being a review, taken on a regular basis, embracing Steps Four to Nine. I especially look out for self-centeredness, dishonesty, resentment and fear. As with all the Steps, I do it mainly for my own benefit to maintain and enhance my spiritual condition. I must stress that I do not always get it right. If we were all perfect, if we were all saints, there would be no need for Step Ten!

It is easy to let up on the spiritual programme of action and rest on our laurels. We are headed for trouble if we do, for alcohol is a subtle foe. We are not cured of alcoholism. What we really have is a daily reprieve contingent on the maintenance of our spiritual condition. Every day is a day when we must carry the vision of God's will into all of our activities. "How can I best serve Thee – Thy will (not mine) be done." These are thoughts which must go with us constantly. We can exercise our will power along this line all we wish. It is the proper use of the will.[27]

11. Sought through prayer and meditation to improve our conscious contact with God *as we understood Him*, praying only for knowledge of His will for us and the power to carry that out.

This is one of my favourite Steps because in an indirect and unconscious way it was responsible for my finding AA and recovery. In being confirmed two months before I stopped drinking, I was, without in any way being aware of the consequences of what I was letting myself in for, seeking help from some sort of contact with God as I understood Him. Shortly afterwards I was to enter treatment and I am sure that this was not mere coincidence.

The Step is asking us to seek 'to improve our conscious contact with God' by way of prayer and meditation. Such prayer and meditation should seek only knowledge of His will for us and the power to carry that out. Throughout my drinking career I did very much as I pleased and made no real attempt to do other than turn my back on God, with what I can now see were inevitable consequences. I totally neglected many things and, under the influence and effect of alcohol, failed to pay any attention to the spiritual disciplines which make life enriching. Deep down, I knew that so much of what I was doing was wrong and over the years I became increasingly terrified of being found out. If ever the parable of the Prodigal Son applied to anyone, it applied to me and, like the younger son in the parable, I did not believe that I deserved forgiveness or that it would be given. 'Father I have sinned against Heaven, and in Thy sight: I am no more worthy to be called thy son.' I was, to say the least, very hesitant about turning to God for help because I did not believe He would listen and hence I denied Him. In the end, however, the only other choice was death and as I somehow never really considered suicide as a viable option, all I could do was rather covertly and deviously turn to Him. The quite wonderful thing I discovered as a result is that my God loves sinners who truly repent as much as He loves anyone. 'All saints have their past and all sinners have their future!' I now believe that all those who deny God, for whatever reason, do so because of their despair at not finding a forgiving and nurturing God. If we do not seek to improve our conscious contact with God, how can we possibly know what He wants of us?

No matter how each of us perceives Him, it is vital that sooner or later we do have a perception of our own God with which we are comfortable; also that we make a sincere effort to form an active partnership with Him. As I have said, my own perception is that of the Christian God albeit stripped of the dogma, theology and cant of organised man-made denominational religion.

'Sought through prayer and meditation'

For me, prayer is very much a question of chatting with God, thanking Him for what I have, most of all for my sobriety, and of listening. He is a great friend or mate and if I listen (learn to listen and listen to learn), the answers do come, though very often not in the form I expect. They come mostly from listening to other people in and out of AA, from reading AA and other literature, and, very occasionally, as a flash of inspiration as if it were directly from above. The Step suggests that we confine our prayer to asking **only** for knowledge of His will for us and the power to carry that out, which I have done for many years now, and if I should pray for something directly, I always add 'if it be Thy will.' I do not believe that we can or should bargain with God.

The Chambers Concise 20th Century Dictionary defines the verb to meditate as 'to consider thoughtfully, to engage in contemplation, especially religious, to consider deeply, to reflect upon'. To me, it is reflecting on some basic truths: I am powerless over alcohol and other mood altering chemicals, and always will be; I am powerless over people, places and things, and, despite its numerous and apparent imperfections, we nevertheless live in a wonderful world.

'And ye shall know the truth and the truth will set you free.' These words of Christ are profoundly true yet many if not most of us spend our lives denying or running away from the truth. I once read somewhere that 'obviously the truth is what's so; not so obviously, it is also so what!' Yes I am an alcoholic but so what? It simply means that to live, I have to refrain from taking alcohol and other mood altering drugs. Abstinence is no big deal, in fact I very much prefer my present life to the drinking life that went before and for that I am profoundly grateful. For over a quarter of a century, I have read most of AA's literature and other spiritual literature as well; I have also listened a great deal. As a result, I and my own personal philosophy have changed greatly. But the last twenty seven years have only been the continuation of the beginning and unless I continue the quest and pursuit of learning, self improvement and personal growth, I shall go backwards. I have been on a fascinating and exciting journey and even now I still believe that the best is yet to come.

Each day, I try to set some time aside for meditation. I can do it at home, in the car, in the loo, wherever. From time to time I set aside longer periods when I read and reflect upon some of the great pieces of writing. It is a good idea for each of us to find a few that we like and which suit us best, and then consider deeply what they are saying and how well or how poorly our own thoughts and actions are in accord with them. The following are four of my own particular favourites which I presently keep in my bedroom. They are full of wisdom and contain nothing that could possibly be described as being contrary to God's Will. Interestingly and to greater or lesser extents, all are paradoxical.

[137]

The Prayer of St. Francis of Assisi

Lord, make me an instrument of thy peace: where there is hatred, let me sow love: where there is injury, pardon; where there is doubt, faith; where there is darkness, light: where there is despair, hope and where there is sadness, joy.
Lord, grant that I may not so much seek to be consoled, as to console, to be understood as to understand, to be loved, as to love.
For it is in giving that we receive, it is in pardoning that we are pardoned, and it is in dying that we are born to eternal life.

I Shall not Pass this Way Again

Expect to pass through this world but once; any good thing, therefore, that I can do, or any kindness that I can show to any fellow-creature, let me do it now; let me not defer or neglect it, for I shall not pass this way again.

Desiderata

Go placidly amid the noise and remember what peace there may be in silence.
As far as possible without surrender, be on good terms with all persons. Speak your truth quietly and clearly; and listen to others, even the dull and the ignorant, they too have their story.
Avoid loud and aggressive persons, they are vexatious to the spirit. If you compare yourself with others you may become vain and bitter, for always there will be greater and lesser persons than yourself.
Enjoy your achievements as well as your plans. Keep interested in your career however humble; it is a real possession in the changing fortunes of time. Exercise caution in your business affairs, for the world is full of trickery. But let this not blind you to what virtue there is; many persons strive for high ideals, and everywhere life is full of heroism. Be yourself, especially do not feign affection. Neither be cynical about love; for in the face of all aridity and disenchantment it is as perennial as the grass. Take kindly the counsel of the years gracefully surrendering the things of youth.
Nurture the strength of spirit to shield you in sudden misfortune. But do not distress yourself with imaginings. Many fears are born of fatigue

and loneliness. Beyond a wholesome discipline, be gentle with yourself.
You are a child of the universe, no less than the trees and the stars. And
whether or not it is clear to you, no doubt the universe is unfolding as it
should.
Therefore be at peace with God, whatever you conceive Him to be; and
whatever your labours and aspirations, in the noisy confusion of life, keep
peace with your soul. With all its shams, drudgery, and broken dreams, it
is still a beautiful world. Be cheerful. Strive to be happy.

Max Ehrmann

If

If you can keep your head when all about you
Are losing theirs and blaming it on you;
If you can trust yourself when all men doubt you,
But make allowance for their doubting too;
If you can wait and not be tired of waiting,
Or being lied about, don't deal in lies,
Or being hated, don't give way to hating,
And yet don't look too good, nor talk too wise:

If you can dream – and not make dreams your master;
If you can think – and not make thought your aim;
If you can meet with triumph and disaster
And treat those two impostors just the same;
If you can bear to hear the truth you've spoken
Twisted by knaves to make a trap for fools,
Or watch the things you gave your life to, broken,
And stoop and build 'em up with worn-out tools:

If you can make one heap of all your winnings
And risk it on one turn of pitch-and-toss,
And lose, and start again at your beginnings
And never breath a word about your loss;
If you can force your heart and nerve and sinew
To serve your turn long after they are gone,
And so hold on when there is nothing in you
Except the will which says to them: "Hold on!"

If you can talk with crowds and keep your virtue,
Or walk with Kings – nor lose the common touch,
If neither foes nor loving friends can hurt you,
If all men count with you but none too much;
If you can fill the unforgiving minute
With sixty seconds' worth of distance run,
Yours is the Earth and everything that's in it,
And – which is more – you'll be a Man, my son.

Rudyard Kipling

When my father died in 1965, I inherited from him 'I Shall not Pass this Way Again', which used to sit on his desk, and the copy of Kipling's 'If', which used to hang in his office and which I now have in my bedroom. They are two of my oldest possessions. Mainly because it has to do with growing up and maturity, 'If' is an apt poem for any alcoholic or addict to reflect upon, particularly the second and third verses. During the last few years of my drinking I would often read the poem, invariably with tears in my eyes, and in my inebriated or semi-inebriated state I would reflect upon what a bad set of cards life had dealt me and how unfair it was that I seemed unable to do any of the things in the poem. Strangely, it was less what my dead father might be thinking of me that really bothered me and more what my own children might be thinking. In some strange and macabre way that I can't explain, the poem, even then, was a friend and somehow gave me comfort and hope. Perhaps it was the 'old boy upstairs' or my own father trying to get through to me. Perhaps it was a subconscious factor in my asking for help and eventually in my finding recovery. I don't know, but all my life the poem has meant a lot to me. What I do know is that when I was drinking I often yearned to be some of things suggested in the poem. Since I put down the glass, I believe that belatedly and at last I have begun to make progress. Some years ago I went to visit 'Batemans', the house in Sussex where Rudyard Kipling lived for many years, and I was interested to discover that he died on the day before I was born.

'... and the power to carry that out'

'I can do all things through Christ [or Higher Power] which strengtheneth me.' For centuries people have found that they are empowered by a Power greater than themselves in whom they can trust and with whom they have a direct and close relationship. Without such a personal relationship, however, they cannot be empowered because, as was my own case when

[140]

drinking, they are cut off from God. In my opinion, it is, therefore, essential that we find a Higher Power for ourselves and have our own personal relationship with Him. In the long run someone else's God will not do. 'Seek and ye shall find.' One of the saddest things in life is that many people wait until life becomes unbearable before they start looking. The real tragedy is that being frightened – perhaps by the fear of not finding Him – to seek a God of their own understanding, they miss so much. I was one of those people, and if pain, hopelessness and despair were what it took for me to seek Him, I am nonetheless very pleased that eventually I did so. It changed my life.

I have known many in AA who, despite saying they were atheists or agnostics, started to pray to a God they did not believe in, only to end up, sooner or later, with a conception of their own Higher Power in which they could believe.

12. Having had a spiritual awakening as the result of these Steps, we tried to carry this message to alcoholics, and to practise these principles in all our affairs.

Perhaps the most important three words in the above statement are: 'the', 'this' and 'these'. It is often overlooked that the qualifying clause of this Step provides us with a promise or guarantee that a spiritual awakening is **the** inevitable consequence of taking the first Eleven Steps. Opinions may vary as to precisely what a spiritual awakening is but for me, spirituality has to do with the change in the way my thinking, attitudes and actions determine how I relate to God, myself and others. When I was drinking, the manner in which I related was negative, self-centred, self-defeating and very destructive. Today, however, as **the** result – not *a* result – of taking and practising the Steps, my life and manner of relating have become much more positive, fulfilling and enhancing. I have moved from being very fearful to being mostly trusting with a strong faith that whatever happens, it will be OK so long as I stay sober – it may not be what I want, but it will be OK. I have moved also from being full of self-pity to being grateful for what I have become and possess, from being resentful to being in the main accepting, and from being almost totally dishonest to being much more honest, particularly with myself. Most importantly of all, I have been relieved of the terrible compulsion to drink against my will that I once had and I am no longer alcohol's compulsive slave. Nor do I any longer have any desire at all to drink and for this gift alone I am eternally grateful. This to me is the great miracle of AA.

I also think that spirituality has to do with how we feel and the spiritual growth, which we inevitably experience as **the** consequence of practising the Twelve Steps, manifests itself in a sense of wholeness, humility, improved self-worth and well being the like of which the alcoholic has never previously known. At last, he has some contentedness and serenity, and he is feeling good about himself and the feelings are coming from within. When this happens the alcoholic is no longer suffering from his illness and he may be said to have recovered. Rightly, however, AA usually talks about recovering as opposed to recovered alcoholics, as none of us is cured and each one of us, whether we have been sober for a week or thirty years, has to maintain our sobriety by continuing on a daily basis to practise AA's spiritual principles. The price of freedom is eternal vigilance.

'**...we tried to carry** *this* **message to alcoholics.**' The message we carry is that we are living proof that anyone who works the first Eleven Steps will have a spiritual awakening and recover from alcoholism. Carrying this message is often referred to as 'Twelfth Stepping' and it is an essential part of the maintenance of continuing recovery and AA life. It happens when a suffering alcoholic asks for help and a recovering alcoholic reaches out to him, sharing his experience, strength and hope with the newcomer and encouraging him to attend an AA meeting. 'To keep it, you have to give it away.' This paradox is a well known AA saying and there is no doubt that, not only may the beginner be helped in his first efforts, but the bearer of the good news also always derives something that is essential for his own continued recovery. So we carry AA's message to others in order to stay sober ourselves. This is the raison d'etre of AA, as its very existence is due to Bill W.'s search for another alcoholic in order that he might stay sober himself. As he himself said when he sat down with Dr. Bob for the first time, '*Bob, I am speaking because I need you as much as you could possibly need me. I am in danger of slipping back down the drain'. (Please see Overture)* Bill W. had his last drink in November 1934 and the first people he subsequently approached did not stay sober. It was not until he met Dr Bob who had his last drink in June 1935 that Bill had his first success in helping another to sober up. Yet throughout this six month period, Bill himself had stayed sober. It is a selfish programme! Dr Bob was perhaps the greatest Twelfth Stepper of all time. When he was four years sober he said:

It is a most wonderful blessing to be relieved of the terrible curse with which I was afflicted. My health is good and I have regained my self-respect and the respect of my colleagues. My home life is ideal and my business is as good as can be expected in these uncertain times.

I spend a great deal of time passing on what I learned to others who want and need it badly. I do it for four reasons:

1. Sense of duty.

2. It is a pleasure.

3. Because in so doing I am repaying my debt to the man who took time to pass it on to me.

4. Because every time I do it I take out a little more insurance for myself against a possible slip.

...If you think you are an atheist, an agnostic, a skeptic, or have any other form of intellectual pride that keeps you from accepting what is in this book, I feel sorry for you. If you still think you are strong enough to beat the game alone, that is your affair. But if you really and truly want to quit drinking liquor for good and all, and sincerely feel that you must have some help, we know that we have an answer for you. It never fails, if you go about it with one half the zeal you have been in the habit of showing when you were getting another drink.

Your Heavenly Father will never let you down![28]

It should be noted that while we are asked to carry the message of recovery, we cannot carry the burden. No alcoholic is responsible for the recovery of another, only himself. All any of us can do is help another to help himself. I would say to a newcomer, 'The good news is that if you want to, you can get well and you will get lots of help and encouragement. The bad news is that no one else can do it for you! I can't take the First Step for you and you can't take it for me. Would that it were otherwise but that is the way it is.' It may be a generalisation, but over many years I have observed that if newcomers want sobriety, I can say no wrong, but if they don't want it, I can say no right! They will argue. Experience has taught me not to waste too much time with people who don't want to stop drinking; it is better to wait until such time as they may change their minds and in the meantime go and help someone else.

There is another way that we carry the message and that is indirectly, for example by giving advice to members of an alcoholic's family or friends. Although I have never gone around shouting to the whole world that I am an alcoholic, neither have I never hidden the fact, and I have always been quite relaxed about breaking my anonymity; pretty nearly everyone who knows me, knows also that I am an alcoholic and a member of AA. As a consequence, I have been able to use this indirect approach to help a number of alcoholics achieve sobriety.

The message we all carry is that life without alcohol and other mood altering substances can be and usually is joyous and happy. That is not to say that it is a bed of roses all the time because there are times when life is very difficult. But by being sober, we are able to confront our difficulties and, a day at a time, overcome them. Given time we are able to form better and loving relationships. We learn to enjoy rather than endure life. Eventually, we start to make a worthwhile contribution to life: miraculously, we become givers and not takers. What I remember most about the message first carried to me by Ed in Broadway Lodge was the hope I was given. A number of people who had what I wanted told me that if they could do it, then I could do it. It was a message I shall never forget and the only way I can ever repay them is by passing on the same message to others; it is one of the reasons why I still go to AA.

"....and practise *these* principles in all our affairs." The last clause of the Step is perhaps the most difficult and probably the one that many of us do least well. For the most part it refers to our lives in the world outside of AA. If we are serious about our recovery, over time the AA way of life increasingly becomes a part of us. It is a way of life that we come to love, yet I believe there is a limit to the personal growth that can be obtained from AA alone. AA is often described as 'a bridge to normal living', and so, while staying fully in AA, it is necessary that we venture forth outside of it, return to and take our rightful places as full and worthwhile members of the wider society in which we live. Having as a result of the Twelve Steps discovered who we are, we must still try to develop further the potential of the natural talents with which we are all blessed, and endeavour to become all that we are capable of becoming, for this is the highest calling of each human being. As long as we try to do this in the spirit of the Ninth Step, without harming others, we are likely to make the world a better place for having been here. Bearing in mind our past, what more could any alcoholic or other addict aspire to?

Chapter 10

My Life in AA

The first AA meeting I ever attended was in early January 1983, in the village of Hutton, on the outskirts of Weston-super-Mare. It was a Step Meeting and the Step being discussed that night was Step Eight. I was at Broadway Lodge at the time and one of the Broadway Lodge trainee counsellors was also there; he shared that he hadn't really got to Step Eight, which astounded me at the time. Apart from that and the fact that the meeting was taken by a quite elderly lady, I remember nothing else about it.

There are currently some forty thousand members of AA in the UK, meeting weekly in approximately four thousand groups. My present 'home group' is the Monday Night 'As Bill Sees It' group at Christ Church, in the Isle of Dogs, in the East End of London. It belongs, along with other groups in the locality, to the Outer East London Intergroup which, together with other intergoups north of the Thames, belongs to the North London Region, one of many regions into which the country is divided up. Each year there is a General Service Convention in York, where the UK AA Head Office is situated, and each region sends delegates. It is at this annual convention that major policy decisions are taken.

Throughout the whole of AA, each group complies with AA's Twelve Traditions (see Appendix 1), basically a set of guidelines within which the whole Fellowship operates. AA does not have any enforceable rules, nor does it have any bosses. Power to direct or govern is the essence of any organisation, yet AA, despite its enormous size, is the exception. Neither its General Service Conference, its Foundation Board nor the humblest group committee, can issue a single directive to an AA member and make it stick, let alone mete out any punishment. It was tried many times in the early days but utter failure was always the result: it was found that whilst an AA member might take advice or suggestions from a more experienced member, he won't take orders. It is probably fair to say that because of this stubborn resistance, both individually and collectively, the Twelve Traditions evolved by trial and error. In the final analysis, the Traditions are no more than suggestions or recommendations which have been shown to work over many years; they are accepted by AA members for one simple reason, which is often overlooked:

Unless each A.A. member follows to the best of his ability our suggested Twelve Steps to recovery, he almost certainly signs his own death warrant. His drunkenness and dissolution are not penalties inflicted by people in authority; they result from personal disobedience to spiritual principles.

The same stern threat applies to the group itself. Unless there is approximate conformity to A.A.'s Twelve Traditions, the group too can deteriorate and die. So we of A.A. do obey spiritual principles, first because we must, and ultimately because we love the kind of life such obedience brings. Great suffering and great love are A.A.'s disciplinarians; we need no others.[18]

My own experience confirms this: I have seen a number of groups deteriorate and cease to exist simply because they did not comply with the Traditions, even refused to comply with them in one or two cases. Those groups were no loss to AA: if they could not or would not comply with AA's Traditions, they were unlikely to help anyone, and may well have done much harm. AA works because all successful groups do comply approximately with the Traditions and because of this I can walk into any AA meeting anywhere in the world, feel at home and be familiar with the proceedings. AA's leaders are, literally, but trusted servants; they do not govern.

As soon as I completed treatment at Broadway Lodge, I followed Ed's suggestion that I go to AA and attend Step meetings, particularly in my early days. It was no accident, therefore, that one of the first meetings I attended when I got back to London was the Tuesday night Step meeting in Wimbledon. I liked the feel of the meeting and decided to make it my home group; it remained so for many years, until we moved to Docklands in December 1999. A home group is the group we attend virtually every week, where often we make close friends and where we probably make our first commitment to service by, for example, making the tea and coffee each week. Other forms of service at group level are being secretary of the group (the secretary is the person who takes the meeting and is normally responsible for arranging the weekly main speakers), group treasurer, literature person, group service representative (GSR) at intergroup meetings (usually held bi-monthly), and greeter(s). It is recommended that a certain length of sobriety is advisable for some of these positions. There are broadly similar positions at both intergroup and region levels.

In my early to middle years I did a lot of service at group, intergroup and region levels, also manning the London telephone office, taking calls from drinking alcoholics and others seeking help. One of the great benefits of doing service is that we get involved and become, as I like to put it, 'playing members'. Another benefit is that it provides us with a greater understanding of how AA operates. But perhaps the greatest benefit is the paradoxical one that the more service we put into AA, the more we get out of AA. There is no doubt that the people who embrace AA and are enthusiastic about service and the Twelve Step Programme, are the ones who get well; on the other hand, those who just turn up at meetings and say little or nothing are those who struggle the most and usually fail to make it. As one very charismatic man, who had been sober for about twenty years, shared in a meeting I was attending some years ago, 'There are no musts in AA but nor are there any alternatives.' He then added, 'Nor is AA a place for wimps or victims who, in reality, are but spectators in their own lives.'

As I have grown older I have opted to take more of a back seat and let others obtain the same great benefits of doing service that I received. I still, however, have a home group on a Monday night in the Isle of Dogs and I still do a bit of service currently as group treasurer. It keeps my hand in, helps me to keep a proper perspective on life and it keeps me in touch.

Thanks particularly to Ed and Eric at Broadway Lodge, I was given a very thorough grounding in the first five Steps and what recovery is generally all about. In effect they were my sponsors and they were the only ones I have ever had. From Step Six onwards, I just had two or three very close friends, more experienced than I, who gave me very considerable help when I asked for it.

I did not find it that difficult to follow AA suggestions on Steps Six to Twelve (as detailed in the Big Book and in the '12 x 12'). I regarded them as instructions and simply did as they suggested. I was very conscientious and when I had a problem it was easy to obtain help and advice. I must emphasise, however, that I am not in any way recommending that this is how all other AAs should do the Steps, merely describing my own experience.

A sponsor's job is to show the newcomer how he took the Steps so that the sponsee can do likewise; thus, in my opinion, the sponsor should be someone who has done all Twelve Steps and is accordingly comfortable with his sobriety; in effect, he has what the newcomer wants. When the sponsee has completed all the Steps, I believe the sponsor's job is finished. Most people then either go their separate ways, often for work or geographical reasons, or they become very good friends. I do not believe it is a sponsor's job to tell a sponsee what to do in respect of any matter other than the Steps; the sponsor should not, for example, advise on marriage or job problems, because rarely is he qualified to do so and even if he were, he might well be wrong. At the end of the day the sponsee has to make up his own mind on such matters.

If I myself have a sponsor today, by which I mean a good and trusted friend with whom I can discuss absolutely anything, it is one of my own former sponsees, Huw T., whom I took through all the Steps in fewer than six months over twelve years ago.

I have only had a handful of sponsees over the years. 'What they want' may not have been apparent in me or they might have known that I did a lot of written work and that I might ask them to do the same – something they might not have wanted to do! Recently, I happened to mention the fact that very few people ask me to sponsor them to one of my very good AA friends, Kevin S. 'Don't worry,' he said, 'you sponsor people in all the meetings you go to.' And it is certainly my hope that through sharing at meetings and drawing on my years of experience I can be of benefit to fellow members.

I had been in AA for six or seven years when a couple of my close AA friends died sober and the thought then struck me that I was no longer a newcomer. It did not occur to me before then because I was still looking to see what I could get out of AA, little realising that I could only ever get out of AA what I put into it and that I can only put in what I have got, namely my experience, strength and hope. There comes a point when the pupil miraculously becomes the teacher and unfortunately it is then that sometimes people will leave AA thinking, quite wrongly and tragically, that AA no longer has anything for them. They just do not seem to realize that when they think they no longer need a meeting, it is then that the meeting needs them, sometimes desperately so. What would AA be without the experience of old timers to give hope, encouragement and help to newcomers, and show them that if the old timer can recover so too can they. As it says in the Big Book, *'Rarely have we seen a person fail who has thoroughly followed our path.'*[14] Exactly one week before my 27th sobriety anniversary, I went with my old friend Huw T. to the East Sheen lunchtime Thursday meeting of AA which I used to regularly attend in the late nineteen eighties and nineties. Of the twenty-four people at the meeting I recognized eight members whom I knew from my earlier days. So out of the twenty-four present, nine of us had been sober for over ten years; in fact, three of us had each been sober for well over twenty years. Between the nine of us, we had some one hundred and fifty years of sobriety and as far as I could see, we all seemed to be grateful, happy and very satisfied 'customers'. It gave me great pleasure seeing my old friends again and I was moved as I reflected how we had all had the same problem and we had all found the same solution simply by helping each other to thoroughly follow AA's suggested (and proven) path to recovery.

Apart from the fact that nearly all people who stop going to AA sooner or later relapse, many to die, those who come back never ever say what a wonderful time they've had! I believe most strongly that not only is continuing to go to AA a necessary part of my own ongoing recovery but I have a duty to remain in AA, as it is the only way that I can repay what I owe to those who helped me. Besides, nothing gives me a bigger thrill than to see a newcomer recover and get well and if I can help him, so much the better. As a wise old timer once told me over twenty years ago, 'Whenever a newcomer walks into an AA room, we may be witnessing the beginning of the restoration of the dignity of a fellow human being.'

I am absolutely clear in my own mind that the AA Twelve Step philosophy has become an integral part of me and I do my best to practise its principles in all my affairs both inside and outside AA. That does not mean I succeed in doing it all the time, but whenever I make a mistake I invariably find that the answer to my problem lies somewhere in the Steps. Most often it is to do with control and not accepting my powerlessness over things other than alcohol, forgetting that I am powerless over everything except my thinking, my attitudes and my behaviour. One of the authors in the 'Personal Stories' section of the Big Book expresses it well:

*At last acceptance proved to be the key to my drinking problem. After I had been around A.A. for seven months, tapering off alcohol and pills, not finding the programme working very well, I was finally able to say, "Okay God. It **is** true that I – of all people, strange as it may seem, and even though I didn't give my permission – really, really am an alcoholic of sorts. And it is all right with me. Now, what am I going to do about it?" When I stopped living in the problem and began living in the answer, the problem went away. From that moment on, I have not had a single compulsion to drink.*

*And acceptance is the answer to **all** my problems today. When I am disturbed, it is because I find some person, place, thing, or situation – some fact of my life – unacceptable to me, and I can find no serenity until I accept that person, place, thing, or situation as being exactly the way it* *is supposed to be at this moment. Nothing, absolutely nothing happens in God's world by mistake. Until I could accept my alcoholism, I could not stay sober; unless I accept life completely on life's terms, I cannot be happy. I need to concentrate not so much on what needs to be changed in the world as on what needs to be changed in me and my attitudes.*[29]

Chapter 11

Chemical Dependency and Other Addictions
Additional facts, thoughts and opinions

My alcoholic progression is probably typical of many others of my generation who did not take other drugs though, unlike some, I never drank to seek oblivion; I loved the effect it had on me far too much to do that. Alcoholics do, however, seem to have different rates of progression or time clocks. For example, there is the lovely young twenty eight year old woman, now enjoying a successful career, whom I heard sharing only this week that she has been sober for seven years (and I remember her well as a twenty one year old when she was a newcomer looking much older and far less glamorous than she does today), almost the same length of time as she drank for. She started drinking at fourteen and as she herself said it was not the actual amount she drank that mattered but the effect that it had on her. Then there is my old friend and AA member, Jeremy Best, who is the same age as me, but did not find the Fellowship until he was sixty one. (It is interesting to note that, like ninety per cent of alcoholics, all three of us smoked.)

Unlike when I stopped drinking in 1982, the vast majority of newcomers in AA today are also addicted to one or more other hard drugs. When I was in treatment at Broadway Lodge we referred to ourselves as being alcoholic and chemically dependent irrespective of whether or not we had taken drugs other than alcohol. Chemical dependency is an umbrella term referring to a primary illness or disease characterised by addiction to a mood altering chemical. By definition, therefore, it includes both what is commonly regarded as drug addiction (both illegal and prescribed) and alcoholism – addiction to the drug alcohol – which in many ways, even though it is legal, is the most dangerous drug of all. I am a chemically dependent person whose drugs of choice were alcohol and tobacco.

Having said that, I doubt if there are many who could accurately and meaningfully define what addiction is. For me the best definition remains the one which I read somewhere twenty six years ago: **Continued compulsive use of a substance or behaviour despite [increasingly] adverse consequences**. It is simple and it is all embracing. As such, it invites us to look again at any misconceptions we may have and to recognize that there are many 'habits' not generally recognised as addictive which fall within this definition. It should first be noted that if the use of a substance or behaviour is not compulsive and there are no increasingly adverse consequences, then it is not addictive. The problem is, however, that, initially, the compulsion may be so mild that neither the sufferer nor anyone else spots it and the increasingly adverse consequences do not manifest until well after the disease has got a hold. In its early stages, it also goes undetected and undiagnosed simply because it is ubiquitous and because it often hides behind the mask of social acceptance and respectability; in other words, it appears to be normal. It is my strong conviction that chemical dependency is the most common and life threatening disease in the Western World today. In one form or another it is to be found literally everywhere and perhaps because of this, it paradoxically is also the most undiagnosed

Alcoholism is a typical case in point. It is to be found amongst men and women of all races, creeds, classes and economic and cultural backgrounds. It does not matter whether you are heterosexual or homosexual, devoutly religious, atheist or agnostic, professional, blue or white collar worker, or unemployed – it can get you just the same. In AA I have met, inter alia, murderers, a French funeral director (bankrupted because he had drunk all the advance payments or deposits for funerals of those yet to die), doctors, nurses, housewives, lawyers (including judges), accountants, insurers, bankers, members of both sexes of the armed forces, journalists, authors, writers, teachers, university dons, university undergraduates, actors, composers, musicians, pop-stars and others in the music business, TV personalities, sportsmen, TV and other celebrities, policemen and women, taxi drivers, bus drivers, prostitutes, estate agents and politicians as well as blue collar and manual workers and of course the unemployed. In the last ten years I have met six London underground train drivers in the Fellowship. Transport for London operates a strict 'no drinking' policy but even so, what concerns me is not the number of drivers who are in AA but the number who are not! An estimated eight percent or one in twelve of the UK population are alcoholics. (Please see A Plea for Common Sense) If this percentage is applied to the six hundred and forty six members of the House of Commons, and judging from the reports of the amounts drunk in the subsidised House of Commons bars there is no reason why it should not be, statistically there are over fifty M.P.s who are alcoholics! No single category, including children who are perhaps the most vulnerable, is immune from it, for it respects no one. The youngest I have met was a seventeen year old girl who was also addicted to heroin and the oldest was a wonderful eighty-nine year old cockney of the old school who first joined the Fellowship in 1964 and is still going strong.

But so often the disease goes unnoticed, not only because it is ubiquitous, but also because it is progressive and often takes decades to manifest. Because it sometimes has a long 'gestation period', many alcoholics, of which I was one, will function adequately and sometimes even brilliantly until well into their thirties, forties, fifties and sixties - even into retirement. It is a bit like a time bomb waiting to explode but when eventually it does go off, it usually does so with an almighty bang!

Clearly, addiction is not merely confined to alcohol and illegal Class A drugs. It extends also to prescribed mood altering medication, cannabis, solvents, eating disorders, nicotine, caffeine, gambling, work, promiscuity/ sex and, of course, power (Many people in government are addicted to power – apart from some of our own politicians, think of Hitler, Stalin and Mugabe to name but three. It is a well known saying that power corrupts and absolute power corrupts absolutely. I suspect that this is true, and it is true because leaders can become 'drunk on power' and because power is addictive.) Addiction is present, too, amongst those with whom the primary sufferer mixes, particularly the family or work colleagues, many of whom may become co-dependent in that they are obsessed with trying to control the addict's behaviour which, because of their own and the addict's powerlessness, they cannot do. As such, they effectively may be said to be addicted to the primary addict.

In a sense it can be argued that all of the above, as well as other addictions, are essentially the same in that they are all compulsive, have increasingly adverse consequences and, unless arrested, are life and/or soul destroying; the only main difference is the substance or behaviour of choice, and most people, having more than one addiction, will be multi or cross addicted. In this context it may be helpful to think of alcohol and other mood altering drugs as being rather like chocolate and sweets, the only main difference between them being that each type has a different flavour. In the last thirty years and following the lead given by AA, many new anonymous fellowships have sprung into being in the UK for a variety of addictions, and all are identically based on AA's Twelve Step programme of abstinence and recovery because of the realization by these other recovering addicts that it is by far the most successful treatment for recovery from any major addiction.

One is either an alcoholic or other addict (chemically dependent) or one is not, and this remains just as true even when one is in recovery; there is no grey area. I say this because I deny my own chemical dependency, alcoholism and powerlessness at my peril. I have absolutely no doubt whatever that if I were to pick up a drink, it would immediately reactivate the physical craving and mental obsession for alcohol and would quickly lead me to an early grave; and I have no desire to go before my time. I have found recovery through AA, but as a citizen of this country it concerns me greatly that most medical opinion and NHS literature on the subject of alcohol and drugs show an almost complete disregard for and/or ignorance of the illness and of the concept of powerlessness. With regard to alcohol, the incessant theme is that those who drink above the 'appropriate' levels should reduce their drinking to the recommended 'sensible' levels and all will be well. In my experience, no alcoholic could ever keep to such levels, nor would he want to. Every means possible seems to be used by medicine and the authorities to blur and confuse the situation with the constant use of such phrases as: 'a bit of a problem', 'a drink problem', 'heavy drinker', (incidentally how heavy is heavy?) 'problem drinker', 'binge drinker', 'alcohol abuser', 'alcohol misuse', 'recreational drugs', 'recreational user', 'problem drug users', 'drug misuse', and so on.

In my own doctor's surgery, some years ago, I picked up a pamphlet (produced in 1993 for the Department of Health by the Central Office of Information) entitled *Drug & Solvent Misuse*. It stated: 'Because the word "addiction" is loaded with ideas about the way society reacts to drug-taking, most medical experts and health professionals don't use the word any more and don't use the term "drug addict".' In the same pamphlet the word 'alcoholic' was not used at all except in the useful addresses section where 'AA (Alcoholics Anonymous)' was listed. In this world of increasing 'political correctness', it seems highly irresponsible and utter folly where human life itself is at stake to soft pedal, minimise and even deny the illness in this way. It would appear that the medical profession and the politicians are as much in denial of their own powerlessness as is the alcoholic/addict who is insane and incapable of being sensible. **Addiction will not go away by trying to pretend it is something else, and, as I have said, the fact remains that chemical dependency is still the most untreated treatable disease in the Western World today.**

Unless an alcoholic is extremely rich, chronic alcoholics invariably have financial, employment and other problems which inevitably have consequential adverse effects on the family. In these circumstances a spouse is inevitably eventually faced with the question of whether he or she should terminate the relationship and this is especially so when children are involved. In my case, I now think that Caroline was very probably right in putting her own and our children's interests first by divorcing me. And it almost certainly hastened my rock bottom so that when, fewer than eighteen months later, I entered treatment, I was fortunately able to find sustained recovery. On the other hand, I have a great friend who similarly and rightly divorced her chronically alcoholic husband, and the poor man died from the illness within six months. Imagine the potential for guilt in this situation; yet it was not her fault that her husband died. He died because he had an incurable illness (over which she had no control) which always proves fatal unless it can be arrested.

Some alcoholics go on benders and disappear for a day, weeks, months or even longer. Many will be in 'black out' for much of this time and 'come to' or wake up in some strange place or even foreign country, having no idea of how they got there. Others become violent and my guess is that most of the domestic and other violence reported almost daily in the Press is carried out by alcoholics/addicts. Occasionally, though, it can be the non-alcoholic spouse or partner who is violent, driven to it by anger and frustration at being unable to control the alcoholic's drinking and irresponsible behaviour. In such cases, the non-alcoholic understandably fails to realize that if the alcoholic cannot control his drinking because of powerlessness, how on earth can a spouse control it? A further point about harm or damage is that because all chronic alcoholics become self-centred, caring only about their drink and where the next one is coming from, they are not capable of love. They may say and think they are but they are not because, if there is a conflict between drink and anything else, always the drink will win out. It is not their fault; it is just the way it is.

For the spouses, family members and close friends of alcoholics, Al-Anon was founded in the late nineteen thirties by Bill W.'s wife Lois, and came to Britain in 1951. It is the sister fellowship to AA and has the same Twelve Step recovery programme. Any family member of an alcoholic would be well advised to contact Al-Anon (it has a comprehensive website) where they may discover much about the disease of alcoholism and, just as importantly, much about themselves.

I am often asked what causes alcoholism (although, strangely, never what causes smoking and nicotine addiction). As an alcoholic in recovery, I am not the slightest bit interested in what caused my alcoholism because it is of no consequence. What matters to me is the knowledge that I am an alcoholic and the only question I had to ask myself when I found that out was not 'Why am I?' but 'What am I going to do about it?' Even today, the only question I have to ask myself is 'How do I maintain my recovery and avoid relapsing?' I am not cured and although I have been sober for a long time I am no more immune from the dangers of the first drink than a newcomer is. Even if a cure were to be found tomorrow, which is unlikely, I would not trade what I have now just for the ability to drink like normal people. What interests me now is how I can help other alcoholics achieve sobriety.

As a member of society, however, who happens to be an alcoholic, I should very much like to know what causes it so that we could perhaps prevent millions from having to endure the agony and stupidity/insanity of alcoholism. There is a school of thought that believes that there is a genetic predisposition to it, and there is some evidence of this, though in my view, it is by no means conclusive; there is another school of thought that believes it is inappropriate learned behaviour. Certainly it often runs in families but this could be due to either or both of these theories. A good friend of mine who has been sober for many years certainly thinks that in his case the answer is both!

The truth is I do not know what causes alcoholism, so I stress that anything I say in this regard is my opinion only, and I could be wrong.

Before developing my own theory, however, let us first consider just what the drug alcohol is. Chambers Concise 20th Century Dictionary definition of the word drug is 'any substance used in the composition of medicine; a substance used to stupefy or poison or for self-indulgence'. As I was taught in treatment, alcohol is a sedative, narcotic drug (C_2H_5OH) very similar to ether, which was often used a hundred or so years ago as an anaesthetic for people undergoing operations. As such, alcohol is **an addictive drug** similar to other narcotics, such as heroin, and other tranquillisers, and it is no coincidence that in his letter to Bill W., Dr. Carl Jung described it as 'the most depraving poison'.[9]

In a relatively short space of time, the body gets used to alcohol or other drugs so that it develops tolerance and needs an increasing amount of the substance to gain the same effect. In the case of alcohol the 'tolerance factor' is three to four whereas with heroin, for example, it is in the region of twenty. This means that a teenager drinking for the first time will become paralytic after three or four drinks but, if they persevere with their drinking, after a time they will need nine to twelve drinks to obtain the same effect.

A heroin user, on the other hand, will, after a relatively short period of time, require twenty times the amount to obtain the same result. This explains why when in the Army doing my National Service, my tolerance increased so that for many years I would normally be showing little or no sign of intoxication after eight or nine drinks. Though I did not know it at the time, and as I have already said, this is a sure symptom of alcoholism. It also explains why the rate of progression of the disease is faster for most drug addicts than it is for alcoholics (those alcoholics that is who only take alcohol and are not cross or multi-addicted). My tolerance did begin to decline towards the end of my drinking, though at the time I was unaware of it.

So why am I an alcoholic? I have yet to meet an alcoholic, (or drug addict for that matter) who, for whatever reason, did not have low self-worth or lack of self-belief and who, though they may not have realized it, were, therefore, in some form of emotional pain when they first picked up a drink. As I have already described, the effect of my first drink on me was one of euphoria and a tremendous sense of well being, feelings which are similar to the initial effects of other narcotic drugs. As such it relieved my feelings of inferiority and because of this I not unnaturally wanted more of it. Quite simply, and like all alcoholics, I drank because in the short term it made me feel good, **and therefore it seemed the sensible thing to do. That was the conscious choice I made in the very beginning as I thought quite logically, albeit wrongly, that it was the answer to life's problems.** I believe that this is why over the years I drank alcoholically, and I use the word 'alcoholically' deliberately: I did not drink every day but I drank relatively heavily when I did drink and I drank like this for some twenty years. Then came that point in 1974, when I was made redundant and for the first time I consciously and deliberately used alcohol as a drug, because I knew it would kill the emotional pain I was feeling. From that moment on, the illness 'upped a gear' and I was well and truly hooked: I could not stop; want became need and alcohol increasingly became its own antidote in that I was both consciously and subconsciously using it to alleviate the withdrawals which, of course, it was forever creating. And the more I needed it, the greater became the obsession, craving and compulsion to drink and the less it worked for me, so that eventually I was drinking only to feel less ill even as it was making me more ill and killing me. I would add that from the word go I was in denial and the more I drank the greater became my denial.

Non-alcoholics do not drink heavily because they do not like the effects (intoxication, loss of control, hangovers and other subsequent withdrawal symptoms) that excessive drinking has on them; in the main they only drink for social reasons and then, more often than not, it is in small or relatively small quantities. Rarely, if ever, do they drink alone and if they do, they stop quickly because they do not like the effect. So, if anyone reading this drinks to change the way they feel and because they like the effect of drink, I would caution them to beware because the more they like it, the more likely they are to continue drinking and, because of denial, the more prone they are to eventually ending up in the same state as I did; especially if they also take other addictive, mood altering drugs, including prescribed drugs, which more and more people seem to be doing these days. Unfortunately, this is the disease that tells sufferers they have not got it, so they will either not believe me or, as I did, lie about it. Despite all the evidence, they will continue to deny that they have a problem until it is too late and the alcohol/drugs have them well and truly addicted. The fact remains, however, that anyone who drinks as much as I did, as often as I did and for as long as I did, will almost certainly sooner or later manifest as I did, namely as a chronic alcoholic. Like it or not, alcohol is an addictive drug.

Since I sobered up, I have talked and listened to literally hundreds of ex-drunks and they all said that they drank to change the way they felt and in order to, initially, feel better. But I cannot reiterate too strongly that because alcohol is a powerful, seductive, addictive and narcotic drug, it should be treated by everyone with the greatest respect and caution, for I am sure that anybody who drinks heavily for long enough will inevitably become so addicted that, without help, they will be unable to stop on their own. When it comes down to it, it is as simple as that. I believe that there is more than a grain of truth in the sayings that I first heard over a quarter of a century ago: 'If it works, it is addictive' and 'if you have to lie about it, it is addictive'. I also think Bill W. was right when he said, *'his drunkenness and dissolution are not penalties inflicted by people in authority; they result from his personal disobedience to spiritual principles.'*[19]

Happiness comes from within and if any of us look for it outside of ourselves and live so that our 'happiness' is dependent on alcohol, drugs, or any other substances or behaviours which we cannot control, we will subsequently experience ever increasing pain. Alcoholics and other addicts will go to any lengths for the avoidance of immediate pain and, when they do, they totally forget or deny the simple formula mentioned in Chapter 6:

[158]

PAIN + ALCOHOL (OR A DRUG) = TEMPORARY RELIEF + **INCREASED PAIN**

In my experience, it would seem to be a fact that there is no long term chemical substitute for legitimate emotional suffering. Pain, emotional or otherwise, is nature's way of telling us that there is something wrong, that we have to change, and it is in order to get away from the constant pain of being sick and tired of being sick and tired that, if we don't die first, some of us eventually seek recovery.

Even though there may be no definitive answer as to what causes alcoholism, it can be recognised and diagnosed long before the illness becomes chronic, if one knows what to look for. There is no greater authority in the world on alcoholism than Alcoholics Anonymous, which has now had seventy five years experience of the disease – very considerably longer than any other person or body. In its pamphlet, *WHO ME?*, the following twenty questions are asked of anyone who thinks they may be an alcoholic.

1. *Is drinking making you unhappy?*
2. *Does drinking make you careless of your family's welfare?*
3. *Do you drink because you are shy with other people?*
4. *Is drinking affecting your reputation?*
5. *Do you drink to escape your worries or trouble?*
6. *Do you drink alone?*
7. *Have you lost time from work due to drinking?*
8. *Has your ambition decreased since drinking?*
9. *Has your efficiency decreased since drinking?*
10. *Is drinking jeopardizing your job or business?*
11. *Have you ever felt remorse after drinking?*
12. *Are you in financial difficulties as a result of drinking?*
13. *Do you turn to or seek an inferior environment when drinking?*
14. *Do you crave a drink at a definite time of day?*
15. *Does drinking cause you to have difficulty in sleeping?*
16. *Do you want a drink next morning?*
17. *Do you drink to build up your self confidence?*
18. *Have you ever had a complete loss of memory as a result of drinking?*
19. *Has your doctor ever treated you for drinking?*
20. *Have you ever been in hospital or prison because of drinking?*

WHAT'S YOUR SCORE?

If you have answered YES to any one of the questions, there is a definite warning that you may be an alcoholic.

If you have answered YES to any two, the chances are that you are an alcoholic.

If you have answered YES to three or more, you are almost certainly an alcoholic.

Why do we say this? Only because the experience of hundreds of thousands of recovering alcoholics has taught us some basic truths about our symptoms – and about ourselves.

How many people do you know who would honestly answer YES to three or more of these questions? And incidentally, anyone who thinks they may be an alcoholic, almost invariably is one because if they weren't, it would not even occur to them to think that they might be.

Speaking for myself and if, as is very doubtful, I had been completely honest, I would have answered YES to questions 3, 17 and possibly 8 by the time I was nineteen, since they were the reasons why I drank in the first place. By the time I was thirty I would have said YES to five or six of them; by the time I was forty it would have risen to about twelve; on the day before I entered Broadway Lodge, it would have risen to nineteen and on the day after to twenty, the full Monty! These answers of mine demonstrate both the progressive nature of the disease and how it also takes time for all the adverse consequences to manifest. Yet despite all the evidence, my denial held firm in Broadway Lodge as I rationalised (using my intelligence to deny the truth) that because, for example, I had never lost my driving licence nor wet the bed, I could not be an alcoholic or powerless over alcohol!

Similar types of questions can be asked in respect of other addictions falling under the chemical dependency umbrella.

Chapter 12

A Miscellany

Bill W. instructed all AAs to 'pass it on' and so it is in this spirit that I pass on to you some of the things that I have learned, both inside and outside AA, that have helped and enabled me to stay sober for the last twenty seven years and, despite the many and various problems that life throws at us all, to generally have a more enriched, contented and happy life. May they also prove beneficial to you.

THE POWER OF POWERLESSNESS

I believe that perhaps AA's greatest gift to the world will eventually prove to be the concept of powerlessness. If people would only stop trying to control all the things over which in reality they have no control at all, and instead take control of the three things they can control, the world would be a much better place.

For the better part of thirty years I was increasingly under the control of alcohol; by the end it had become my complete and utter master. But I would not admit this because alcohol poisons not only the liver and other organs but it also attacks the brain which is why alcoholism is a mental illness as well as a physical and spiritual one. Many have difficulty accepting it is a mental illness simply because they don't want to think about it; but if you watch anyone who has had a few drinks, it is readily apparent that not only can't they walk straight, but they can't think straight either. They become deluded into thinking they are having a great time and have the answers to all of the world's problems, which they never tire of telling you about. Such people may or not be alcoholics but all the same when they have had even a couple of drinks they are handing over to alcohol some of the control of themselves that they exercise when sober, and this, of course, is why, for example, we have drink driving restrictions.

Those of us who are alcoholics become deluded into thinking that, whether drunk or sober, we are the masters of drink. Though I had lost virtually everything and was truly disempowered, this delusion persisted right to the bitter end. Once my denial was broken, however, and I accepted and surrendered to my powerlessness, I regained the power of choice and became empowered again. **This is the power of powerlessness: the total** recognition, surrender to and acceptance of the fact that, clean and sober, we are powerless over everything except our thinking, our attitudes and our behaviour. Intoxication and denial of powerlessness disempowers the mind whereas acceptance of and surrender to our powerlessness empowers the mind so that it once again has the ability to choose and, if we want it enough, to choose recovery and the consequent liberation from the shackles of the illness which have for so long enslaved us.

WILLINGNESS, HONESTY AND OPEN MINDEDNESS

AA says that the indispensable essentials of recovery are willingness, honesty and open mindedness but I had been sober for some considerable time before I realized just how true this statement is. I well remember hearing someone sharing about the importance of willingness and it prompted me to ask myself just what was it that I had been willing to do. The answer was that I had been willing to stick around and not pick up a drink until something happened. ('Stick-ability' or 'stick-to-itiveness' as Dr Bob referred to it, is a very important quality as without it our chances of ever achieving recovery are greatly reduced.) It was not something that I particularly wanted to do, but at Broadway Lodge I was told that if I did not, I would die. In the beginning it was not easy because I still wanted to drink; but not drinking was undoubtedly a better option than dying. In effect, I was also being told to open my tightly closed mind to new facts and ideas, especially to the fact that despite everything I had lost control of my drinking and I was powerless over alcohol. As you may recall, when I was in Broadway Lodge I found it very difficult to take on board what I was learning because it was contrary to everything I had ever thought or believed about alcohol. Even so, I was intrigued and wanted to know more and this certainly helped me to try to keep an open mind and stick around.

My biggest problem, though, was my pride, which, because of the awful shame I felt, was preventing me from being honest. (The verbal I had to say for a whole week – 'I am not a gentleman drunk but a sick person trying to get well. If I don't get honest, my pride will kill me' – was so true.) Even though, throughout the first six weeks in treatment, my very inflated ego was taking quite a battering as my denial (a defence mechanism to prevent an over-inflated ego from facing the truth) was continually being confronted, that denial still held firm. In many ways, when I was told that Broadway Lodge thought there was nothing more that they could do for me and that I might have to drink again, it was similar to what Carl Jung had told Rowland H. and Dr Silkworth had told Bill W. But it deeply deflated my ego and softened me up, making me ready for the gift that came when I saw the slogan in the NA meeting. Only then was my ego sufficiently deflated for me to become honest enough to surrender to and accept without reservation my complete powerlessness over alcohol. This recognition of 'The Power of Powerlessness' was the great truth for me and it was the turning point: the spiritual experience that was the beginning of recovery, of spiritual growth and of the rest of my life.

For me it was also serendipity. The Oxford English Dictionary defines serendipity as 'the faculty of making happy and unexpected discoveries by accident', and Webster's Dictionary defines it as 'the gift of finding valuable or agreeable things not sought for'. Both of these definitions more than adequately describe what happened to me. You could argue that I was just lucky to be in the right place at the right time. I think, however, that there was probably a bit more to it than that: it might have had something to do with the fact that by sticking around, not walking out of treatment and not drinking, I had put myself in a position where I had a much greater chance of being aware of the presence of serendipity and of accepting the gift of sobriety when, in an NA room of all places, I, at last, felt and understood the true importance and meaning of powerlessness.

It is my experience that those AA newcomers who are first willing to stick around and to keep coming back for long enough will, sooner or later, become honest and open minded enough to be able to surrender to and accept their powerlessness. If they do this, and even though they may not realise it, they will then experience the power of powerlessness and, at the same time, they will also experience serendipity. If they then continue to stick around and follow the rest of the AA programme, they will recover.

LOVE AND EVIL

In his farewell talk delivered in 1950, when he was in the terminal stages of cancer shortly before his death, Dr Bob, AA's co-founder said, *'Our Twelve Steps, when simmered down to the last, resolve themselves into the words "love" and "service." We understand what love is, and we understand what service is. So let's bear those two things in mind.'* (See the full text in Appendix 6) Far be it from me to quarrel with anything Dr

Bob said, but, speaking for myself, I never had a proper understanding of what love is or what it involved (in the sense that I am now sure he meant), until I read *The Road Less Travelled* by Dr. M. Scott Peck, in which he defines love as: *The will to extend one's self for the purpose of nurturing one's own or another's spiritual growth.*

This definition, defining love in terms of the purpose or desired goal of spiritual growth, is certainly in accord with the Big Book which, referring to the Twelve Steps, says: *The point is we are willing to grow along spiritual lines. The principles we have set down are guides to spiritual progress. We claim spiritual progress rather than spiritual perfection.*[14] The 'will' in Scott Peck's definition covers rather more than just mere desire because the desire or intention has to be sufficiently strong for the will to convert it into action – the possibly painful act of extending one's self for the purpose of growing. Real love is, therefore, an intention, an action and a commitment to grow, to evolve. At the same time, however, it is also a choice which, until the moment an alcoholic or addict surrenders to and accepts his powerlessness he is not free to make: a drinking alcoholic or using addict has lost the power of choice and cannot love because he is in the grip of the poisonous drug intent on ultimately killing him.

The way that loving parents nurture their children is easy to understand and observe in action and it is this type of nurturing to which the definition refers. There are many other parents, however, who would say that they love their children but who make little or no attempt to nurture and discipline them; this is neglect, and they may exercise other forms of what, to a greater or lesser extent, can only be described as cruelty. Knowingly or unknowingly such parents are wicked or evil and we read about them in the papers almost daily. What adds to the sadness of this, and what others seemingly fail to take due notice of, is that many, if not most, of them are probably drinking and/or taking other drugs of one sort or another, and that therein lies a major part the problem.

In a very real sense, love is about winning the battle to overcome the downward forces of entropy and laziness (which some would say is the original sin) from which we all suffer. To grow spiritually we have to extend our limits and the only way to do that is by exceeding them. Love is effortful, often very hard work and sometimes very difficult. It is also very rewarding.

From the time I stopped drinking, I was mentored, nurtured and loved by counsellors, fellow patients and sober AA members until such time as I had grown enough spiritually to start similarly giving to other AA newcomers.

The amazing thing was that in nurturing another's spiritual growth, I myself benefited and grew spiritually. To me this is what AA is all about, and I am sure others in AA, who have sponsored or taken newcomers through the Twelve Steps, would say the same. It is a loving programme.

The opposite of love is anti-love or evil. Speaking of evil in *The Road Less Travelled*, Scott Peck says:

First I have come to conclude that evil is real. It is not the figment of the imagination of a primitive religious mind feebly attempting to explain the unknown. There really are people, and institutions made up of people, who respond with hatred in the presence of goodness and would destroy the good in so far as it is in their power to do so. They do this not with conscious malice but blindly, lacking awareness of their own evil – indeed, seeking to avoid any such awareness. As has been described of the devil in religious literature, they hate the light and instinctively will do anything to avoid it, including attempting to extinguish it. They will destroy the light in their own children and in all other beings subject to their power.

Evil people hate the light because it reveals themselves to themselves. They hate goodness because it reveals their badness; they hate love because it reveals their laziness. They will destroy the light, the goodness, the love in order to avoid the pain of such self-awareness. My second conclusion, then, is that evil is laziness carried to its ultimate, extraordinary extreme. As I have defined it, love is the antithesis of laziness. Ordinary laziness is a passive failure to love. Some ordinarily lazy people may not lift a finger to extend themselves unless they are compelled to do so. Their being is a manifestation of nonlove; still, they are not evil. Truly evil people, on the other hand, actively rather than passively avoid extending themselves. They will take any action in their power to protect their own laziness, to preserve the integrity of their sick self. Rather than nurturing others, they will actually destroy others in this cause. If necessary, they will even kill to escape the pain of their own spiritual growth. As the integrity of their sick self is threatened by the spiritual health of those around them, they will seek by all manner of means to crush and demolish the spiritual health that may exist near them. I define evil, then, as the exercise of political power – that is, the imposition of one's will upon others by overt or covert coercion – in order to avoid extending one's self for the purpose of nurturing spiritual growth. Ordinary laziness is nonlove; evil is antilove.

I have quoted Scott Peck at some length because not only is his work on love and evil outstanding but also because of the clarity of thought and reasoning with which he presents his case. In the above passage he was describing me when I was drinking: I have not the slightest doubt that what chronic alcoholics do to themselves and to those around them is evil. I remember reading this for the first time and thinking just how strong was my own denial whenever exposure of my alcoholism was threatened, how I dreaded having the light shone upon me. It was then that I began to realize that addiction and evil were perhaps synonymous, and if not, they certainly go hand in hand and are very closely related. It seems to me that wherever you find evil, addiction in one or more of its forms is invariably present too. Nevertheless, I am now certain that once the problem is accepted, full recovery from alcoholism and other forms of drug addiction can be achieved by abstinence and – as a consequence of love – the will to extend oneself for the purpose of nurturing one's own or another's spiritual growth.

FORGIVENESS AND RESENTMENT

Love is really an endless series of little acts of forgiveness. Forgiveness removes both resentment and conflict. Serenity or contentment, which we are all seeking, is the absence of resentment and conflict. **The great paradox of forgiveness is that it is something we do to be free of resentment and to get well; it is, therefore, every bit as much for ourselves as it is for other people. Without it, it is almost impossible to let go of the past and to move on.**

'Father forgive them, for they know not what they do.' You do not have to be a Christian to accept the wisdom of Christ's words as he was dying on the cross. In my own rather childlike and naïve way I think that Jesus said these words because he did not want to die hating or holding resentment against the perpetrators of the crime against him. To me this is proof that the final act of love is forgiveness.

'Love thine enemy' is another command which I sometimes find almost impossible to carry out but even though I might hate what someone has done, at least I need not hate them. Sometimes this is the best that I can do and I have to be content with that.

On the other side of the forgiveness coin is resentment, probably best defined as an unwillingness to forgive or a desire still to punish. I have also heard it described as taking poison and hoping the other person dies! The point is that it is the person holding the resentment who suffers, not the other person, who may well be blissfully unaware of being the object of such resentment. Others have described resentment as being a spiritual cancer which is a complete block to spiritual growth. What does AA have to say about it?

Resentment is the "number one" offender. It destroys more alcoholics than anything else. From it stem all forms of spiritual disease, for we have been not only mentally and physically ill, we have been spiritually sick. When the spiritual malady has been overcome, we straighten out mentally and physically. In dealing with resentments, we set them down on paper. We listed people, institutions or principles with whom we were angry. We asked ourselves why we were angry. In most cases it was found that our self-esteem, our pocket books, our ambitions, our personal relationships (including sex) were hurt or threatened. So we were sore. We were "burned up."……It is plain that a life which includes deep resentment leads only to futility and unhappiness. To the precise extent that we permit these, do we squander the hours that might have been worthwhile. But with the alcoholic, whose hope is the maintenance and growth of a spiritual experience, this business of resentment is infinitely grave. We found that it is fatal. For when harbouring such feelings we shut ourselves off from the sunlight of the Spirit. The insanity of alcohol returns and we drink again. And with us, to drink is to die.

If we were to live, we had to be free of anger. The grouch and the brainstorm were not for us. They may be the dubious luxury of normal men, but for alcoholics these things are poison.[30]

So we alcoholics have to be free of resentments. The reality is that we are prisoners of our own resentments and it is forgiveness which unlocks the door to be free of them. Even so, how do we get rid of them? How do we forgive? The only sure way that I know is to give up the idea of revenge and punishment and instead pray for the person against whom we hold the resentment. This is not always easy but nonetheless it always works if we do so. As an unknown clergyman once said, 'If you do this (and it does not matter whether or not you believe in a God) you will be free. If you pray for everything that you want for yourself to be given to them, you will be free. Ask for their health their prosperity and their happiness, even if you don't really mean it, and you will be free. If you do this every day for a couple of weeks you will realize that where you used to feel bitterness, resentment and hatred, you will now feel compassion, understanding and love.' I think that this is a good example of how prayer does not always change the world, but it does change me.

What I also find helpful is to remember that evil is done not by bad people but by sick people, as I myself was once sick, and further, that there is absolutely nothing about resentment that is in any way loving.

ASPECTS OF LOVE

There are three main aspects of love, of nurturing, which at first glance seem obvious but which often receive scant attention. The first of these is to show kindness to the person we love (be that ourselves or another), to show that we care about them, that we value them and that we are on their side and not against them.

Secondly when kindness has been shown, it becomes necessary to encourage them to believe in themselves and what they are capable of by creating a vision and learning, so that they can think and choose for themselves. From early childhood so many of us are taught by our elders and supposedly betters 'you can't do this and you must do that'. This is not loving; it is the opposite.

Thirdly we have to challenge the loved one to develop their talents and to go ahead and achieve their goals. This is the moment of commitment. Sometimes this can be painful and difficult but it may help to think of how birds teach their young to fly the nest. In AA terms, if the newcomer wants what I have, namely contented sobriety, then I can only tell him what I did, show him kindness, encourage him and then challenge him to stay sober and work the programme. I cannot make him do it or do it for him, and if he refuses, as many do, and chooses to drink again, that is his affair. I can only carry the message; I cannot and should not ever try to carry the burden. In such circumstances I have to let go, always remembering that I may have sown a seed which may enable the sufferer to come back again to AA later on.

TOUGH LOVE AND LETTING GO

We must not enable the alcoholic to avoid the consequences of his drinking. This is often difficult and contrary to our natural instincts. For example, if an alcoholic passes out in the sitting room, rather than putting him to bed, it is much better to leave him lying on the floor so that when he wakes up, he might just wonder what on earth he is doing there and how the hell he got there. If he wakes up in bed, he will have neither of these thoughts and will be unaware that he was put to bed. In AA we call this 'tough love': never rescue the alcoholic from the consequences of his drinking.

Some examples of letting go with love particularly with regard to addiction, which were printed on a card I was given very early in my own sobriety, are:

TO LET GO WITH LOVE

- To let go does not mean to stop caring, it means I can't do it for someone else.

- To let go is not to cut myself off, it's the realization I can't control another.

- To let go is not to enable, but to allow learning from natural consequences.

- To let go is to admit powerlessness, which means the outcome is not in my hands.

- To let go is not to try to change or blame another, it's to make the most of myself.

- To let go is not to care for, it's to care about.

- To let go is not to fix, but to be supportive.

- To let go is not to judge, but to allow another to be a human being.

- To let go is not to be in the middle arranging all the outcomes, but to allow others to effect their own destinies.

- To let go is not to be protective, it's to permit another to face reality.

- To love is not to deny, but to accept.

- To let go is not to nag, scold or argue, but instead to search out my own shortcomings and correct them.

- To let go is not to adjust everything to my desires, but to take each day as it comes, and cherish myself in it.

- To let go is not to regret the past, but to grow and live for the future.

- To let go is to fear less and love more.

THE SERENITY PRAYER

God grant me the serenity to accept the things I cannot change;
Courage to change the things I can, and
Wisdom to know the difference.

This prayer, written by the American theologian Reihold Niebuhr in 1934, was adopted by AA in its early days and it is said at every AA meeting. Legend has it that it was adopted by AA as 'never has so much AA been expressed in just three lines'!

The prayer of course is not exclusive to AA and has been the subject of many books; it is not my intention to analyse it in any great detail here other than to explain what it means to me and why it such a favourite of mine. Although I was vaguely familiar with it, the first time I can remember hearing it was on the first morning that I was in treatment in Broadway Lodge. It is a prayer which over the years I have grown to love, the more so because I have come to appreciate and comprehend more fully its incredible beauty and simplicity. I use it regularly, particularly when times are uncertain or when I am facing some difficulty or other. At such times it gives me comfort and settles me down.

If I have a quibble with it – and it is only a quibble – it is that I have never been able to get any serenity until I have sensed and accepted powerlessness. I remember very clearly the serenity, calmness and peace I felt after I first surrendered to and accepted my powerlessness: the serenity, however, came after the acceptance of my powerlessness and not before it. So I think of the prayer as beginning 'God bestow upon me the sense of powerlessness so that I can be granted the serenity to accept the things I cannot change … etc.'

My understanding of it in the simplest of terms and in relation to me (and all alcoholics) is that I must accept my powerlessness over alcohol and all other mood altering chemicals together with everything else and whatever happens (first line), except courage to change, where appropriate, the only things I can: my thinking, my attitude and my behaviour (second line) and never to forget that (third line).

There is a shortened version of the prayer that I hesitate to mention here as I don't want to lower the tone, but as I use it frequently, I will! It should be used only when things are not going your way and it is very important that it should be said with a smile on the face and with a shrug of the shoulders. It is, 'Oh fuck it!'

DECISION: WHAT DO I WANT, WILL I GET IT and DO I WANT IT ENOUGH?

As I look back on my life, I have come to realize that one of the most important things in life is to know what you want. Aided and abetted by alcohol, I went through life not knowing what I really wanted to do and as a result I drifted and did not make the success of my life that my education, talents and intelligence warranted. It was not until I was forty-seven years old that I accepted my alcoholism and then realized that I wanted above all else to be sober and to live.

Want. An alcoholic may want to be sober but does he want it enough to follow the AA programme which would guarantee him sobriety? Does he think he could do it, is it worth the risk and does he believe he would do it?

It is a fact of life that if we want something we are invariably going to have to do things we don't want to do in order to get it. If, for example, a woman wants to be a doctor, she is going to have to be a student for some seven years before she qualifies and starts earning significant money, and even then she will only be on the lowest rungs of the medical ladder. She may not want to undergo all those years of training and relative hardship, so she must decide if she wants to be a doctor enough to do them. I want to publish this book but first I have to endure the work and frustrations of researching and actually writing it before that's possible. What we want in life will always be equal to what we don't want to do or put up with in order to get it! So arguably, what we have got is what we want!

Can/can't belief. Henry Ford said, 'Whether I think I can or whether I think I can't, I am right either way.' If an alcoholic thinks he can follow the AA programme and achieve sobriety, he can; if he thinks he can't, he can't - though he may well start only to give up later.

This thinking is of course closely tied up with believing or not believing. Speaking at AA's Twentieth anniversary celebration in St Louis in 1955, Bill W's spiritual advisor, Father Ed Dowling said, 'Belief is capitalising on the experience of others. Blessed are the lazy for they shall find their short cuts. The world can now capitalise on the A.A. experience of two decades'[31] I don't know about the world, but when I made the decision to commit to AA and its recovery programme, I had seen enough people in AA, who were sober, working the programme and obviously happy, to know that if I were to do what they were doing, it would work for me too. In other words, I believed that I could capitalise on their experiences in order to get well. As far as the short cuts were concerned, I knew there was no point in trying to reinvent the wheel by looking for easier, softer ways; the short cut was the Twelve Step programme which worked. I remember thinking at the time, *I can bloody well do this,* and so it has proved to be.

Decision. Knowing we want something enough and confidently believing we can do what is necessary to get it, we nonetheless have to make the decision to go ahead. In this regard, people fall into one of two categories, the decisive or the indecisive. Decisive people are quick to make up their minds and slow to change them; whereas, indecisive people take ages to make up their minds and as soon as they have done so they want to change them. Decisive or indecisive, an alcoholic will never get well unless he makes the decision to practise the Twelve Steps. It is a decision which, if followed through, he will never regret

PRINCIPLES OF HUMAN BEHAVIOUR

When I was in Broadway Lodge I read a book on anger in which I learned of the **pleasure** principle and the **reality** principle. These principles originate in Freud's phychoanalytic theory of human behaviour. The pleasure principle refers to the drive for immediate gratification of all needs and wants and the avoidance of pain, and it generally dominates in early life; for example, a baby crying to be fed, or a small child screaming with frustration and anger when denied something he wants. In adults it can translate into 'I want my pleasure and I want it now and I don't give a damn how I get it or on whose toes I tread.'

The reality principle, on the other hand, refers to deferred gratification and is what the child grows towards, learning that he is not the axis around which everyone and everything revolves. Growing up and maturing, human beings learn patience and the ability to be realistic, to consider consequences and acceptable ways of getting what we want. 'I want it but I am prepared to be patient or to work for it, and I will try not to harm anyone as a result of getting it.'

As chronic drinking alcoholics we undoubtedly operated selfishly and self-centredly according to the pleasure principle since, for us, absolutely nothing else mattered except the next drink and where it was coming from. (There is a joke about the dying chronic alcoholic whose last words were, 'I wonder around whom the world is going to revolve now?'!) But in recovery we often move quite quickly and increasingly to operating according to the reality principle. Indeed, our primary purpose is to stay sober and help other alcoholics to achieve sobriety. This dual purpose is selfish in so far as we put our own sobriety first, but it is otherwise altruistic in respect of our desire and willingness to help others.

Chapter 13

My Sobriety

If I had been asked when I left Broadway Lodge back in 1983 what I thought life would be like from then on, I would have got it wrong on just about every count. Somewhat unrealistically and ever the optimist, I thought that if I were to stay sober everything in the garden would be lovely; that, despite my many problems, we all would live happily ever after, and the nation's problems of alcoholism and drug addiction would soon be solved. What follows is a small selection of a few of the more important and some of the more memorable things that I have done and not done, things which have happened to me, good and bad, mostly in the latter half of my sobriety. Had I been drinking, I would not have experienced any of them, and they demonstrate that through sobriety – thanks to the Twelve Step Programme – recovered alcoholics can live life as abundantly as any non-alcoholic. In doing so, we discover that neither joy nor sadness is *ever* a reason to pick up a drink or drug. We also discover that once alcoholism and powerlessness are accepted without reservation, recovery is not difficult if one thoroughly follows AA's programme: today I am no more bothered about not being able to drink alcohol sensibly than I am about not being able to drink arsenic sensibly. For me there is no difference.

Early in sobriety, as I've already mentioned, all alcoholics find themselves confronted with many problems which have their origins in their drinking days. To some it seems as if we are reaping a whirlwind and in this regard I was no exception. My biggest problems were in finding employment, attempting to restore my second marriage and my other relationships generally, but particularly with my children who had suffered as a result of their parents' divorce, though, I am pleased to say, nothing like as much as many others. Nevertheless, I could have dealt with *none* of these problems had I picked up a drink. For a recovering alcoholic, picking up a drink never has nor ever will solve any problem, and as Scott Peck says on the very first page of *The Road Less Travelled*, *'Life is difficult. This is a great truth because once we truly see this truth, we transcend it. Once we truly know that life is difficult – once we truly understand and accept it – then life is no longer difficult. Because once it is accepted, the fact that life is difficult no longer matters.'*

It has been said that the greatest mistake a man can make is to be afraid to make one, and also that the man who never made a mistake, never made anything. Having said that, I did make a number of mistakes, one of the biggest perhaps being that I did not pay anything like sufficient attention to my pensions. When I was with UDT, I was a member of their very good pension scheme but when I was made redundant in 1974 it ceased, and I made no serious attempts to pay attention to providing for my retirement. Even when I sobered up in 1982, pensionable age seemed such a long way off that it did not matter. But it most definitely did: now at the age of seventy-four, I am still paying the penalty for such neglect and I will continue paying for it for the rest of my life. I have my statutory old age pension, but I am now reaping what I sowed both in my drinking days and in sobriety, as my other pensions are meagre. So whether an alcoholic or not, it is imperative for everyone to pay attention *now* to providing for old age, before it is too late. The years go by very quickly and pensionable age creeps up with a great rush! It is today's problem, not tomorrow's!

Possibly, the other big mistake I made was in not looking, in my early years of sobriety, at what I really wanted to do in life. I am not completely sure about this as if I had changed my career at that point, I would have missed so many of the good things that have since happened to me. But my heart was never really in insolvency because I felt more empathy with and compassion for those who went bankrupt or insolvent than ever I did for their principle creditors who were my paymasters; in the main these were the banks who frequently lent quite unbelievably irresponsibly. The speed with which they then blamed and sometimes humiliated the debtor, rather than looking at their own foolishness, was often amazing – and with the credit crunch, it's still just the same.

In spite of this there was much that I enjoyed about insolvency, particularly meeting many interesting people, some of whom I may have been able to help. In this respect, insolvency is not always the disaster it seems and very often, though not by any means always, it does afford people the opportunity to change their lives. Insolvency, of course, flourishes in times of economic downturns and slumps, but it ceases to thrive when the economy starts to recover. Despite knowing this, it still came as a surprise to me when in 1994 I was made redundant for the second time. It had been obvious for some time as the country came out of recession that our volume of business was going down, but since I was the most senior member of staff, I thought my position was relatively secure. In the event, however, I was the first to go because I was the most expensive and least affordable!

[175]

This time, I did not go home and pick up a drink; the thought actually never crossed my mind. All the same, I did make the serious mistake of thinking that at fifty-eight I was too old to get another job. I was also guilty of thinking that if I were to apply for jobs I would be rejected; fear of rejection can be literally paralysing. My redundancy of course caused considerable financial difficulties but fortunately Sarah was working and, thanks mainly to her, one way or another we did manage to get by.

In 1999 we decided to sell our house in Wimbledon and move to Docklands which was then and still is a very much up and coming area. Most of our friends, thinking Docklands is on the other side of the world, thought we were quite mad! In fact, it is only about fourteen miles away. When we moved here in December 1999 there was only one tall building standing in Canary Wharf, but now when we look west from our kitchen or bedroom windows, the skyline, especially when lit up at night, looks like a not-so-mini-Manhattan. To the east, our fourth floor flat overlooks the river, including the Thames Barrier, to well past the Woolwich Ferry (surprisingly still operating free of charge) over a mile away. This is the fantastic ever changing view I see whenever I look up from my laptop. We love living here and being so close to Canary Wharf, which is very fresh, clean and modern.

Having moved to the East End, I found that even when I was well past normal retirement age, I was quickly able to get part time temporary work selling new build property. In doing this, I discovered that I am a very good salesman and that, far from being a handicap, having a few grey hairs and being a bit of a 'father figure' was a distinct advantage. (As Norman Vincent Peale wrote in *The Power of Positive Thinking:* 'Every problem has in it the seeds of its own solution. If you don't have any problems, you don't get any seeds.') Often a temporary assignment quickly turned into a more permanent one, including one with Taylor Woodrow when I was well over sixty-five. More recently work has proved more difficult to find because of the economic downturn, which has hit the housing market particularly badly.

Until I was stricken down with arthritis, I was also able to do some part time work in a residential home for homeless alcoholics and addicts run by Kairos Community Trust (Kairos), a charity in South London. Kairos was founded in 1991 by John Kitchen, a Catholic priest; with Tony Walsh he set up home for a few homeless people in an old derelict Church of England property in north London. Today it has grown to a point where it now offers a unique service that provides an opportunity for mostly homeless

[176]

men and women to come to terms with and recover from their addictions. The service provided is in four progressive main stages:

- Residential community detox at 'Linden Grove', a hostel providing twenty four bed accommodation.

- Residential primary care Minnesota Model type treatment at 'Bethwin Road'.

- Move-On supported accommodation for about one hundred and fifty homeless people completing rehabilitation in thirty houses (including an all female one and one for armed forces veterans) in five London boroughs.

- Post rehabilitation Aftercare Programme in Peckham.

In October 2009 I attended the Annual General Meeting and it is remarkable that in the two weeks prior to the meeting an astonishing twenty two people obtained the keys to move into their own individual flats. Kairos obtains just over fifty percent of its overall funding from housing benefits and it is a classic example of the type of organisation which, like Broadway Lodge and other Minnesota Models treatment centres, the government should be encouraging, supporting and funding.

When I was there, I was working in 'Linden Grove', and there one saw alcoholism and addiction 'in the raw' from the front line. The home is abstinence based and whilst it is not a Minnesota Model Treatment Centre, it is AA and NA conscious and encourages all the residents well enough, to attend meetings. Like Broadway Lodge and other such treatment centres, it is a place full of tough love and discipline (things which most of them have never before experienced in their lives), under which conditions these very sick patients/residents respond very well. Without alcohol and hard drugs to intoxicate them, their mostly good behaviour is little short of remarkable, especially considering that only a few days or short weeks previously the majority of them were homeless and getting into all sorts of trouble with the law. I enjoyed the work, especially the counselling and taking groups which I had not done for many years, but I was frustrated by the very slow rates of some residents' detoxification. In Broadway Lodge, 'straight-up' alcoholics are now de-toxed over three days and, with the very odd exception, everyone else over a period of three weeks. At 'Linden Grove', however, detox still often takes weeks or months and practically every one can have a 'calmer' or a sleeping pill if they ask for one. This is not in any way a criticism of Kairos, but it is a criticism of the doctors, who should know better. Until a resident or patient is completely clean and sober, it is very difficult to make any worthwhile start on the recovery process. Because of this, the drop out or relapse rate is, I believe, higher than it would otherwise be.

In September 2006, soon after I had started work with Kairos, I suffered an attack of shingles which was to last for about four months. It attacked me on the left hand side of my body and at that time it was one of the most continuously painful experiences of my life. The pain, which was searing at times, moved around and as it is pretty much untreatable there was no option but to grin and bear it. And I'm pleased to say that, apart from the day on which I was diagnosed, I did not have any time off work because of it. Whether or not I transcended it I am not sure, but in some ways it did not seem to matter that much as I was determined that it should not interfere with my life if I could possibly help it. After about three months of never ceasing, the pain gradually eased until by January 2007 it had more or less gone completely.

2007 was one of the best years of my sobriety. Egged on by a very good friend in the Fellowship who wishes to remain anonymous but to whom I shall always be very grateful, I was not only encouraged to start playing golf again after a lapse of twelve years or so (I had had to give up in 1994 when I broke two toes and despite operations, walking was extremely painful) but also to think about rewriting this book, the original draft of which had been lying on the shelf gathering dust for an equally long time. The golf went well and I was soon hitting as many good shots as I was poor ones, especially at the driving range and on the practice ground. I still could not walk far without pain in my foot, but with a buggy I was easily able to play eighteen holes and I began playing quite regularly with my aforementioned AA friend Huw T.

For many years my son Charles, who played for the Cambridge Stymies against the Oxford Divots (he also played for the Blues side, though not against Oxford) when he was up at Cambridge in the 1990s, had talked of our having a few days playing golf in Scotland. It seemed that October 2007 might be the best chance to fulfil what to me had for a long time been only a dream. We were terribly spoilt for choice as there are wonderful courses all over Scotland, but we eventually settled for playing on the West Coast on the Kintyre Course at Turnberry which had been designed by my brother Donald, at Machrihanish on the Kintyre Peninsula which I had for years wanted to play, and finally on the Old Course at Prestwick where the first Open Championship had been played in 1860.

[178]

Shortly before going to Scotland I had experienced intermittent pain in my groin which I suspected might be the beginnings of an inguinal hernia but I certainly did not think it was serious enough to prevent me from going to Scotland. I drove up to Prestwick, Charlie came by air, and I met him at the airport in the early evening. The next day we played on the Kintyre Course at Turnberry which has probably the finest views I have ever seen on a golf course. It was a glorious autumn day and we both played quite well on a very good course we had never played before. An added bonus was that Donald had kindly arranged for us to play 'courtesy of the club' with a free buggy thrown in for good measure.

After lunch it was off to Machrihanish. Although it is only some thirty or so miles away as the crow flies, by road it is about one hundred and fifty miles: first to Glasgow and then north to Tarbet on Loch Lomond, across to Inverary on Loch Fyne and then south down the Kintyre Peninsula. The consolation for having to make such a long drive was, of course, the beautiful scenery seen on a glorious day from a very good, fast and near deserted road. The driving was also enormous fun (for me at any rate) and it reminded me of what driving used to be like in my youth, only this was much better because I was driving fast in a much more powerful 3.3 litre modern car. I felt young again and it was sheer bliss!

As we walked into the club house at Machrihanish the following morning it was like going back a hundred years or more, almost to what golf must have been like when the ten hole course was first established in 1876. It was redesigned and subsequently increased to eighteen holes by no less than four and three time Open Champions, Old Tom Morris and J.H.Taylor. The course itself is a true links course laid out amongst the dunes with an opening hole which has been described as 'the best opening hole in the world'. The hole is a four hundred and thirty six yard, left handed dog-leg with an intimidating drive across the sea and beach to the fairway beyond. On the days we played it was relatively easy to carry to the fairway, though into a strong wind it might be an altogether different proposition. The club house itself was wonderfully old fashioned and the staff members were extremely hospitable and friendly. Though in need of some refurbishment, it was both welcoming and comfortable – and we had haggis, bashed neaps and tatties for lunch!

Our morning round started promisingly enough but after a few holes I began to feel slight pains in my groin. In themselves they did not amount to much but they were enough for me to be conscious of them; consequently, I did not have the confidence to 'trust my swing': I began backing off when playing a full shot. This not only greatly reduced the distance I could hit the ball but it caused me to hit it with a slightly open face, thereby producing a slice as well. As a result, my play deteriorated badly and I was unable to give Charlie a proper game. Nevertheless, I got round and could appreciate just what a good and enjoyable course Machrihanish is. Were it not in such a remote location, I am sure it would attract more tournaments and amateur championships. It is, however, well worth making the effort to play there.

After watching England unexpectedly beating Australia in the Rugby World Cup on television in the afternoon, we went out for a second round about five o'clock by which time the weather was beginning to close in a bit. Being late in the day and with no one in front of us, we got round in about two and a half hours and the fine drizzle held off until the last few holes. We played again the next morning and after lunch we explored Kintyre and went down to the famous Mull, from where we could easily see the coast of Northern Ireland to the south-west.

On our last day we drove all morning in pouring rain to Prestwick, but this time we took the ferry from Tarbert across Loch Fyne to Portavadie and then again from Dunoon across the Clyde to Gourock. We arrived at Prestwick in time for lunch and in time to meet Alistair Pickles, who had been a sometime member at Denham and is currently a member at Prestwick; he was, at the time, also the Honorary Secretary of the Old Fettesian Golfing Society. He kindly agreed to introduce us to the club and play with us in the afternoon.

Although the clubhouse has been modernised, Prestwick was very much as I remembered it when I first played it in the 1950s and there is a great sense of golfing history about the place. It is sad, though, that in the lovely old 'Smoking Room', which looks out at the eighteenth green, each table still has a gleaming copper ashtray on it even though nobody is now allowed to smoke. I am a tolerant chronic ex-smoker who has not lit a cigarette for over twenty-three years, but I am not convinced by the evidence of the harmful effects of passive smoking. I think they are hugely exaggerated and I am very doubtful if there will be significant health benefits from the indiscriminate blanket banning of smoking in all public places which, alas, has now taken effect. So much of it is unnecessary and the 'health fascists' may yet have much to answer for.

Happily the rain ceased as we got on to the first tee after lunch, but unfortunately after only a few holes I felt pain in my groin again and also in my right knee after I had slightly twisted it on the bank of a bunker on the third hole. As I drove off from the seventh tee, the pain in my groin was agonising and I had to stop playing altogether, leaving Alistair and Charlie to continue on their own. Sad to say that was the last shot I played on a golf course – but I still live in hope!

One curious and unusual feature which the three courses we played have in common is airports: on parts of the course at Turnberry, the remains of the long since disused wartime runway can be seen; at the far end of the course at Machrihanish is the runway of the Machrihanish airport, while again at the far end of the course at Prestwick is the much used Prestwick International Airport.

After tea, I dropped Charlie off at the airport for his flight back to London and so ended a memorable four days. For me the best part of it was being able to spend some time with my thirty-two year old son. There was never a cross word between us and during those four days we had much interesting conversation. I got to know him and what makes him tick so much better, and he may also have found out a bit about me that he did not know before! The break was an absolute delight for me and I genuinely thank him for putting up with his old dad for so long. Like his sister Clare, he has a fine career and I am justifiably very proud of them both.

After I got home, I was duly diagnosed with an inguinal hernia and though I had to wait almost all of the statutory eighteen weeks maximum before I was operated on, the keyhole surgery went well, I was in and out of the hospital within the day and I have had no trouble of that kind since. In mid January 2008, however, I awoke one morning practically unable to walk as my right knee was so painful. I was diagnosed with osteoarthritis, given a prescription for paracetamol and told that nothing else could be done about it. Two or three days later a client walked into the property sales office where I was working and, seeing me hobbling, asked what was wrong. He turned out to be an osteopath and said he might be able to help. He did some manipulation on me which certainly did help but, even so, I hobbled around in great pain for a few weeks until Sarah introduced me to the senior consultant rheumatologist at Whipps Cross Hospital in North London. I saw him privately and following an x-ray he told me that due to wear and tear I had no cartilage left in my right knee and 'ouch' that I had bone scraping on bone! He gave me a cortisone injection which the next day eased much of the pain and told me that I should have to have a total right knee replacement operation. He referred me to his preferred surgeon and the operation was duly carried out at the end of April; the artificial knee has proved a complete success.

I was in hospital for a week, after which I was on crutches, not allowed to drive and effectively a prisoner in our flat. I could, though, make a cup of coffee in the kitchen; but the trouble was that, on crutches, I could not then take it back into the sitting room! Eventually the problem was solved by putting the coffee into a small thermos flask and hooking one finger round the handle of the cup screwed on to the top of the flask. I was still in pain, however, as by this time my left leg was also playing up, in part due to compensating for my gammy right leg. So as one leg was getting better, the other was getting worse. Then in September my rheumatologist drew off thirty millilitres of fluid from my left knee, gave me another injection of cortisone and, touch wood, I have had no trouble from it since. But by then I had developed very painful swellings in my feet, wrists and elbows. My osteopath suggested I have some blood tests done for rheumatoid arthritis and as soon as I saw the results it was clear what this latest problem was. So back I went to my rheumatologist, who has been treating me for rheumatoid arthritis ever since. The medication he has given me has been very effective and the condition would appear to have stabilised and thankfully is now in remission. Accordingly and providing the disease remains in remission, I am hopeful that one day I may be able to play golf again. Even if I can't, I am sure that I will be able to live without golf for I still have an awful lot going for me and unless I can play reasonably well, I would rather not play at all.

So one way or another, I was pretty much in acute pain for the whole of 2008, not said to evoke sympathy but to make the point that whilst from time to time I might have become a bit grumpy, irritable and fed up, at no time did I become depressed or miserable – and the thought of having a drink never occurred to me. That to me is the magic of the power of powerlessness [acceptance and surrender] and of practising the AA recovery programme. In spite of all that physical pain, I did not want to drink – and some people don't believe in miracles!

In July 2006, my daughter Clare who had married two years previously, made me a grandfather and my granddaughter was followed by her brother in November 2008. I usually see them every two or three weeks and they are a great joy. My only wish is that I was a bit more mobile so that I could get on the floor and play with them more than I do. When I look at them it seems strange to think that they are both twenty-five percent of me and that when I die a bit of me will live on in them. But then, that is what life and death are all about.

Clare is very much a working mother: having gained a first class degree in Mechanical Engineering at Birmingham University and then passing the

ACA Chartered Accountancy exams, she is now a director of an established investment management company for institutional clients.

Friends whom I would never have made had I continued drinking are a big component of my sobriety for which I'm certainly very grateful. One of them was Nigel A. I first met him in Broadway Lodge and I shall never forget the confused and bewildered look on his face when he arrived there in January 1983. As he surveyed the strange mixture of middle-aged alcoholics and young drug addicts of both sexes to whom he was about to be introduced, I could 'hear' him thinking, *What on earth am I doing here?* He was about to share a room with me and he was the first person I had met since stopping drinking who really made me laugh, something that made a huge difference and had much to do with the bond we subsequently developed as fellow sufferers. He was a year or two younger than me but we had quite similar backgrounds: he went to school at Marlborough and did his National Service in, and was commissioned in the Royal Marines whose 45 Commando I had been attached to briefly when I was in Cyprus. He was a very good mimic and had an inexhaustible fund of funny stories.

After completing treatment, we went our separate ways but we always kept in touch. I would be lying if I said that Nigel embraced the AA programme in his early days because probably all he did in addition to not drinking was to attend a few AA meetings. He used to tell a story against himself of how he complained to his sponsor of the time that no one ever asked him to do the main share at an AA meeting. 'Well Nigel,' his sponsor replied, 'the object is to carry the message, not spread the disease!'

Another of his stories was about the self-made man who had everything: a beautiful wife, lovely children, money, fantastic house, swimming pool, Rolls Royce car and so on. Then one day there was a fire and he lost the lot. Being uninsured, he decided to start again, this time in California, and in no time at all he was successful once more with a beautiful new wife, lovely children, house and so on. This time there was an earthquake and again he lost everything. Undeterred he went to the West Indies and did it all again, only for a hurricane to again destroy everything. As he sat on the beach surveying the wreckage, he looked towards the sky and cried out, 'Why me, Lord? Why me?' Not once, not twice, but three times: 'Why me?' Suddenly a great shaft of light shone down from the heavens and a voice said, 'Some guys just piss me off!'

After a few years, Nigel went with his fairly new second wife to live in Spain and in the early 1990s I went to visit them on a number of occasions, sometimes with Sarah. All his old complaints about everything were still there but so too was the humour and his hopelessly ambitious and grandiose plans for making a fortune. Then one day in the mid nineties, by which time he and his wife had separated, he returned to England and, following some seemingly inexplicable falls, was diagnosed with Motor Neurone Disease (MND). I had taken him to the hospital so I was with him when he received the terrible news. He looked at me with that same look he had had on his face when he entered Broadway Lodge; and then, after a pause, he said, *'Some guys just piss me off!'* It was typical of him and we both burst out laughing, or perhaps crying would be nearer the truth for we both knew that MND was incurable. Of all diseases, MND is the nastiest I have ever come across and Nigel's decline was pretty quick. With the help of the Motor Neurone Disease Association (MNDA) and the Royal British Legion (RBL) a place was found for him in the RBL's then relatively new hospice in Aylesford, Kent. Probably all his life, Nigel had obsessed and worried about money and to me the great irony was that near the end, when he had not a penny and was completely physically incapacitated, all his keep and treatment were paid for by MNDA, RBL and the State, whilst he, because of his disease, was unable to spend even the £50 a week he was given as pocket money.

I visited him regularly, as did many other AA members in the Kent area, and it was painful to see him deteriorating so fast. In the beginning, I could, with some difficulty, take him out for a pub lunch but as the months went by his condition worsened until not only could he not move, but neither could he speak, and communication became almost impossible. For an alcoholic not to be able to speak is just about the end and it must have been so frustrating for him to understand what I was saying without being able to convey any sensible reply. In the end I had to ask him to wink if the answer was 'yes' but even then I could not be sure whether the wink was intentional or involuntary.

I am sure that some people do not die until they are ready to go and while there is unfinished business still to be done. Nigel was one of these. At the beginning of December 1997 there were three things which Nigel was still living for: his sixtieth birthday early in December, Christmas (his younger daughter and grandchild lived nearby) and his fifteenth AA sobriety anniversary on 2nd January 1998. The hospice arranged a sixtieth birthday party for him, which Sarah and I attended and which despite everything I am sure he enjoyed. This was the last time I saw him and my final memory of him is of him sitting helplessly in a wheel chair as I kissed him for the first and only time, and said goodbye. In early January, less than fifteen months since the initial diagnosis, I had a telephone call from the hospice to say that he had passed peacefully away the day after his fifteenth AA anniversary. He had no more business left to do.

He was an extraordinary man, absolutely infuriating at times, especially when he would ask my opinion on something and then almost invariably go and do the opposite of what I had suggested. He professed to adore women but treated them pretty badly; while I knew him he had a string of mostly unsuitable and unsuccessful relationships which in itself was a symptom of his untreated co-dependency. He was a wonderful salesman and managed to persuade many to part with large sums of money to back his highly speculative entrepreneurial projects but, when he had money, he was a kind and very generous host. He couldn't boil an egg or make a sandwich, yet, like so many men of my generation he mistakenly fancied his chances on a barbecue, where he was expert in producing burnt but underdone sausages! In spite of all this, he remained a very loyal friend to me for what we had between us was forged out of our common suffering and, at a time when I still thought that perhaps life held nothing more for me than doom, gloom, ginger ale and Jesus, he made me laugh, and laughing is very therapeutic and healing. There is good and bad in us all, but no one deserves what he had to put up with. He faced his last losing battle with very great courage – the Royal Marines would have been proud of him – but at the end when all was lost, he surrendered, and I like to think he died at peace.

Nigel was the third of close AA friends from my early days to die sober. The other two, Barbara B. and Dick N., both of whom helped and influenced me a great deal, died of cancer some years earlier. Dick, who was very good to my children, had his moment of fame when he was the Grenadier Guards' subaltern who trooped the Grenadier's Colour in 1951 at the King's Birthday parade. For the first of many times since, the salute was taken that day by our present Queen, then Princess Elizabeth, who was standing in for her sick father, King George VI.

From people to pets: Laurel and Hardy were Burmese cats given to Sarah shortly before she and I got together. They were dark brown brothers from the same litter and still kittens when I first met them. Like my first wife Caroline, Sarah is a 'cat person' and Laurel and Hardy were always a much loved and integral part of the family. Hardy was Sarah's cat and Laurel was mine. Hardy was the boss cat and although I am sure Sarah would disagree, I always thought Laurel was the more intelligent. Both were very friendly and had wonderful temperaments. When we moved to Docklands, we bought a ground floor flat so that they could go out, but by then they were becoming old boys and, as it turned out, they no longer went out very much. So, fifteen months later, when we moved to our present fourth floor flat in the same development, they were quite content simply to go out on to the balcony and drink from the fountain. At the age of seventeen, Hardy started having fits and sadly had to be put down; a year later, so too did Laurel when he went blind and became completely disoriented. They had had good lives and had been with us for a long time. We still miss them both but we have very good memories of them and talk about them often.

Then there was Augusta, or Gussy as we called her for short. All of my life I had wanted a dog but never really had the chance to have one. In 2007 I thought that it would finally be possible and after some research, Sarah and I decided on a Labradoodle which, as the name implies, is a cross between a Labrador and a poodle. As such, they tend to combine the calmness and trainability of the Labrador with the exuberance of the poodle. Generally, they also have much better hips than Labradors and like poodles they do not moult. Having first seen her as a tiny black pup with some silver streaks, we bought Gussy as an eleven week old puppy and we only had a few minor accidents house training her as she was a quick learner. She was very much my dog and I adored her. She went practically everywhere with me and loved being in the car. I took her to work with me at Kairos, where she was very popular with most, though not all, of the residents, and every day I would take her for walks in the park just below our flat and adjacent to the river.

All was going well until I got this bloody arthritis and very soon it became clear that I could no longer take her for her walks or generally look after her. In the end, when I could barely walk, we decided to return her to her breeder as we were both determined that she should have a happy life. It was not a difficult decision to make because the reality was that it was the only one to make, but it nonetheless almost broke my heart. The morning I took her back in March 2008, I awoke to find her on my bed trying to lick me all over in a way that none of my three wives ever did! It was not something she had ever done before and it was as if she knew what was about to happen.

From time to time I still keep in touch with her breeder Steve, and the last time we spoke he told me that Gussy is very well and happy, especially when she is in his field running around with her mates, which, at the end

[186]

of the day, is all that matters. Perhaps it was a mistake having her at my age and I think now that it was definitely a case of the heart overruling the head, but I have no regrets. I would much rather have loved and lost – for that is what it was – than never to have loved at all.

In the spring of 2008, I was sitting in an AA meeting in Canary Wharf listening to a lady who was talking about change and how much she feared it. I suspect that many, indeed perhaps most people fear change but it is what life and growing are all about. I began to think of all the changes that had happened to me since I sobered up in December 1982. The more I thought about it, the more I realized that everything in my life had changed except for one thing. My wives had changed, my home had changed many times as had my jobs and my cars. In December 1982, David Cameron was a sixteen year old boy at Eton, Tony Blair and Gordon Brown had yet to become M.P.s and were unheard of, Concorde still had many thousands of miles to fly, the Berlin Wall was still up, telexes and typewriters were still in general use, the digital revolution was still in the future, mobile phones were in their commercial infancy and there certainly was no internet. During the last twenty seven years my children have grown up and have become successful adults, my mother has died and my two grandchildren have been born. I could go on, but the one thing that has not changed is my commitment to Alcoholics Anonymous and sobriety.

A number of my old AA friends have died sober and one or two sadly from their alcoholism; my meetings have changed and I have changed but I can truthfully say that because of my commitment to AA and its Twelve Step programme, I have been supported, sustained, encouraged and loved throughout, in a way that would not otherwise have been possible. I am certain that without AA, I would have been dead long, long ago. As Bill W. himself opined:

If I drew a line between active alcoholism on the one side, and life as God wants me to live it and has equipped me to on the other, then I am somewhere in the middle, striving towards the ideal. If I allow my character defects to rule my life again and forget the AA program, forget where the power to change for the better comes from, I will, in the long run, inevitably drink again.[32]

For myself I must be and am very content to continue to follow the simple suggestions I first heard back in 1982, for despite my many years of sobriety, I still have to remain sober; it remains as true for me today as it always has done: 'One drink is too many and one hundred not enough – it's the first drink that does the damage!' So

REMEMBER YOUR POWERLESSNESS, ALWAYS REMEMBER THE POWER OF POWERLESSNESS

A Plea for Common Sense

Everything that I have learned in the last twenty seven years about chemical dependency leads me to the conclusion that one will never begin to recover from alcoholism or drug addiction unless one first abstains from taking any form of mood altering chemical. One of the things I am passionately interested in is in helping others to find and achieve recovery, so what follows is concerned only with recovery and not with how the illness can be prevented or otherwise controlled. My purpose in writing it is to try to reach those people who have the power and are in a position to make a difference.

ESTIMATED NUMBER OF PEOPLE DEPENDENT/ADDICTED

		(Percent of population)
Nicotine	15 million	(25%)
Caffeine	12 million	(20%)
Alcohol	4.6 million	(8%)
Tranquillisers	1.5 million	(2.5%)
Heroin	150,000	(0.25%)
Cocaine	20,000	(0.03%)

(Sources: Ash, Drug Scope, Alcohol Concern, Department of Health, NHS)

Quite how these recent estimates were arrived at I am not sure: how, for example, do they define an alcoholic and would they include people like me who are in recovery? How are people who are multi-addicted, counted? Nor do they include cannabis addiction as I have been unable to ascertain any reliable estimates. My own guess, however, is that the number of cannabis addicts probably exceeds the number of heroin addicts. When I was training to be a chemical dependency counsellor in 1989, there were a surprising number of chemically dependent patients who said that cannabis was their drug of choice. Be that as it may, these estimated figures do give a reasonable indication as to the extent of the problem. Ignoring nicotine and caffeine, the last four categories are chemical dependency and drug addicts pale into insignificance compared with alcoholics. Even the number of tranquilliser addicts far exceeds the number of heroin and cocaine addicts combined, which means that the doctors who prescribe the tranquilisers are staggeringly the biggest drug pushers of all! (Although it did not happen here, in my opinion, Michael Jackson would never have died as he did, had it not been for numerous doctors prescribing for him, over a period of many years, vast doses of narcotic drugs. In fact, all they were really doing was subjecting him to further misery and feeding his addiction until he died from it.)

The following extracts (mostly regarding treatment) from a report published in May 2009 by the Centre for Policy Studies entitled 'The Phoney War on Drugs' make very depressing reading.

'*Between 1998 and 2007 the Government spent more on its war against drugs than on its combined operations in Iraq and Afghanistan. Spending continues to rise.*' *The sources of this information were: the Prime Minister who stated that the cost of the combined operation in Iraq and Afghanistan was £6 billion (Today Programme BBC Radio Four, 12th May 2007) and Ian Martin, Head of the Drug Strategy, Home Office, who stated that the spending on drug strategy budget to date was £7 billion (Future of the Drugs Strategy, Home Office, London Conference. 13th March 2007)...* (Page 17)

The Nationalisation of Harm Reduction

'*We are in the business of providing services to users, not in the business of providing users to services.*' *(From a letter to Kathy Gyngell, the author of the report from the National Treatment Agency, quoting Paul Hayes (head of the NTA) 16th December 2008)...* (Page 25)

In 2001 Labour set up a new Special Health Authority, the National Treatment Agency (NTA,) to process as many Problem Drug Users (PDUs) into treatment as quickly as possible. Since then, the actions of the NTA have been defined and driven by targets. 50% of the then estimated 200,000 PDU population was targeted for treatment. In 2002 an even more ambitious target was set – to increase the number in treatment by 100% by 2008. In 2005 new 'waiting time' and 'retention in treatment targets' were key elements of the NTA's 'treatment effectiveness' strategy.

Through hundreds of commissioning edicts and care protocols dictated to the 150 Drug Action Teams (DATs), the NTA soon had the requisites of a harm reduction strategy in place. Any DAT not meeting its target did so at its peril. Future funding allocations became contingent on local needs assessments and treatment plans tailored to NTA demands.

Excluded from this new treatment funding was the existing network of charitable and private residential centres and programmes that provided time intensive abstinence based recovery and rehabilitation programmes. Similarly ignored by the government and the NTA were the country-wide 24/7 non profit fellowships (recovery groups) of Narcotics Anonymous (NA) and Alcoholics Anonymous (AA). Abstinence and recovery had no place in Labour's new 'evidence based' drug treatment business.

Today the NTA is the pinnacle of a monolithic bureaucracy. Its original staff of 30 has expanded to 150. Its operating (administrative costs) stand at over £14.5 million a year. On its advice, the pooled treatment budget of £655 million a year is distributed to purchase treatment, a figure that has more than doubled since 2002. Senior staff are rewarded with performance-related bonuses if they meet their targets.

The emperor's new clothes

The Public Service Agreement target to increase numbers in treatment to 170,000 by 2008 was achieved in 2006.

The numbers of clients in 'treatment contact' rose to over 200,000 in 2007/08. 147,000 were prescribed opiate substitutes even though some two thirds of the original problem using population had been defined as crack cocaine addicts for whom there is no approved pharmacological treatment interventions. According to the NTA, only 4,300 people (fewer than 2% of the total in treatment) accessed residential rehabilitation and just 6,700 (just over 3%) had inpatient detoxification.

But this of course was a success: the NTA had beaten the original target of getting 50% of PDUs into some form of treatment.

The apparent pointlessness of the national treatment bureaucracy was first exposed by Mark Easton, the BBC's Home Affairs Editor, on The Today programme in 2007. He revealed that the numbers emerging from treatment free of addiction had barely changed from 5,759 to 5,829 despite a £130 million rise in the budget. This was the equivalent of £1.5 million for getting each person off drugs over this three-year period. Not only were fewer than 3% of PDUs free of drugs after treatment but this proportion had actually fallen from 3.5% three years previously. It should *be noted that the Drugs Outcome Research Project in Scotland has shown that this is the proportion of PDUs that would become drug free without any treatment intervention at all.* (Pages 25-28)

Finally, in the Conclusion to the report, which is thorough and wide ranging under the heading of 'Treatment' it says:

The UK's default treatment of methadone substitution is only appropriate (if at all) for opiate addicts. This is despite rising numbers of cocaine and cannabis addicts, polydrug and alcohol abusers. The UK treatment goal is harm reduction, not abstinence or recovery.

The goal of treatment in both Sweden and the Netherlands is abstinence. Treatment in Sweden and the Netherlands is based on the notion of addiction care, is needs driven and does not discriminate between alcohol and drugs.

Abstinence-based treatment is not provided at all by the State in the UK and is only supported for very few patients. Of the treatment targets set out in the latest drugs strategy, there were still none for numbers becoming free of drugs, despite some lip-service being paid to abstinence-based treatment.

Yet abstinence-based approaches to addiction can work... (Page 65)

You couldn't make it up if you tried!

But it gets even worse. In April 2010 it was revealed by The Sun newspaper that there is now a new NHS treatment strangely called "**retoxification**" which apparently has been going on for some five years. Chambers dictionary defines 'detoxify' as 'to rid of poison or the effects of it'. It follows, therefore, that this new word 'retoxification' which unsurprisingly is not listed in my dictionary must mean poisoning again. 'Retoxification' is apparently administered to prison inmates who came into prison as, for example, heroin addicts and even though they may be drug free prior to their release, they are nonetheless given substitute drugs such as methadone because once released, they are deemed likely to use heroin again. The quite ludicrous and insane reasoning behind it is that it gets their bodies used to drugs again by building up tolerance thus 'slashing' the risk of overdose deaths. As Kathy Gyngell observed "It gives the impression the Government is giving up on tackling drug addiction. This doesn't get people off drugs – but captures them in the grip of methadone instead." A senior police source was also quoted in The Sun as saying: "We have enough difficulties coping with drug-fuelled crime without ministers sanctioning this. It's one of the craziest ideas from any government."

The NHS and the government would appear to be completely uninterested in recovery, only in allowing the disease of drug addiction to flourish. Indeed, you could say that they are spreading the disease and, far from reducing the harmful effects, they are actively prolonging and increasing them. Their default treatment of methadone substitution is condemning addicts to remain addicted users and shows a complete lack of concern for the harmful effects that all mood altering drugs have on the human brain: far from freeing it from these harmful effects, the NHS further drugs the brain into submission with methadone, which to my mind can only be called cruel and evil. All drugs, by definition are toxic and poisonous. All attack one part of the body or another, but for alcoholics and drug addicts the major problem with mood altering drugs is that initially they create pleasurable sensations. This is why we take them in the first place and why we want more and more of them. Such pleasurable sensations, however, are delusional and short-lived before the poison really gets to work and starts destroying parts of the brain and other organs such as the liver and pancreas.

Methadone is a synthetic, narcotic drug similar to morphine; it 'shuts you down' or 'blinkers you' so that you don't fully experience bad feelings but neither do you feel good feelings. It is also an extremely dangerous drug. In America, for instance, according to the National Centre for Drug Statistics, the number of methadone deaths nationwide rose from 786 in 1999 to 4,462 in 2005, a nearly six-fold increase. This compares with fatal cocaine overdoses rising 63% from 3,382 in 1999 to 6,228 in 2005. In Scotland statistics from the General Register Office revealed that in the Lothian Region **there were actually more methadone-related deaths in 2007 than heroin associated deaths,** the respective comparative figures being 22 and 20. In Scotland as a whole the figures were 114 and 289 respectively. These figures show that methadone is no harmless drug and that giving it to a heroin addict (heroin itself being a derivative of morphine) is rather like giving wine or beer to an alcoholic whose drink of choice is whisky or vodka! Additionally, methadone substitution is no guarantee that the addict will stop using his drug of choice: many sell their methadone so that they have the money to go to their dealer and buy whatever other hard drugs they may want. In such instances, the tax payer

[193]

is simply financing the addict's habit and it is difficult to see how this can possibly be described as either sensible economics or 'harm reduction'. It is madness and can in no way be described as treatment of drug addiction. Methadone substitution is not treatment; it is maltreatment and as such is surely at variance with the tenets of both the Hippocratic Oath and the Convention of Geneva.

H.M. PRISONS

Prisons are mostly awash with drugs and to a lesser extent alcohol. Quite why this should be so and why they are not drug and alcohol free, I cannot understand.

In February 2009, the prison population amounted to 82,190 of which 4,273 (5%) were women. According to audited accounts of the Prison Service, the operating costs of the prison service for the year to 31st March 2008 were over two thousand million pounds! This means that the overall annual cost of keeping a person in prison amounts to approximately £25,000. And a very large part of the prison population is made up of alcoholics/drug addicts; some estimates have put it as high as seventy per cent. According to HM Inspector of Prisons, **£77.3 million** was provided for custodial drug treatment during 2006/07. I believe that this treatment was almost identical to that referred to in the report prepared by the Centre for Policy Studies above. Further, according to The Centre for Social Justice – Prison Reform, 64.6% of all released prisoners re-offend within two years. I think it is fair to assume that the vast majority of these will be the drug/alcohol addicts who have received methadone substitution treatment but who are still not in recovery and who make up the 70% or so of all prisoners. As hardly any of them are clean and sober or in recovery when they leave prison, it is a racing certainty that practically all of them will re-offend and the cost of crime committed by such ex-prisoners is £11 billion per year. This is a staggering figure and makes one wonder what on earth was the real point of putting them in prison in the first place. Little or nothing appears to be spent on treating alcoholism.

If, as indicated in the 'The Phoney War on Drugs', there are some 200,000 PDUs (presumably these are all addicts but with government-speak you can never be quite sure what they mean) there are, therefore, some 57,000 in prison (70% of 82,000) which means that 28%, or more than one in four of all drug addicts, are in prison; this is quite a thought.

What is absolutely clear from these extracts from the Centre for Policy

Studies' report and the Prison statistics is that the government's so called drug policy of methadone substitution simply does not work and is a complete waste of huge sums of money. What really puzzles me is who is it that recommends and approves such ignorant and daft treatment policies? Whoever they may be, I am sure that they are not chemically dependent people in recovery, who in my opinion are the real experts and whose opinions should be listened to before all others, including the so-called health/addiction experts.

More generally and with regard to alcohol and alcoholism, the Department of Health would seem to base all its policies on helping people to drink sensibly by not consuming more than the 'safe' number of units of alcohol per week. I have no wish to be the spreader of gloom but if the figures quoted above are correct and 8% of the population are alcoholics, statistically that means that one in every twelve people will turn out to be alcoholic.

The government and some doctors also talk about increasing the price of drink and I would accept that if the price of drink goes up, the amount consumed by the nation may well go down. But it is the alcoholics who probably drink up to 50% of the total consumed, and their consumption will remain unaffected because they will continue to drink at the same high levels whatever the price. If necessary they will steal to finance their habit, and I know because, like countless others, I myself did so. The one thing that alcoholics will never be able to do is control their drinking and drink sensibly. It is this that defines us as alcoholics. It should also be remembered that anyone who tries to control his drinking has already lost control! As with drug addiction there seems to be no emphasis on or even mention of abstinence, without which recovery is impossible. Additionally, they just do not seem to be able to understand that we are dealing with an illness which is part spiritual. How on earth can you beneficially treat the human spirit long term with any sort of drug?

The strange thing about all this is the total lack of consistency and logic in treatment policy making. With drug addiction the illness is treated with yet more drugs; with alcoholism it is treated by beseeching and expecting alcoholics to drink sensibly and control the amounts they drink – something they cannot do. With cigarette smoking, however, not only are smokers banished from almost everywhere, they are encouraged and helped to give it up. **They are actually encouraged to abstain!** These are three very different and contradictory ways of dealing with three different drug addictions. How illogical and what madness!

THE MEDICAL PROFESSION

Back in 1980 I went to see a leading psychiatrist at one of the London teaching hospitals who failed to diagnose my alcoholism when to anyone who knew anything about the disease, it was staring them in the face. On the other hand, a couple of years later I was extremely lucky in that I saw a G.P. in private practice who fortunately knew about chemical dependency and Minnesota Model treatment centres; he diagnosed me as a chronic alcoholic almost straight away and immediately arranged for me to go to Broadway Lodge. I don't think it is mere coincidence that I have not had a drink since that day.

In 2008 I had two operations under general anaesthetic. During this time I was told by no less than four different doctors – my local doctor's locum, two different anaesthetists and the doctor in charge of night medication at the hospital where I had one of the operations – that because I had not had a drink for over twenty-five years I could not be an alcoholic. I was told this not once, not twice, not thrice, but four times. I find this level of ignorance quite astonishing, especially from three doctors who administer drugs. All three had asked if I was allergic to anything and they all looked surprised when I replied on each occasion that I was allergic to alcohol and that not only was I an alcoholic but that I was also chemically dependent. I am not sure, but I strongly suspect from their reactions that they did not even know what chemical dependency was.

Because I am chemically dependent, I have to be very careful about what medication I am given by doctors. The following account highlights the necessity for this: in 2007 an AA member in south London, who had been sober for almost nine years, had had the same operation as I had had for a total knee replacement; unfortunately he became 'hooked' on an opiate based pain killing drug that was prescribed for him post operatively, and shortly after he left hospital he relapsed on alcohol. Although he subsequently got back to AA, at the time of writing he has been back out again, drinking this time for over three months; although I hope he will, it is by no means certain that he will ever recover. This is a true story and it is a good example of how, if we take another mood altering substance, in this case a subscribed opiate, it can lead us back to our original drug of choice. It is also proof that once an alcoholic, always an alcoholic – something doctors do not seem to be generally aware of. Yet G.P.s meet addiction every day in their surgeries. They don't usually spot it because they are not looking for it and know next to nothing about it. As a result, most will prescribe tranquilisers or antidepressants, which are drugs and, apart from the fact that over any length of time they don't work, they are addictive and if given to an addict of any kind, they have the almost identical effect as giving alcohol to an alcoholic!

The shocking and sad thing is that none of this is very surprising because, as far as I have been able to ascertain, doctors are not taught about alcoholism, chemical dependency or any other form of addiction; nor are there any Minnesota Model type treatment centres based on abstinence and the Twelve Steps in the whole of the NHS. Quite simply, the NHS does not do abstinence. Abstinence based treatment programmes of existing charitable and private treatment centres, both residential and non-residential, AA and NA were all specifically excluded from the NTA's new treatment funding referred to above. In point of fact, neither AA nor NA can accept money from outside agencies but both would be more than willing to accept referrals, and treatment would be free of charge. So why are these dreadfully bureaucratic, expensive and useless so called substitution treatments continually pursued when it has been proven time and time again that they do not and cannot work? Why is this, when it has been proven that recovery can often be achieved with the Minnesota Model treatment based on abstinence and the AA Twelve Step Recovery Programme? If ever there was a better example of insanity – making the same mistake twice and expecting a different result – I can't think of one.

In Sweden and the Netherlands the treatment goal is abstinence. And the attitude of the medical profession in America is also different from ours, particularly with regard to AA and NA: any AA member in America, who has a period of sobriety under his belt, is a respected member of society and, unlike here, gets 'brownie points' for mentioning this on his CV; judges in American Courts will often give an offending alcoholic the option of attending AA and staying sober as an alternative to a custodial or other sentence. From its very early days starting in 1935, the fledgling fellowship of AA received great support from Medicine and the Press, who wrote about it and spread its good news extensively. After Dr. Silkworth's first endorsement of AA (see Overture), medical societies and physicians in the US set the seals of their approval upon AA. The following are some excerpts from comments of doctors present at the 1944 annual meeting of the Medical Society of the State of New York where a paper on AA was read:

Dr Foster Kennedy, neurologist: "This organization of Alcoholics

Anonymous calls on two of the greatest reservoirs of power known to man, religion and that instinct for association with one's fellows … the 'herd instinct.' I think our profession must take appreciative cognizance of this great therapeutic weapon. If we do not do so, we shall stand convicted of emotional sterility and of having lost faith that moves mountains, without which medicine can do little.'

Dr G. Kirby Collier, psychiatrist: "I have felt that A.A. is a group unto themselves and their best results can be had under their own guidance, as a result of their philosophy. Any therapeutic or philosophic procedure which can prove a recovery rate of 50% to 60% must merit our consideration."

Dr. Harry M. Tiebout, psychiatrist [a non-alcoholic trustee on the General Service Board of AA for many years and the author of a number of outstanding papers particularly with regard to alcoholism and surrender]: *"As a psychiatrist, I have thought a great deal about the relationship of my speciality to A.A. and I have come to the conclusion that our particular function can very often lie in preparing the way for the patient to accept any sort of treatment or outside help. I now conceive the psychiatrist's job to be the task of breaking down the patient's inner resistance so that which is inside him will flower, as under the activity of the A.A. program."*

Dr W.W. Bauer, broadcasting under the auspices of The American Medical Association, in 1946, over the NBC network said in part: "Alcoholics Anonymous are no crusaders: not a temperance society. They know that they must never drink. They help others with similar problems … In this atmosphere the alcoholic often overcomes his excessive concentration upon himself. Learning to depend on a higher power and absorb himself in his work with other alcoholics, he remains sober day by day. The days add up into weeks, the weeks into months and years."

Dr John F. Stouffer, Chief Psychiatrist, Philadelphia General Hospital, citing his experience with AA: "The alcoholics we get here at Philadelphia General are mostly those who cannot afford private treatment, and A.A. is by far the greatest thing we have been able to offer them. Even among those who occasionally land back in here again, we observe a profound change in personality. You would hardly recognise them." [33]

In 1951 [four years after AA came to England] the Lasker Award was given to Alcoholics Anonymous. The citation reads in part as follows:

"The American Public Health Association presents a Lasker Group Award for 1951 to Alcoholics Anonymous in recognition of its unique and highly successful approach to that age-old public health and social problem,

alcoholism … In emphasizing alcoholism as an illness, the social stigma associated with this condition is being blotted out … Historians may one day recognize Alcoholics Anonymous to have been a great venture in social pioneering which forged a new instrument for social action; a new therapy based on the kinship of common suffering; one having a vast potential for the myriad other ills of mankind." [34]

These early medical endorsements of AA, made at a time when AA was in its infancy and when its membership was but a tiny fraction of the two million plus it is today, are not only important, they were also prophetic; yet, to this day, in the UK there is still so much ignorance about AA, alcoholism and other drug addictions. AA had its genesis in the consulting rooms of Dr Carl Jung, one of the great pioneering psychiatrists, and its co-founders, one of whom was also a doctor, were greatly influenced by yet another doctor specialising in alcoholism (Dr Silkworth); yet, in Britain the BMA seems hardly aware of AA's existence, and if it is, knows almost nothing about it. Why haven't the medical profession, the Department of Health and the government followed the Americans' lead in backing AA and its treatment programme? Over the years, literally many millions have recovered from alcoholism in AA. Instead of ignoring it, why are they not learning about it and championing its very considerable successes? Why are they not recommending it and its younger sister anonymous fellowships to anyone who thinks they may be alcoholic or suffering from other forms of addiction? Instead of leaving successful methods of treatment to charities, why don't they invest in the development of Minnesota Model Twelve Step based treatment centres throughout the NHS and in the prisons? If they were do so, it would be an awful lot cheaper and it would contribute hugely to the saving of many lives. I repeat, yet again, that any alcoholic or addict who thoroughly follows the Twelve Step programme of AA will recover and get well. I and countless others like me are living testament to this simple fact.

I believe that the time has now come for the NHS and the medical profession to recognise and accept the limitations of the assistance they can give in the treatment of chemical dependency. Doctors can be of great help first of all in diagnosing the illness much earlier than is commonly the case (huge numbers die from it without having ever been diagnosed at all), secondly in administering detoxification which in the case of prescribed drug addiction and alcoholism can otherwise be particularly dangerous, and, thirdly in the treatment of the physical consequences of the disease such as sclerosis of the liver and some cancers which are perhaps attributable to the primary disease. In my experience, however, and those of many others who are in long term recovery, virtually all recovery throughout the Western World takes place outside the purview of clinical medical treatment in the context almost exclusively of multi help support groups of which, as I have said, by far the most successful are the proven abstinence based Twelve Step spiritual and ongoing programmes of Alcoholics Anonymous and the other anonymous fellowships.

So to those in positions of authority and who have the power to make a difference in Government, in Medicine and in the Department of Health, I make this heartfelt plea on behalf of all alcoholics and other drug addicts both those in recovery and those who are still suffering:

With open minds, please look again at what you are presently doing and at last follow the lead given around seventy years ago by the doctors Jung, Silkworth, Smith (AA's co-founder), Tiebout and the other pioneering doctors referred to above; look at what others are presently doing and change this country's existing insane policies in respect of the treatment of alcoholism and drug addiction (including prescribed drugs), which manifestly have failed and continue to fail. Please think again, change direction and pursue those abstinence treatment policies which both here and in other countries have been proven to work.

As 'The phoney War on Drugs' makes clear: *The goal of treatment in both Sweden and the Netherlands is abstinence. Treatment in Sweden and the Netherlands is based on the notion of addictive care, is needs driven and does not discriminate between alcohol and drugs.* **If the Swedes and the Dutch can pursue policies based on abstinence, so can we. Given the will and a proper understanding of what is involved, there is no earthly reason why this cannot be done in the UK, and done quite quickly.**

Epilogue

'The Law of Unintended Consequences'

In December 1982, a friend of mine took a risk in agreeing to pay for the cost of my six weeks residential treatment at Broadway Lodge, which ended up being a fraction over £2,000, a lot of money at the time. The chances of his ever getting his money back were pretty slim and must have appeared the more so when at the end of six weeks I was told that there was nothing more they could do for me and that they thought I might have to drink again.

My friend, who is not an alcoholic, always wished to remain anonymous; in fact, I don't think he intended that even I should ever know who he was, but I found out and it was one of the best moments of my life when I was able to repay him the £2,000 which he had invested in me. Indeed, I should really say gambled on me for his 'investment' was very high risk!

I have no intention of breaking his anonymity, but if he should read this, as I hope he will, I would ask him to consider and reflect upon just how enormously beneficial his very generous act towards me has proved to be. In helping me to find sobriety and recovery, I in turn have helped many others to achieve sobriety, and they in their turn have helped still others and so on into the future pretty well ad infinitum. As an example of this, one of our East End cockney members of AA, who had returned to London on leave from his job in South Korea, told me in a meeting that some of the things I had once shared in his early days had helped him, and consequently he was passing them on in the AA meetings he attended in Korea. As he told me afterwards in his broad cockney accent, 'What you told me 'ere, is now being shared all over Korea!'

So my friend's gamble on me has paid off far, far more than I suspect he ever dreamed, for it is still causing and hopefully will continue to cause ripple effects, not just here, but all over the world. Usually the Law of Unintended Consequences is associated with negative consequences but in this case it is the opposite, and it is for this reason that I shall always be eternally grateful to him. It gives real and added meaning to one of the quotations already given in Chapter 9:

Expect to pass through this world but once; therefore, any good thing

that I can do, or any kindness I can show to any fellow-creature, let me do it now; let me not defer or neglect it, for I shall not pass this way again.

As I look back, I can see that I have been very fortunate and blessed. I have been from the palace to within an inch or so of the gutter and I have had experiences that are not given to many, for it remains a sad fact that only a few ever recover from this incurable disease which, though I no longer suffer from it, I still have. I am not cured of alcoholism; all I really have is a daily reprieve and even though I have now had over 10,000 of them, these reprieves still remain contingent on the maintenance of my spiritual condition. This is why I continue to go to one or two AA meetings a week and practise the AA programme as best I can. But it is no hardship because, apart from being able to carry the AA message, it is invariably very enjoyable and I regularly get to meet some of my best friends. It is now only a small (in terms of time) but very important part of my life and it is still the only way I can repay those who helped me in my early days.

The Big Book movingly and much more eloquently expresses just how I presently see things.

...I wish everyone could be in AA, and if everyone were there would be no need for jails, in my opinion.

For I am happy. I thought I could never be happy. A happy man is not likely to do harm to another human being. Harm is done by sick people, as I was sick, and doing dreadful harm to myself and to my loved ones.

For me, AA is a synthesis of all the philosophy I've ever read, all the positive, good philosophy, all of it based on love. I have seen that there is only one law, the law of love, and there are only two sins; the first is to interfere with the growth of another human being, and the second is to interfere with one's own growth.

I still want to write a fine play and to get it on. I'd gladly do it anonymously, as I have done this brief account of my struggle with alcohol – merely to present certain ideas for the consideration of the reader. I don't care too much about personal fame or glory, and I want only enough money to enable me to do the work I feel I can perhaps do best. I stood off and took a long look at life and the values I found in it: I saw a paradox; that he who loses his life does indeed find it. The more you give, the more you get. The less you think of yourself the more of a person you become.

In AA we can begin again no matter how late it may be. I have begun again. At fifty-four, I have had come true the old wish, "If only I could live my life over, knowing what I know." That's what I am doing, living again, knowing what I know. I hope I have been able to impart to you, the reader, at least a bit of what I know; the joy of living, the irresistible power of divine love and its healing strength, and the fact that we, as sentient beings, have the knowledge to choose between good and evil, and, choosing good, are made happy.[35]

Postscript

Caroline

Shortly before publication of this book and at the comparatively young age of sixty five my first wife died of cancer on the 3rd June, coincidentally the fifteenth anniversary of my marriage with Sarah. In the summer of 2008, Caroline was diagnosed with cancer of the peritoneum but following chemotherapy and an eight hour operation in January 2009, she was declared cancer free. The disease continued to stalk her, however, and it reappeared in the autumn of 2009. Sadly, this time, the chemotherapy failed to make an impression and slowly she began to deteriorate. I last saw her on Easter Sunday, when she was in good form; to all outward appearances there seemed to be no trace of her illness. But such was the final rapacious rate of the progression of her disease that within two months she had died. It was almost twenty nine years since we had parted company and although we had had our run-ins and certainly did not by any means always see eye to eye, I was sad and still felt compassion for her. She had, after all, been an important part of my life for fourteen years and she had borne me two wonderful children who, as I have already said, are both now in their mid-thirties.

It is a strange irony that, statistically, many cancer patients have a far greater chance of recovery than alcoholics, of whom only two or three per cent recover. Caroline was almost ten years my junior, and in 1981 when we were divorced, I was still drinking, thus making the odds against my surviving her very long indeed. Yet again, I cannot help but be reminded of just how lucky I am to be alive and free of the otherwise progressively fatal consequences of my alcoholism simply by, a day at a time, not picking up a drink and by following a few very simple suggestions. What, I wonder, would Caroline have given to be able to do that? May she rest in peace.

NOTES

1. *The Language of the Heart*, pages 281-286
2. *Alcoholics Anonymous* (The Big Book), 'The Doctor's Opinion'
3. AA pamphlet '15 Points...'
4. www.broadwaylodge.org.uk/treatment.htm 10/04/2007
5. William Glasser, *Reality Therapy*
6. The Big Book, pages 83-84
7. Dr. Vernon E. Johnson, *I'll Quit Tomorrow*, page 2. (Dr Johnson was founder of The Johnson Institute in Minneapolis, Minnesota, which offered one of America's most successful training programmes for the treatment of alcoholism.)
8. *Twelve Steps and Twelve Traditions*, 11th Edition, page 143
9. *The Language of the Heart*, Part Three: 1958-70, page 281
10. 1947 AA Grapevine Inc.
11. *The Language of the Heart*, 'The Bill W. – Carl Jung Letters', pages 276-281
12. *As Bill Sees It (*an anthology of extracts from many of Bill W.'s writings), page *1*
13. *Twelve Steps and Twelve Traditions*, page 15
14. The Big Book, pages 58-60
15. The Big Book, Appendix II
16. The Big Book (4th Edition) page 180
17. The Big Book, (4th Edition) page 564
18. *Twelve Steps and Twelve Traditions*, page 178
19. *Alcoholics Anonymous Comes of Age*, pages 38-40
20. The Big Book, page 30
21. The Big Book, pages 35 to 37
22. The Big Book, page 60
23. *Twelve Steps and Twelve Traditions*, page 59
24. The Big Book, page 83
25. Ibid.
26. *Twelve Steps and Twelve Traditions*, page 92
27. Big Book, page 85.
28. The Big Book, 3rd Edition, 'Dr Bob's Nightmare', pages 180-181
29. The Big Book, 4th Edition, 'Acceptance was the Answer', pages 416-417,
30. The Big Book, page 64

31. *Alcoholics Anonymous Comes of Age*, page 257

32. *Best of The Grapevine*, Vol. 3, page 187

33. The Big Book, Appendix III

34. The Big Book, Appendix IV

35. The Big Book, 3rd Edition, 'He Who Loses His Life', pages 542-543

APPENDICES

APPENDIX 1

The Twelve Traditions of AA

I.   Our common welfare should come first; personal recovery depends on A.A. unity.

II.   For our group purpose there is but one ultimate authority – a loving God as He may express Himself in our group conscience. Our leaders are but trusted servants; they do not govern.

III.   The only requirement for A.A. membership is a desire to stop drinking.

IV.   Each group should be autonomous except in matters affecting other groups or A.A. as a whole.

V.   Each group has but one primary purpose – to carry its message to the alcoholic who still suffers.

VI.   An A.A. group ought never endorse, finance, or lend the A.A. name to any related facility or outside enterprise lest problems of money, property, and prestige divert us from our primary purpose.

VII.   Every A.A. group ought to be fully self-supporting, declining outside contributions.

VIII. Alcoholics Anonymous should remain forever non-professional, but our service centres may employ special workers.

IX.   A.A., as such, ought never be organized; but we may create service boards or committees directly responsible to those they serve.

X.   Alcoholics Anonymous has no opinion on outside issues; hence the A.A. name ought never be drawn into public controversy.

XI.   Our public relations policy is based on attraction rather that promotion; we need always maintain personal anonymity at the level of press, radio and films.

XII.   Anonymity is the spiritual foundation of all our Traditions, ever reminding us to place principles before personalities.

APPENDIX 2

Spiritual Experience

(Reprinted from pages 567-568 of the Fourth Edition of the Big Book)

The terms "spiritual experience" and spiritual awakening" are used many times in this book which, upon careful reading, shows that the personality change sufficient to bring about recovery from alcoholism has manifested itself among us in many different forms.

Yet it is true that our first printing gave many readers the impression that these personality changes, or religious experiences, must be in the nature of sudden and spectacular upheavals. Happily for everyone, this conclusion is erroneous.

In the first few chapters a number of sudden revolutionary changes are described. Though it was not our intention to create such an impression, many alcoholics have nevertheless concluded that in order to recover they must acquire an immediate and overwhelming "God-consciousness" followed at once by a vast change in feeling and outlook.

Among our rapidly growing membership of thousands of alcoholics such transformations, though frequent, are by no means the rule. Most of our experiences are what the psychologist William James calls the "educational variety" because they develop slowly over a period of time. Quite often friends of the newcomer are aware of the difference long before he is himself. He finally realizes that he has undergone a profound alteration in his reaction to life; that such change could hardly have been brought about by himself alone. What often takes place in a few months could seldom have been accomplished by years of self-discipline. With few exceptions our members find that they have tapped an unsuspected inner resource which they presently identify with their own conception of a Power greater than themselves.

Most of us think this awareness of a Power greater than ourselves is the essence of spiritual experience. Our more religious members call it "God-consciousness."

Most emphatically we wish to say that any alcoholic capable of honestly facing his problems in the light of our experience can recover, provided he does not close his mind to all spiritual concepts. He can only be defeated by an attitude of intolerance or belligerent denial.

We find that no one need have difficulty with the spirituality of the program. *Willingness, honesty and open mindedness are the essentials for recovery. But these are indispensable.*

[209]

"There is a principle which is a bar to all information, which is proof against all arguments and which cannot fail to keep a man in everlasting ignorance – that principle is contempt prior to investigation."

–HERBERT SPENCER

APPENDIX 3

Some AA Milestones

1935	Bill W. and Dr. Bob met in Akron, Ohio. Alcoholics Anonymous was founded on 10th June when Dr. Bob had his last drink.
1937	The Twelve Steps of Recovery was written.
1938	The Alcoholic Foundation was established as a trusteeship for AA
1939	*Alcoholics Anonymous* (The Big Book) was published.
1940	First AA World Service Office was opened in Vesey Street, New York.
1941	Saturday Evening Post article boosted AA membership from 2,000 to 8,000.
1942	First AA prison group in San Quentin, California.
1944	First issue of the AA magazine Grapevine was published.
1947	AA came to England on 30th March at the Dorchester Hotel, London.
1949	First issue of the AA magazine Grapevine was published.
1950	Twelve Traditions were adopted at first International Convention in Cleveland, Ohio. Dr. Bob died on 16th November aged 71.
1951	First General Service Conference, U.S.A.
1953	The book, *Twelve Steps and Twelve Traditions,* was published.
1957	General Service Board, UK, formed.
1960	100 groups in England
1966	First UK General Conference held in Manchester.
1969	First World Service Meeting held in New York.
1971	Bill W. died on 24th January at Miami Beach, Florida aged 75.
1972	UK Newsletter became SHARE.
1974	First World Service Meeting held outside of America held in London.
1977	1,000 groups in UK
1978	European Information Centre opened in London.
1981	1,500 groups in UK
1985	2,000 groups in AA
1986	UK General Service Office move from London to York.
1992	3,000 groups in UK
2001	21 million copies of the first three editions of The Big Book sold.
2008	4,000 groups in UK
2009	30 million copies of the first four editions of The Big Book sold.

APPENDIX 4

Fourth Step Inventory

In taking my inventory I first considered under 'A' my personality defects by giving two examples of each whilst drinking (I could have given many, many more) and one of 'what it is like now'. This was followed by similar examples under 'B' and 'C', respectively, of the 7 Cardinal Sins and the 10 Commandments. Finally and every bit as importantly, I considered under 'D' my virtues, attitudes and responsibilities. Throughout my Fourth Step I made brief notes sufficient only to remind me of the incidents concerned, in order for me to be able to talk about them in Step Five. Where comments appear in brackets, they are my own.

A.   PERSONALITY DEFECTS

1.   **Selfishness – (self-centeredness) egocentric – Taking care of one's own comfort, advantage, etc. without regard for the interest of others.**

2.   **Alibis: - The highly developed art of justifying our drinking and behaviour through mental gymnastics.** Excuses for drinking – the alcoholic calls them reasons. Phoney as a $3.00 bill.

3.   **Dishonest Thinking** – Another way of lying. We may even take truths or facts as our hypothesis, and then through some phoney mental hop-scotch, come up with exactly the conclusions we had planned to arrive at. No wonder we drank.

4.   **Pride** – One of the 7 Cardinal Sins and a serious character defect. Egotistical vanity – too great admiration of one's self. Inordinate self-esteem, arrogance, ostentatious display, bragging. (And as I have since learned from C.S. Lewis, **'Pride gets no pleasure out of having something, only of having more of it than the next man.'**)

5.   **Resentment:** Under **Anger** in the 7 Cardinal Sins and, for many alcoholics the most damning fault in the entire repertoire. It is the displeasure aroused by a real or imagined wrong or injury, accompanied with irritation, exasperation or hate. It brings out the worst of our immaturity and produces misery to ourselves and all concerned.

6.   **Intolerance:** Refusal to put up with beliefs, religious or political, practices, customs or habits that differ from our own.

7. **Impatience:** Unwillingness to bear delay, opposition, pain, bother, etc. calmly. ('God grant me patience but hurry!')

8. **Envy:** Sadness at another's good fortune.

9. **Phoniness:** A manifestation of our great false pride; a form of lying; rank and brash dishonesty. It's the old false front.

10. **Procrastination:** Putting off...postponing things that need to be done...the familiar 'I'll do it tomorrow.'

11. **Self-Pity:** An insidious personality defect and a danger signal to look for. Stop it in a hurry – it's the build up to a drink. **(In my opinion it is a very unattractive defect and sometimes difficult to self-diagnose. Poor me, poor me, pour me a drink! It is also very akin to, if not the same as, depression. If ever I find myself saying 'Why me, 'If only', 'But for', I know that I am being self-piteous and I must change my thinking and attitude.)**

12. **Feelings Easily Hurt:** Sensitive, touchy, thin-skinned.

13. **Fear:** An inner foreboding, real or imagined, of doom ahead. (Fear is an implicit faith in the negative result.) We suspect our drinking, overt acts, negligence, etc. are catching up with us. We fear the worst. (Fear). When we learn to accept Step One, ask God's help and face ourselves with honesty, the nightmare of fear will be gone.

B.   THE 7 CARDINAL SINS

Pride: Egotistical vanity – too great admiration of one's self. (See Character Defects)
Covetousness or Avarice: Perversion of man's God-given right to own things.
Lust: Inordinate love and desires of the pleasures of the flesh.
Envy: Sadness at another's good fortune. (See Character Defects)
Anger: A violent desire to punish others.
Gluttony: Abuse of lawful pleasures God attached to eating and drinking of foods required for self-preservation.
Sloth: Illness of the will which causes neglect of duty. (Laziness, procrastination).

C.   THE 10 COMMANDMENTS

1.   **I am the Lord, thy God, thou shalt not have any Gods before me.** Is God omnipotent to me, or are my Gods money, fame, position? Does He come first, or do I? Do I seek His will?

2.   **Thou shalt not take the name of the Lord, thy God, in vain.** Am I profane, and would I be to God's face? Isn't that pretty phoney respect?

3.   **Remember to keep holy the Sabbath Day.** Would my attitude towards 'religion' and church perpetuate that spirituality?

4.   **Honour thy father and thy mother.** The law of love, respect and obedience. Have I as a parent earned that honour?

5.   **Thou shalt not kill.** Here include hate, anger, resentment and hurt through our misdeeds.

6.   **Thou shalt not commit adultery.** Have we violated another's marriage under any circumstances?

7.   **Thou shalt not steal.** How about cheating, misrepresenting, pressure deals, debts, etc.?

8.   **Thou shalt not bear false witness against thy neighbour.** Include slander, gossip, and using dubious testimony.

9.   **Thou shalt not covet thy neighbour's wife.** Not immoral acts alone, but the thinking, temporizing and condoning as well. The mental, emotional and spiritual misery I imposed upon myself and others.

10.   **Thou shalt not covet thy neighbour's goods.** Remember envy, competitive dishonesty, 'dog eats dog' tactics.

D.   VIRTUES, ATTITUDES and RESPONSIBILITIES

1.   **The Divine Virtues – Faith, Hope and Charity (Love)**

a.   **Faith:** The act of leaving that part of our destiny we cannot control, i.e. our future, to the care of a power greater than ourselves, or God, with assurance that it will work out for our well-being. Shaky at first, it becomes a deep conviction.

1.   Faith is a gift, but one acquired through application: acceptance, daily prayer, daily meditation and our own effort.

2.   We depend on faith. We have faith that dinner will be served, that the car will start, that our co-workers will handle their end. If we had no faith, we would come apart at the seams.

3.   Spiritual faith is the accepting of our gifts, limitations, problems and trials with equal gratitude, knowing God has His plan for us. With 'Thy will be done' as our daily guide, we will lose our fear, find ourselves, find our destiny.

b.   **Hope:**   Faith suggests reliance: 'We came to believe...' Hope assumes faith but also aims for objectives. We hope for sobriety, for self respect, for love of family. Hope resolves itself into a driving force; it gives purpose to our daily living.

1.   Faith gives us direction; Hope the head of steam.

2.   Hope reflects attitude. Remove hope and our attitude becomes insipid.

c.   **Charity (Love):** 'So there abide faith, hope and charity (love), these three; but the greatest of these is charity (love).'

1.   'Charity is patient, is kind; charity does not envy, is not pretentious, is not puffed up, is not ambitious, is not self-seeking, is not provoked; thinks no evil, does not rejoice over wickedness, but rejoices with the truth; bears with all things, hopes all things, endures all things...'

2.   In its deeper sense, charity is the art of living realistically and fully, guided by spiritual awareness of our responsibilities and our debt of gratitude to Almighty God and to others.

Analysis: Have I utilised the qualities of Faith, Hope and Charity (Love) in my past living? How would they apply to my new life?

2.   The Little Virtues – the Building Material

a.   Courtesy: Some of us are actually afraid to be gentlemen. We'd rather be boors, the self pampering type.

b.   Cheerfulness: Circumstances don't determine our frame of mind. We do. Today I will be cheerful. I will look for the beauty in life.

c.   Order: Live today only; organise this day. Order is the first law of Heaven.

d.   Loyalty: The test of a man's sense of obligation.

e.   Use of time: Time can be productive, abused or desecrated.

f.   Punctuality: Self-discipline, order; consideration of others.

g.   Sincerity: The mark of self respect and genuineness. Sincerity carries conviction, generates enthusiasm, is contagious.

h.   Caution in speech: Watch thy erring member, the tongue. We can be vicious or thoughtless. Too often the damage is irreparable.

i.   Kindness: One of life's great satisfactions. We haven't known real happiness until we have given of ourselves. Practise daily.

j.   Patience: The antidote to resentments, self-pity, impulsiveness.

k.   Tolerance: Requires common courtesy, courage, live and let live.

l.   Integrity: The ultimate qualification of a man; honest, loyal, sincere.

m.   Balance: Don't take yourself too seriously. We get better perspective if we can laugh at ourselves. (Take your illness/recovery seriously but don't take yourself too seriously). It will cure the piques.

n.   Gratitude: The man without gratitude is stupid, arrogant or both. Gratitude is simply honest recognition of help received. Use it in your prayers, 12th Step work, our family relationship. **(Gratitude is the antidote to everything).**

Analysis: In considering the Little Virtues, where did I fail particularly and how did that contribute to my accumulated problem? What virtues should I pay attention to in this rebuilding problem? Have I used them at home and with those that love me?

How about starting NOW, applying little acts of consideration, unselfishness, and gratitude today? Don't make a production of it: three or four little acts every day is far better than running the gamut one day and 'resting up' the next.

3.   Just for Today (Card) – A Plan for Living

(The **"Just for Today"** card was written shortly before her death in 1935 by the nun Sybil Partridge and has been adopted almost in its entirety by A.A. It is one of the most useful ready aids to joyful living there is. If one uses it at any time when one is feeling down and acts on any one or more of the suggestions on the card, one is guaranteed to feel better. It has never failed me and it can be as useful to me today as it was in 1983 when I first experienced its simple wisdom. I carry it still in my diary.)

a.   A beautifully designed plan of action to handle today. Don't let its simplicity fool you. This hits us where we used to live.

b.   Live one day at a time: handle our drinking problem for today only. Yesterday's gone; tomorrow may never come. Today is ours. (Today is the tomorrow we worried about yesterday!)

Just for today I will try to live through this day only and not tackle my whole life problem at once. I can do something for twelve hours that would appaul me if I felt I had to keep it up for a lifetime.

Just for today I will be happy. This assumes to be true what Abraham Lincoln said that 'Most folks are as happy as they make up their minds to be.'

Just for Today I will adjust myself to what is, and not try to adjust everything to my own desires. I will take my luck as it comes, and fit myself to it.

Just for Today I will try to strengthen my mind. I will study. I will learn something useful. I will not be a mental loafer. I will read something which requires effort, thought and concentration. (e.g. The Big Book)

Just for Today I will exercise my soul in three ways. I will do someone a good turn, and not get found out; if anybody knows of it, it will not count. I will do at least two things I don't want to do – just for exercise. I will not show anyone my feelings are hurt; they may be hurt, but today I will not show it.

Just for Today I will have a programme. I may not follow it exactly, but I will have it. I will save myself from two pests: hurry and indecision.

Just for Today I will have a quiet half hour all by myself, and relax. During this half hour, sometime, I will try to get a better perspective of my life

Just for Today I will be unafraid. Especially I will not be afraid to enjoy what is beautiful, and to believe that as I give to the world, so the world will give to me.

[217]

Just for Today I will be agreeable. I will look as good as I can, dress becomingly, talk low, act courteously, criticize not one bit, not find fault with anything and try not to improve or regulate anybody except myself.

4. Attitudes

a. To God

1. Have I based my concept, or refusal, of God principally through my early training, hearsay, disappointments or emotional approaches? Would I prepare for a career or even a hobby in the same manner? In other words, have I sought God?

2. Do I appreciate the magnitude of the spiritual as applied to;

   a. My daily living?

   b. My problems, frustrations, despair, bitterness and boredom?

   c. My present mess? Can I accept God's judgment as better than my own?

3. Conceding the possible importance of spiritual development, can I honestly say I have given it time, study, and pursuit? Have I given myself a fair shake, or have I drifted and procrastinated?

4. For those of us who claim religious adherence, just who has come first in our lives, the great I Am or God? Have we really accepted God?

5. Am I willing to turn my will and my life over to the care of God as I understand Him?

b. To myself

1. Have I honestly faced myself or have I sidestepped through daydreaming, wishful thinking, resentments, self-pity, and the bottle?

2. Am I satisfied with myself, my responsibilities, morals, disposition, the examples I set, my family relations?

3. Haven't I been cheated, short changed through dishonesty to myself? How badly?

4. A change of attitude from the old alibi 'I can't take anymore' to 'I can take this and a lot more for this day'.

c. **To my family**

1. Do I recall my marriage vows? Have I lived up to them? – be careful, don't start taking your spouse's inventory.

2. Have I gained the love and respect of my children? Do I want them to be honourable, happy and well adjusted? Has my training and example emphasized those aims? Has my drinking helped my children?

3. Do I dictate to my family, or have I created trust and love through unselfishness, interest, and examples?

4. Do I want my children to turn out like me?

d. **To my Work**

1. 'No matter what the job, do it well.' Is that for others, or do I apply it to myself as well?

2. Am I carrying my weight in my work, or have I been 50% man on the job due to my drinking? Am I producing or just getting by?

3. Has my relationship with my boss and fellow workers, associates, been on an honest level, or has it been filled with resentments, pettiness, deceit, and self-pity?

4. Have I discharged my responsibilities well to my associates, clients, and others involved in my work?

5. Are there any ethical considerations in my work that clash with my moral standards, or do I excuse it on the basis that it is "business"?

6. Am I doing the kind of a job I would expect if someone was working for me?

e. **To my Friends, Neighbours, and Community**

1. Do I cultivate friends for what I can get out of them? Does friendship have my price tag attached?

2. Frankly, am I interested in my neighbour, their kids, the welfare of our churches, schools, and community projects or don't I give a hoot?

3. Do I consider myself a worthy citizen of city and country, or am I taking a free ride? Am I a respected member of my community?

4. Does the Golden Rule apply in my relationships with people, or is it me first, last and always?

5. Responsibilities

a. To God
1. The daily pursuit and daily practise of faith through proper prayer, meditation and attitude.
2. Applying Step 3: Let go – let God.
3. Practising the precepts of spirituality, reverence, love, charity and moral responsibility.
4. Learning and exercising gratitude as one of the greatest of graces and the key to happiness.
5. Picking myself up when I fall.
6. Interest in welfare of others

b. To myself
1. To determine what I want in life and to seek the necessary help to realize it. Required: honesty, intellect, effort, and time.
2. To become cognizant of my daily obligations, recognising their fulfilment is essential to my peace of mind and sobriety.
3. To put First Things First, (my sobriety) to accept what must be accepted (powerlessness over alcohol), and never again to short change or deceive myself (Step 1).
4. To look for the wonders and beauty in life, instead of facing the wrong direction.
5. A change of attitude to the old alibi 'I can't take this anymore' to 'I can take this and a lot more for this day'.

c. To my family
1. To cherish: they are mine and a part of me. They look to me for love, guidance, example, admonition, leadership, and spiritual and material care. Almighty God and I shape their destiny.
2. My love: Not only the self-indulgent type, but more to plan for, fight for, sacrifice for – to make them finer people.
3. To provide: our families come first; we, second. Their needs, worries, interests come before ours. That's as it should be.
4. To enjoy: family outings, family interests, shows together, games with the kids, finally praying together. Those are cherished memories.

[220]

d. To my work

1. Above all to seek balance. If I am lazy, to put more effort into the job and establish order; if I am unrealistic, to seek work in keeping with my capabilities; if I am gifted, to utilize those abilities, but never to the exclusion of spiritual, personal and family obligations.

2. To keep an eagle eye beamed on Money for Money's sake, power, position, and personal acclaim. They are the alcoholic's poison.

3. To deal with people in my work as ethically as I do in any phase of living – if I want peace with myself.

4. To be less demanding and more producing; business is always looking for a better man. Our rewards will come if we want them.

5. Am I doing the kind of job I would expect if someone was working for me?

e. To A.A.

1. To remember always: 'To God and A.A. I owe my deliverance.' My obligation is twofold – to be the best A.A. I can and to help make it available to others.

2. My knowledge of alcoholism and A.A. principles means nothing, unless applied constantly. One 'must' to my continued sobriety is regular attendance at group meetings. (my underlining)

3. My sobriety is contingent not on admittance, but on acceptance and undertaking of all 12 Steps. (my underlining)

4. To contribute to my group's betterment. If their idea of a meeting is a bragging contest on history making binges, suggest more solid material, such as one of the Steps. The calibre of the meeting is all important – to me and to each member.

5. Be careful how you live. You may be the only copy of the Big Book other people have read. (my underlining)

APPENDIX 5

Some Suggested AA Reading

'Alcoholics Anonymous'

'Twelve Steps and Twelve Traditions'

'Alcoholics Anonymous Comes of Age'

'Dr Bob and the Good Old Timers'

'Pass It On'

'The Language of the Heart'

'Came to Believe'

'Living Sober'

NB. AA literature can be obtained in the UK from AA's General Service Office in York, PO Box 1, 10 Toft Green, York YO1 7NJ. Tel 01904 644026

APPENDIX 6

Dr. Bob's Farewell Talk

The following text is taken from Dr Bob's remarks made at the First International Convention in Cleveland, Ohio on 3rd July 1950 just over four months before he died from cancer on the 16th November 1950.

My good friends in AA and of AA...

I get a big thrill out of looking over a vast sea of faces like this with a feeling that possibly some small thing I did a number of years ago played an infinitely small part in making this meeting possible. I also get quite a thrill when I think we all had the same problem. We all did the same things. We all get the same results in proportion to our zeal and enthusiasm and stick-to-itiveness. If you will pardon the injection of a personal note at this time, let me say that I have been in bed for five of the last seven months and my strength hasn't returned as I would like, so my remarks of necessity will be brief.

There are two or three things that flashed into my mind on which it would be fitting to lay emphasis. One is the simplicity of our program. Let's not louse it all up with Freudian complexes and things that are interesting to the scientific mind, but very little to do with our actual AA work. Our Twelve Steps when simmered down to the last, resolve themselves into the words "love" and "service". We understand what love is, and we understand what service is. So let's bear those two things in mind.

Let us also remember to guard that erring member the tongue, and if we must, let's use it with kindness and consideration and tolerance.

And one more thing: None of us would be here today if somebody hadn't taken time to explain things to us, to give us a little pat on the back, to take us to a meeting or two, to do numerous little kind and thoughtful acts in our behalf. So let us never get such a degree of smug complacency that we're not willing to extend, or attempt to extend, to our less fortunate brothers that help that has been so beneficial to us.

Thank you very much.

APPENDIX 7

Bill W.'s Last Meeting with Dr. Bob

The following text is taken from page 214 of 'Alcoholics Anonymous Comes of Age'.

...I took my leave of Dr. Bob, knowing that the following week he was to undergo a very serious operation. Neither of us dared say what was in our hearts. We both knew that this might well be the last decision we would ever make together. I went down the steps and then turned to look back. Bob stood in the doorway, tall and upright as ever. Some color had come back to his cheeks, and he was carefully dressed in a light gray suit. This was my partner, the man with whom I had never had a hard word. The wonderful, old, broad smile was on his face as he said almost jokingly, "Remember, Bill, let's not louse this thing up. Let's keep it simple!" I turned away, unable to say a word. That was the last time I ever saw him.

Lightning Source UK Ltd.
Milton Keynes UK
01 November 2010

162210UK00007B/93/P